Oxford Junio
Teache

Second edition

Oliver Gregory

Oxford

Oxford University Press, Walton Street, Oxford OX2 6DP

Oxford New York Toronto
Delhi Bombay Calcutta Madras Karachi
Petaling Jaya Singapore Hong Kong Tokyo
Nairobi Dar es Salaam Cape Town
Melbourne Auckland

and associated companies in
Beirut Berlin Ibadan Nicosia

Oxford is a trade mark of Oxford University Press

Second edition first published 1980
Reprinted 1982, 1983, 1986, 1988

Printed in Hong Kong

Contents

Introduction

The OXFORD JUNIOR ENGLISH COURSE is a programme of English language for the primary or Primary/Middle School age range. It includes many of the elements that will be familiar to teachers but attempts to break new ground in that the work in each book centres round a theme or topic. The complete course is as follows:

Book 1:	Introductory Book	
Book 2:	Food and Farms	Extension Book 2
Book 3:	The Coastline	Extension Book 3
Book 4:	Homes and Shelters	Extension Book 4
Book 5:	Our Language	Extension Book 5

The subject matter of the themes is treated comprehensively and is supported, where appropriate, by illustrations that both adorn and illuminate the text. Together they provide material that is interesting and relevant and able to capture and hold the attention of the pupils. The language work that follows is always derived from the basic theme in one of two ways:

(a) In some cases the subject matter is expanded and explored and in that form is incorporated into questions and exercises.
(b) An important language point in the opening section is taken out, explained, developed and used as exercise material.

In a number of instances methods (a) and (b) are combined. This theme-based technique thus avoids bringing in matter arbitrarily and helps to make the work – reading, writing, finding out and discussing – meaningful and having a unity and direction that the pupils themselves can see and to which they can contribute.

Book 1 lays the groundwork of the method of approach that is more fully exploited in Books 2–5. Each of these, therefore, is really two books in one – a topic book in which a theme is carefully introduced and logically developed, and an English language textbook where the work centres round related aspects of the topic in hand. In order to cater for the needs of those who require further work on more formal matters a special feature of Books 2–5 is the provision of what are called Practice Pages. As the name implies these are revision items and are based closely on points that have been previously introduced. No completely new material is included in the Practice Pages. These occur at regular intervals, in some instances – notably in Books 2, 3 and 4 – dividing up the topic work into various convenient sub-sections.

From an early stage in the course the arrangement of the work generally follows the same pattern and layout in order to facilitate learning and teaching. Some variations have been introduced in Book 5 because it was felt that some changes in the layout of a longer book were both desirable and appropriate. In all cases, each section of work is identified by a letter of the alphabet. Except in the case of the Practice Pages these run from a to e and usually begin with the more straightforward type of exercise. Some of the intermediate sections may require additional support (e.g. from dictionaries and other reference books) but it is the sections marked e that are usually of the more demanding variety. Some of the e sections are suitable for discussion and debate and extended pieces of continuous writing.

Each Extension Book follows up the theme of the parent book of the same number. The four books (there is no Extension Book 1) offer more detailed information about the topic, more advanced language exercises and a wide range of suggestions and ideas for further work. In particular they provide comprehension exercises that call for more than simply identifying and reproducing given facts. Pupils will sometimes need to be able to 'read between the lines', to anticipate, predict, evaluate and offer opinions. Even where all the necessary information is given, pupils will often be called upon to reorganise and rearrange the data in order to present it as an acceptable answer. In other words, the exact form of the answer will not usually be found 'ready made' in the text, merely awaiting extraction. The Extension Books are therefore particularly suitable for the more able pupils who need to be stretched and kept busy.

It was primarily because of the nature and extent of some of the e sections in the parent books and many items in the Extension Books that this answers book has been provided. In many instances, however, the kind of 'answers' supplied are intended as reference material for the teacher rather than suggesting a model that all pupils would be expected to provide. It is hoped that these answers will be useful in suggesting at least some of the points that could be covered in discussion. The more routine one-word and other objective responses are given in accordance with the instructions in the pupils' books and therefore in the form that pupils can be expected to provide. Where considerable variation in the wording is possible this is indicated. Because of the possibility of pupils in the same class working at different levels it was decided to produce one answers book to cover the whole course. Repeater headings on each page promptly identify which part of the scheme is being covered at any point.

An outline of the complete scheme of work follows. This is presented under five broad headings, but it should be noted that many exercises and assignments touch on more than one skill and could therefore be shown in more than one column. The integrated nature of Oxford Junior English makes it particularly difficult to classify every item exclusively under one heading. Nevertheless, the chart does give some idea of the scope and variety of the many ingredients of the course.

	Sentence Work	Comprehension and Vocabulary	
BOOK 1 **Introductory Book**	Matching sentences and pictures Divided sentences True/false sentences Arranging sentences in correct order Choose the right ending Sentences for winter/summer	Literal comprehension Names of things we eat or drink Some 'doing' words Making compound words Names of things we use Odd word out Pairs of words Puzzles, to, two Names of things we wear Things we see and do in the park Names of animals	
BOOK 2 **Food and Farms**	True/false sentences Puzzles in sentence form Divided sentences Arranging sentences in correct order Multiple choice Completing sentences Sentences about animal noises/gender/young Mixed up sentences Using given words in sentences Sentence construction	Literal comprehension Names of farm machines, buildings etc. Things seen on a farm Identifying words whose meanings are given Collective names	
Extension Book 2	Completing sentences Arranging sentences in correct order	Harder literal comprehension Identifying words whose meanings are given	
BOOK 3 **The Coastline**	Arranging sentences in correct order Completing sentences Joining sentences Divided sentences Arranging phrases into sentences Multiple choice Sentence construction	Literal comprehension Identifying words whose meanings are given Identifying sentences expressed in other words Animal homes One word for several	
Extension Book 3	True/false sentences	Identifying words whose meanings are given Harder literal comprehension Inferential comprehension Explaining meanings of phrases	

Grammar, Punctuation and Spelling	Work involving continuous writing	Follow-up and Revision
Capital letters and full stops **Is, are** **A, an** **Is, his** Singular and plural **There, their** **There is, there are** **To, two** **As, has** **And, but** **Where, were**	Developing and completing a story	How much can you remember?
For, four Alphabetical order **By, buy** Verbs Adjectives Nouns Homophones **Has, have** Singular and plural Use of commas Punctuating a given paragraph Prepositions Spelling – silent **l** and silent **w** **Of, off** **And, but** Opposites **To, too**	Writing about life on a farm Writing about combine harvesters Former use of old farm buildings Things made from flour/wool Filling in blanks in passage Writing about sheep dogs Ways of using eggs Battery hens Writing about coffee Ways of using cocoa and chocolate Multiple choice to complete paragraph Ways of using butter Ways of using fruit Writing about less common vegetables Writing about kippers and bloaters	Choosing suitable books Alternative headings The Country Code Practice pages (7) Breeds of cattle and sheep Different kinds of cheese Different kinds of fruit Anagrams of names of vegetables Shell-fish
	Picture questions – labelling, identifying, interpreting etc. Write the stories that the pictures tell	Things to find out Making a chart
Singular and plural Words ending in **–ing** Homophones Punctuating a given paragraph Words beginning with silent **k** **Was, were** **Were, where** Making nouns from verbs **We, us, our** Verbs – past tense Words ending in **–ful** **Its** and **it's** Comparison of adjectives Use of commas	Filling in blanks in passage Writing about holidays Writing about cliffs Writing about caves Writing about coins and Treasure Trove Writing about Martello towers Rewriting paragraph to improve style Writing about smugglers Writing about oil pollution Writing about lifeboats Completing paragraph from pairs of words Writing about crustaceans Completing paragraph from list of words Writing about Starfish Multiple choice to complete paragraph Writing a paragraph, outline given	Puzzle about coins Coastal defence Practice pages (7) Lightships, buoys and lighthouses Precautions to take when walking, climbing, bathing or sailing Shore zones Univalve molluscs Bivalve molluscs Identifying pictures Jellyfish Mammals on the beach Waders A venomous fish
	More things to write about Filling in blanks in paragraph (cloze procedure) Picture questions – identifying, explaining, interpreting	Things to find out Identifying objects from clues or information given

	Sentence Work	Comprehension and Vocabulary
BOOK 4 **Homes and Shelters**	Arranging sentences in correct order Completing sentences Divided sentences Sentence construction Joining sentences	Literal comprehension Identifying words whose meanings are given Adjectives formed from names of countries and continents One word for several Words beginning with **en–** Identifying sentences expressed in other words Collective nouns Using adjectives Explaining meanings of words Rhyming words Trades associated with house building Compound words Other ways of saying **put** Odd word out Shortened words
Extension Book 4	Multiple choice	Identifying words whose meanings are given Alternative words Harder literal comprehension Inferential comprehension Explaining meanings of words
BOOK 5 **Our Language**	Writing sentences about pictures Sentence construction Divided sentences Arranging sentences in correct order Rewriting sentences, improving style Rewriting ambiguous sentences	Compound words Animal sounds Literal comprehension Harder literal comprehension Sounds Identifying words whose meanings are given One word for several Meaning altered by change of stress Words beginning with **tele–** Occupations Acronyms Materials named after places Words borrowed from other languages Alternatives to overworked words Words that may be confused Eponyms Words of similar meaning
Extension Book 5	True/false sentences	Identifying words whose meanings are given Harder literal comprehension Inferential comprehension Idiomatic expressions Alternatives to overworked words and expressions Alternatives to slang expressions Words that may be confused Avoiding ambiguities Latin words and expressions

Grammar, Punctuation and Spelling	Work involving continuous writing	Follow-up and Revision
Singular and plural Adverbs Spelling – c sounded as s Punctuating a given paragraph Verbs – past tense Making adjectives from nouns Punctuating sentences Opposites Apostrophe s Spelling – **ch** sounding like **k** Making nouns from verbs Homonyms Conjunctions Comparison of adjectives Spelling – silent **b** Inverted commas Contractions	Writing about shelter and our other needs Writing about lake villages Completing paragraph from list of words Multiple choice to complete paragraph Rewriting paragraph to improve style Completing paragraph from pairs of words	Things to find out Questions about Roman houses Questions about the Saxons and other invaders of Britain Questions about Normans Practice pages (11) Questions about Tudors Questions about architecture and building Questions about famous houses, services to the home, different types of houses at home and abroad
Punctuating a given passage Abbreviations	Completing paragraph from pairs of words Filling in blanks in paragraph (cloze procedure) Picture questions – identifying, explaining, interpreting Describing houses	More things to write about Things to find out Questions based on plan of house
Words ending in **–gue** Words ending in **–fied** Words ending in **–dge** Nouns, verbs, adjectives Punctuating a given paragraph Spelling – **ph** sounding as **f** Alphabetical order Adjectives and adverbs Abbreviations (Latin) Words ending in **–er** and **–or** Passed and past Plurals Spelling – omissions, additions, words spelt phonetically Homophones Apostrophe s Adjectives from names Common and proper nouns Verbs from nouns	Writing about: non-verbal communication stone age and bronze age cuneiform the Rosetta Stone early forms of writing the Phoenicians letters of the alphabet parchment the Normans printing the spread of English simplified spelling – for and against the calendar Ambiguous notices Surnames Letter writing Signs and symbols Gesture Summarising a passage Combining two accounts into one Writing contrasting accounts of the same thing Completing paragraph from pairs of words	Comparing animal sounds with human speech Picture writing Practice pages (15) The alphabet Words derived from Greek, Latin Old and Middle English Chinese as a world language Made-up words Special days (e.g. Good Friday) Names of the days Names of the months Names of places Word puzzles Headlines Braille Heraldry Mime Using reference material Care of books Onomatopoeia The language of poetry Book titles
Punctuating a given passage Spelling – omissions, additions, transpositions, phonetic spelling	Completing paragraph from pairs of words Picture questions Writing about spelling Writing about ways of using words Explaining advertising slogans Explaining symbols used in communication	More things to write about Questions about: language and communication speech Morse Code Teleprinters Post Office Tower Things to find out Rhyming slang Origins of slang words and expressions Rebuses Some well-known books

Book 1

Book 1 begins by introducing some of the characters and then uses the same layout to name some familiar objects, most of which reappear later on in the book. At page 10 the layout changes to a simpler version of the one that will carry much of the information and many of the exercises throughout the course. Here it is used to describe and explore a series of activities and items of related interest, beginning with a typical breakfast scene and then following the same children through part of a typical day. Additional sections on work and play complete the book. Each double-page spread is complete in itself, though related to the whole.

Plenty of work is provided at each stage, but the settings in the book are such that will give opportunity for further observation and discussion. This will lead to further use and acquisition of language as well as bringing the printed page to life. The life-like characters in the illustrations are based on real people in real situations so that the children can readily identify with them.

page 3

1 This is Sara.
2 This is Paul.
3 This is Mark.
4 This is Julie.
5 This is Kay.
6 This is George.

1 Sara has a bicycle.
2 Paul has a gun.
3 Mark has a comic.
4 Julie has a swing.
5 Kay has a kite.
6 George has a football.

page 5

1 Sara is swimming.
2 Paul is sleeping.
3 Mark is fishing.
4 Julie is skipping.
5 Kay is digging.
6 George is eating.

1 Sara is in the water.
2 Paul is in the bedroom.
3 Mark is by the river.
4 Julie is in the playground.
5 Kay is in the garden.
6 George is at the table.

page 7

1 This is a clock.
2 This is a jug.
3 This is a table.
4 This is a bed.
5 This is a desk.
6 This is a tree.

1 The clock is on the wall.
2 The jug is on the table.
3 The table is in the kitchen.
4 The bed is in the bedroom.
5 The desk is in the classroom.
6 The tree is in the park.

page 9

1 This is a knife.
2 This is a spoon.
3 This is a spade.
4 This is a brush.
5 This is a pencil.
6 This is a ruler.

1 We cut with a knife.
2 We eat with a spoon.
3 We dig with a spade.
4 We paint with a brush.
5 We write with a pencil.
6 We measure with a ruler.

Breakfast time *pages 10–11*

a 1 It is half past eight.
2 Sara and Mum are in the kitchen.
3 Sara is eating cornflakes.
4 Mum is drinking tea.
5 Paul is late for breakfast.

b 1 The food is on the table.
2 Sara and Mum sit facing each other.
3 Sara sits on the left.
4 Mum sits on the right.
5 The clock is on the wall.

c milk bread sugar butter cornflakes

d 1 Sara and Mum are in the kitchen.
2 Sara and Mum are sitting at the table.
3 Sara is holding a spoon.
4 There are three chairs in the picture.
5 It is half past eight in the morning.

e 1 The food is on the table.
2 It is breakfast time.
3 Soon it will be time to go to school.

Going to school *pages 12–13*

a 1 Sara and Paul are going to school.
2 They see two buses.
3 They see three vans.
4 They see seven cars.
5 It takes ten minutes to get to school.

b 1 Sara and Paul walk to school.
2 They see cars on the road.
3 They meet Mark and Julie.
4 The children cross the road carefully.
5 They wait in the playground.

c Sara and Paul had their breakfast.
After breakfast they set out for school.
On the way they met Julie and Mark.
When they got to school they waited in the playground.

d 1 The children are going to school.
2 They meet their friends at the corner.
3 They see traffic on the road.
4 It doesn't take long to get to school.
5 At school they wait outside.

e football
breakfast
bedroom
cornflakes
playground

In the playground *pages 14–15*

a 1 The children are in the playground.
2 Sara is eating an apple.
3 Paul is eating crisps.
4 Mark is kicking a ball.
5 Julie and Kay are running across the playground.

b 1 The children are at school.
2 Sara is holding an apple.
3 George is near the gate.
4 Two girls are running across the playground.
5 Some of the boys are playing football.

c an orange a cake
a bus an uncle
a car a horse
an apple an elephant
a dog an island

d 1 The children are outside.
2 It is daytime.
3 Sara has an apple.
4 Mark kicks the ball.
5 George is not running.

e 1 I would eat the cake.
2 I would read the book.
3 I would wear the coat.
4 I would ride the bicycle.
5 I would drink the milk.

In the classroom *pages 16–17*

a 1 The children are in the classroom.
2 Sara sits next to Julie.
3 George sits next to Andy.
4 The girls are writing stories.
5 Andy is drawing a picture.

b 1 The boy reads his book.
2 The desk is in the classroom.
3 Andy has finished his writing.
4 Now he is drawing a picture.
5 Paul goes to school with his sister.

c We read books.
We draw pictures.
We sing songs.
We write stories.
We watch television.

d 1 The children are in school.
2 Julie sits next to Sara
3 Andy and George sit next to each other.
4 George is reading.
5 One of the boys is drawing a picture.

e 1 The boys and girls are in school.
2 Andy sits next to George.
3 The children are working hard.
4 Sara and Julie are writing.

A story *pages 18–19*

a 1 The teacher is reading the story.
2 The story is called The Gentle Tiger.
3 The tiger lived in a forest.
4 The tiger wanted to be kind and gentle and make friends with people.
5 The other tigers wanted to be fierce.

b 1 We say one book but two books.
2 We say one girl but two girls.
3 We say one song but two songs.
4 We say one boy but two boys.
5 We say one car but two cars.

c 1 A tiger has stripes.
2 A giraffe has a long neck.
3 An elephant has a trunk.
4 A camel has a hump.
5 A tortoise has a shell.
6 Most fish have scales.

d 1 The teacher is reading a story.
2 The teacher is reading to the class.
3 The story is about a tiger.
4 One tiger wanted to be friendly with people.
5 The gentle tiger was left on his own.

e Completing the story about the gentle tiger.
Various answers possible.

Dinner time *pages 20–21*

a 1 It is half past twelve.
2 Paul and Mark sit with Kay and Lyn.
3 The children are eating meat, potatoes and carrots.
4 After dinner the children play outside.
5 George and Andy go home for their dinner.

b 1 The children are eating their dinner.
2 Sara and Julie are sitting over there.
3 If there is time the children will play.
4 George and Andy have dinner with their parents.
5 They will return to their class after dinner.

c 1 jam 3 fruit
2 picnic 4 butter

d 1 It is half past twelve.
2 Some of the children are in school.
3 It is dinner time.
4 It is noisy in the hall.
5 Some children go home at dinner time.

e fish and chips
knife and fork
cup and saucer
salt and pepper
bread and butter

Things to do at home *pages 22–23*

a 1 Sara and Paul are at home.
2 The table is by the wall.
3 Sara is cutting out pictures.
4 Paul is writing in his book.
5 Dad has fallen asleep.

b 1 There is a table in the room.
2 There are two big chairs in the room.
3 There are four people in the room.
4 There is a carpet on the floor.
5 There are two children at the table.

c 1 I am a table.
2 I am a clock.
3 I am a comb.
4 I am a potato.
5 I am a river.

d 1 It is seven o'clock in the evening.
2 There is a table by the wall.
3 Sara and Paul are sitting.
4 Sara is holding a pair of scissors.
5 Paul is using a pencil.

e shoes coat dress trousers shirt

People at work *pages 24–25*

a 1 Julie's father drives a police car.
2 Julie's mother works in an office.
3 Kay's mother works in a shop.
4 George's father drives a bus.
5 Lyn's father is a painter.

b 1 Fishermen catch fish.
2 Miners dig for coal.
3 Nurses look after people who are ill.
4 Dentists look after our teeth.
5 Artists paint pictures.

c 1 A typist uses a typewriter.
2 A painter uses a paint brush.
3 A farmer uses a plough.
4 A baker uses flour.
5 A fireman uses a hose pipe.
6 A hairdresser uses scissors.
7 A bricklayer uses bricks.

d 1 Mr Rider is a jockey.
2 Mr Flowers is a gardener.
2 Mr Field is a farmer.
4 Mr Lamb is a shepherd.
5 Mr Burns is a fireman.
6 Mr Wall is a builder.
7 Mr Stamp is a postman.
8 Mr Pound is a bank manager.

e rubber pen paper typewriter envelopes

In the park *pages 26–27*

a 1 Sara and Paul went to the park on Saturday.
2 The two boys were playing football.
3 The two girls were playing tennis.
4 The children were paddling in the first pond.
5 The ducks were on the second pond.

b 1 The children went to the park.
2 There were two boys playing football.
3 The lady threw crumbs to the ducks.
4 The two ducks ate the crumbs.
5 At last it was time to go home.

c *In Summer*
It is very warm.
There are leaves on the trees.
Children are paddling in the pond.
Some people are sunbathing.
There are lots of flowers in bloom.

In Winter
It is very cold.
The trees are bare.
The pond is frozen.
There is snow on the ground.
People are wearing coats and scarves.

d 1 We fly a kite.
2 We kick a ball.
3 We climb a tree.
4 We sail a boat.
5 We play a game.

e trees birds grass water flowers

The supermarket *pages 28–29*

a 1 Sara and Paul are in the park.
2 Mum and Dad go to the supermarket.
3 They go to the supermarket to buy things to eat.
4 Dad pushes a trolley.
5 Mum has the money.

b 1 Mum has a purse.
2 Dad has the trolley.
3 They walk round as quickly as they can.
4 The supermarket has run out of bread.
5 Mum and Dad pay the girl as soon as they have finished.

c 1 Mum and Dad go shopping but the children would rather go to the park.
2 The shop is busy and it takes time to get round.
3 They look for some bread but cannot find any.
4 Mum opens her purse and takes out the money.
5 They finish their shopping and go back home.

d 1 Sara and Paul are not with their parents.
2 Mum and Dad have gone shopping.
3 Dad pushes a trolley.
4 The money is in Mum's purse.
5 The girl sits at the desk.

e 1 True.
2 Not true.
3 True.
4 Not true.
5 True.

At the zoo *pages 30–31*

a 1 Sara and Paul went to the zoo during the holidays.
2 First of all they saw some moneys.
3 The monkeys were in a cage.
4 They saw some snakes in the reptile house.
5 In another part of the zoo they saw a young giraffe with its mother.

b 1 Sara and Paul were on holiday.
2 A zoo is a place where animals are kept.
3 There were many animals at the zoo.
4 The giraffes were standing side by side.
5 Later, the children went to the aviary where they saw some birds.

c 1 Monkeys chatter.
2 Snakes hiss.
3 Cats purr.
4 Dogs bark.
5 Lions roar.
6 Donkeys bray.
7 Horses neigh.
8 Pigs grunt.
9 Hens cluck.
10 Ducks quack.
11 Frogs croak.
12 Mice squeak.

d 1 Sara and Paul went to a zoo.
2 They saw lots of animals.
3 There were monkeys in the zoo.
4 The snakes were in the reptile house.
5 The children saw a young giraffe.

e rat goat snail weasel mink

How much can you remember? *page 32*

1 Sara and Paul go to school together.
2 They meet Mark and Julie on the way.
3 Sara and Julie are writing a story.
4 Sometimes the children go to the park.

5 The tables are in the hall.
6 The carpet is on the floor.
7 George reads his book.
8 Andy is drawing a picture.
9 I think there are two ponds in the park.
10 The children are eating their dinner.
11 Sara and Paul went to the zoo.
12 They saw two giraffes there.

13 Sara has a bicycle.
14 They went as soon as they were ready.
15 They walked to the corner where they met their friends.
16 The ducks were on the pond.

17 We say one dog but two dogs.
18 We say one bun but two buns.
19 We say one tin but two tins.
20 We say one coat but two coats.

Book 2

It is in Book 2 where the thematic approach begins in earnest. This is begun through the eyes of four of the children we met in Book 1. They are in their classroom about to begin studying farms and food and we take it from there. The idea of gleaning information from reference books is introduced at an early stage and there are exercises that cover some of the skills that are needed to do this work effectively. These will be called upon to do some of the sections that follow, but such assignments are limited in number so as to avoid making too many demands on whatever reference material is available.

Topics covered in Book 2 include farm machinery, buildings, crops and animals, together with dairy products and some items that are imported. Beverages are included. All these are dealt with at reasonable length, but there is ample scope for pupils and teachers to draw further leads from the material, working these up into a large-scale topic if desired and bringing in other activities such as art and craft. Such work would have to be discussed, identified, labelled and described and this would reinforce and expand the groundwork that is covered in Book 2.

Among the many useful books on this topic are

Farms and Farming	J. C. Gagg	Blackwell
The Farmer	I. and J. Havenhand	Ladybird
The Dairy Farmer	John Blackie	Macmillan
Farming	Frank Huggett	Black
Farms and Farm Life	G. A. Perry	Blandford
Farms and Farmers		Macdonald
I-Spy On the Farm		

Topic work *pages 2–3*

a 1 The children are in the classroom.
2 They are doing topic work about farms and food.
3 There are four children in each group.
4 The children find things out from books.
5 Lyn said 'Farmers are very important people'.
6 Paul said 'I wish I lived on a farm'.

b 1 Farmers keep pigs for their meat.
2 A tractor has four wheels.
3 The tractor is used for all sorts of work.
4 Sheep have four legs.
5 Hilly country is often best for sheep.

c 1 tractor plough
2 sty barn
3 wheat potatoes
4 pigs cows
5 apples pears

d 1 Farms are usually in open country.
2 Farmers have to get up early.
3 There is work to be done at the week-end.
4 Farmers have to go out in all kinds of weather.
5 Farm animals are sometimes called livestock.

e *Life on the Farm*

Farming is important because Britain's farms produce more than half of the nation's food. The work can be hard at times and it is important to be very fit. The weather is very important to the farmer, not only while his crops are growing, but when the time comes to gather them in. There is work to be done all the year round, but the farmer is especially busy in June (haymaking time) and in the late summer and early autumn (harvesting wheat, oats and barley). The use of machinery and automation means that more food is now produced by fewer farm workers. Most farm workers live on or near the farm and the working day is long and begins early. But the life of a farm never really stops. Cows must be milked at the week-end and on Christmas day. The farmer cannot have a day off or a holiday unless there is someone to take his place.

Using books *pages 4–5*

a 1 The children use various books to help them.
2 The books contain information and pictures about farms and food.
3 The list of contents is at the front.
4 The contents are arranged in the order in which they appear in the book.
5 The index is at the back.
6 The index is arranged in alphabetical order.

b barley ducks eggs fruit hay
milk oats pigs rice wheat

c seeds sheep straw sugar swede
cabbages calves carrots cattle cauliflowers

d Farm Machinery and How It Works
The Crops We Eat
Fish and Fishing
Farming Round the World
Fruit and Vegetables
All About Dairy Products

e

fruit	vegetables
poultry	pigs
dairy products	root crops
cattle	farm machinery
grain	fish

Farms and food *pages 6–7*

a 1 We buy most of our food from shops and supermarkets.
2 In the first place most of our food is produced by farmers.
3 Bread is made from flour.
4 The flour comes from wheat.
5 Meat and milk come from animals.
6 Milk can be made into cheese, butter, cream and ice-cream.

b 1 Cows are milked by machine.
2 We buy meat from the butcher.
3 Wheat is grown by farmers.
4 Farmers buy machines such as tractors.
5 Sheep are kept by farmers for meat and wool.

c tractor cows gates grass barn

d
1 cow
2 pig
3 sheep
4 hen
5 horse
6 mouse
7 hay
8 oats
9 pear
10 barn

e *The Country Code*

1 Guard against starting fires.
2 Be sure to fasten all gates.
3 Keep your dog under proper control. (Every year thousands of sheep are killed by marauding dogs.)
4 Keep to public footpaths. No short cuts across the middle of fields.
5 Don't damage hedges, fences or walls.
6 Don't leave litter. Take empty bags, packets, boxes and bottles back with you.
7 Don't foul water supplies (river, lakes, ponds).
8 Protect all forms of wild life–plants and animals.
9 Go carefully along country roads. When walking, keep to the right if there is no footpath.
10 Respect the life of the countryside in all its forms.

Farm machines *pages 8–9*

a
1 Horses used to be kept by farmers to help them do their work.
2 The most important machine on the farm is the tractor.
3 The tractor is important because it pulls other machines that the farmer uses, such as a plough, harrow or drill.
4 A plough turns the ground over.
5 A harrow breaks up lumps of soil.
6 A drill is used for planting seeds.

b
1 The farmer drives the tractor.
2 The tractor pulls the plough.
3 A drill plants the seeds.
4 A big machine cuts the corn.
5 The same machine separates the grain from the straw.

c
1 A tractor has four wheels.
2 The back wheels are bigger than the front.
3 The back tyres have a thick tread.
4 The thick tread helps the tyres to grip.
5 A tractor is driven by a diesel engine.

d The farmer uses a plough to turn the ground over.
The plough cuts into the ground and turns the soil over in strips.
The strips are called furrows.
Another machine is used to break up the furrows.
This makes the soil fine and level and ready for sowing.
The sowing is done by a machine called a drill.

e The big machine that cuts the wheat and threshes the grain as it goes along is called a combine harvester. As the machine is driven forward into the standing corn the crop is cut and drawn into the main body of the machine. There it is threshed so as to shake the grain out of the ears. A blast of air is blown through to get rid of the chaff. The grain then passes to a storage tank on top of the combine so that it can be passed into a trailer (drawn by a tractor) by means of an overhead chute. The load of grain is then taken to be dried and stored. Meanwhile, the straw passes through to the back of the combine where it is dropped onto the ground, ready to be picked up later by a baler. Most combine harvesters are self-propelled,–that is to say they have their own engines. They are large, complicated machines, and driving one calls for great skill and concentration. They are best suited to large fields, and for this reason hedges and fences have sometimes been taken down. Combine harvesters were first used in North America, where early models were pulled by teams of horses.
(Note: In some combines the threshed grain is delivered into bags which, when full, are dropped onto the field.)

Farm buildings *pages 10–11*

a 1 A milking parlour is a building where cows are milked.
2 Everything in the milking parlour must be clean because milk can soon be spoiled by germs.
3 The cows are milked by machine.
4 A barn is a big building with wide doors.
5 Barns are useful for storing things and keeping them dry.
6 Things such as hay and straw can be kept under the Dutch barn.

b 1 A milking parlour must be kept clean.
2 A barn has wide doors.
3 A Dutch barn has a curved roof.
4 The roof is held up by tall pillars.
5 The roof keeps the hay dry.

c 1 airy
2 germs
3 storing
4 supported
5 hay

d 1 The farmhouse is where the farmer lives.
2 A dairy is where the milk is kept.
3 A sty is where pigs are kept.
4 A loft is a room over a stable.
5 A Dutch barn has a roof, but no walls.

e stable: mainly for horses
granary: for grain or corn
shippen (or shippon): a cowshed or cattle-shed
byre: another name for a cowshed or cowhouse
cote: a place where animals are kept (as dove-cote or dove-cot, sheep-cote)

Practice pages *pages 12–13*

a 1 We were waiting for two hours.
2 There were four passengers in the car.
3 The cake was cut into four pieces.
4 'What are you doing that for?' she asked.
5 We asked a policeman for help.
6 They left school at four o'clock.
7 The plane had a crew of four.
8 I couldn't decide what to have for supper.
9 Some of the houses have four bedrooms.
10 James was blamed for breaking the window.

b (a)	ant	cat	gorilla	horse	lion
	monkey	rabbit	squirrel	tiger	zebra
(b)	baby	bird	cake	colour	flower
	football	man	money	paint	present
(c)	afternoon	boat	book	cake	dog
	doll	game	garden	lady	watch

c 1 We went to Scotland by train.
2 I called at the shop to buy a newspaper.
3 We buy some of our food from other countries.
4 The work was finished by dinner time.
5 They sat down by the river.
6 Cows can be milked by hand.
7 The meat was too dear to buy.
8 It was only by chance that I saw him.
9 The children had to buy their own books.
10 She doesn't buy many cakes.

d 1 Julie ran as fast as she could.
2 The plane landed at five o'clock.
3 We followed the tracks through the forest.
4 The dog chased the cat across the lawn.
5 He poured the milk into a jug.
6 She chopped the meat into small pieces.
7 Mrs Brown sharpened the pencils.
8 The horses galloped round the field.
9 I called out but nobody seemed to hear.
10 Tim whispered so that no one else could hear.

e 1 We walked slowly up the steep hill.
2 It was difficult to dig the hard ground.
3 Mother had a new coat for her birthday.
4 The old man was very tired.
5 The pirates dug a deep hole.
6 She had a hot bath and went to bed.
7 There was an oval mirror on the wall.
8 Some of the young animals were quite tame.
9 It can be dangerous to swim in the river.
10 Some of the currents are very strong.

Cereals *pages 14–15*

a 1 By cereals, a farmer means different kinds of grasses such as wheat, maize, oats, barley and rice.
2 The seeds are called grains.
3 The seeds are sometimes ground into flour.
4 The most important cereals are rice, wheat and maize.
5 Rice is the most important cereal in China, India and Japan.
6 If there were no cereals many people would starve.

b flour farmer rice grasses breakfast

c 1 Maize is sometimes called Indian corn.
2 We got lost in the maze.
3 The daisy is a small flower.
4 The seeds are ground into flour.
5 The flour is made into bread.
6 A maid opened the door.
7 We watched the serial on television.
8 Cereal crops are sometimes called grain crops.
9 A farmer must know the right time to sow his seeds.
10 If there were no cereals people would go hungry.

d 1 Barley is used in the making of beer.
2 Oats can be made into porridge.
3 Rice grows best in flooded fields.
4 Grains of maize grow on a cob.
5 Wheat flour makes the best bread.

e

bread	rolls	cakes	pancakes
buns	scones	tarts	tea cakes
pies	muffins	biscuits	choux pastry
pikelets	crumpets	puddings	short pastry
flapjacks	batter	sauces	flaky pastry
cookies	dumplings	shortbread	puff pastry
macaroni	spaghetti	macaroons	sausage rolls

(The pupil is asked to say which he or she likes best.)

Cows *pages 16–17*

a 1 We can make leather from the skins of cows.
2 In summer cows eat grass.
3 In winter cows eat hay and cattle food.
4 Cows are sometimes given extra food to help them give more milk.
5 When the cow is grazing it swallows its food quickly.
6 When the cow is at rest the food is brought back to the mouth and then well chewed before being swallowed again.

b 1 Cows and bulls have all come from wild cattle.
2 Some cows have horns.
3 A cow's stomach has four parts.
4 A cow usually has one young at a time.
5 India has a lot of cattle.

c 1 A young cow is called a calf.
2 A young cat is called a kitten.
3 A young duck is called a duckling.
4 A young hen is called a chicken.
5 A young dog is called a pup.
6 A young pig is called a piglet.
7 A young sheep is called a lamb.
8 A young horse is called a foal.
9 A young fox is called a cub.
10 A young goat is called a kid.

d 1 Cows are milked every day.
2 They are usually milked by machine.
3 Cream is made from milk.
4 In summer the cows are mostly outside.
5 Meat from cows is called beef.

e

Dairy cattle	*Beef cattle*	*Dual purpose*
Ayrshire	Highland	Redpoll
British Friesian	Hereford	Lincoln Red Shorthorn
Jersey	Aberdeen Angus	South Devon
Guernsey	Beef Shorthorn	Welsh Black
Kerry	Galloway	Dairy Shorthorn*

* listed under Dairy Cattle in some books

Pigs *pages 18–19*

a 1 Pigs are kept chiefly for their meat, but we also use the skin, bristles, bones and fat.
2 The mother pig is called a sow.
3 She has her first litter when she is about a year old.
4 She has two litters a year.
5 There are about 8–10 piglets in each litter.
6 They are usually fed twice a day.

b 1 A litter of kittens.
2 A flock of sheep.
3 A herd of cattle.
4 A pack of wolves.
5 A swarm of bees.
6 A troop of monkeys.

c 1 The female pig is called a sow.
2 The male pig is called a boar.
3 Young pigs are called piglets.
4 The fat of pigs is made into lard.
5 The skin of pigs is made into leather.
6 The pig's bristles are used for brushes.

d 1 Pigs must be kept warm and dry.
2 Pigs will eat all sorts of things.
3 Wild boars can be dangerous.
4 Farm pigs are fat animals.
5 Pigs are sometimes called swine.

e 1 Fresh meat from a pig is called pork.
2 Cured and smoked meat from the upper part of a pig's back leg is called ham.
3 Cured and smoked meat from the back and sides of a pig is called bacon.
Other types of meat from pigs:
sausages, luncheon meat, pork pies

Sheep *pages 20–21*

a 1 Farmers keep sheep for their meat and their wool.
2 The wool is made into things that we wear and things we use in the home.
3 Merino sheep give the best wool.
4 There are lots of Merino sheep in Australia.
5 Wet ground is not good for sheep.
6 Sheep are often kept on hills and moors.

b 1 blankets 2 carpets 3 hills
4 plants 5 biscuits 6 shops
7 farmers 8 animals
9 pigs 10 cows

c Young sheep are called lambs. They are born at the end of winter or early in spring. At first they drink their mother's milk but later on they eat grass. From time to time the sheep are dipped to keep them free of insects. Shearing is done in early summer. The wool is cut with electric shears and is taken off in one piece. Each piece is called a fleece.

d 1 The meat from sheep is called mutton.
2 Meat from a young sheep is called lamb.
3 Fresh meat from a pig is called pork.
4 Meat from cows is called beef.
5 Meat from a calf is called veal.

e 1 Clothes, blankets, carpets, rugs, felt
2 In Britain farmers or shepherds use sheep dogs, such as collies, to help them control and herd the sheep. In some places–hills farms, for example, where the sheep may be widely scattered–a man on his own could not gather his flock so he will work with one or two dogs. Sheep dogs have to be specially trained. They are essentially working dogs and are not regarded as pets.
3 Cheviot, Herdwick, Shetland, Scottish Blackface, Welsh Mountain, Border Leicester, Kent or Romney Marsh, Lincoln Longwool, South Devon, Hampshire Down, Oxford Down, Southdown.

Poultry *pages 22–23*

a 1 The word poultry means hens, ducks, geese and turkeys.
2 These birds are kept for meat and for the eggs they lay.
3 Hens begin to lay when they are about six months old.
4 A hen will lay about 300 eggs a year.
5 Free range hens are kept in the open.
6 Battery hens are kept indoors in cages.

b 1 Hens, ducks, geese and turkeys lay eggs.
2 Cereals grown by farmers include wheat, maize, barley and oats.
3 Carrots, parsnips, turnips and sugar beet are sometimes called root crops.
4 Sheep are raised in Australia, New Zealand, Britain and many other countries.
5 Butchers sell mutton, lamb, beef and pork.

c *Ducks*:
Ducks quack.
The male bird is called a drake.
The female bird is called a duck.
A young duck is called a duckling.
Geese:
Geese cackle.
The male bird is called a gander.
The female bird is called a goose.
A young goose is called a gosling.

d 1 Ducks have webbed feet.
2 Some hens are a browny-red colour.
3 Chickens are hatched from eggs.
4 Eggs can be hatched in incubators.
5 Chickens hatch from eggs in about three weeks.
6 Farmyard geese make good watchdogs.
7 The first turkeys came from America.
8 Turkeys must be looked after carefully.
9 The male turkey makes a gobbling noise.
10 Wild turkeys are good fliers.

e 1 Ways of cooking and using eggs:
hard boiled, boiled, fried, poached, scrambled;
in omelets, meringues, custard, pancakes, cakes, Yorkshire pudding, lemon cheese, mayonnaise, advocaat.
2 It is less common nowadays to find poultry on 'free range' where, during the day, they move about in the open, scratching and foraging. Instead, many birds are kept indoors all the time in sheds where artificial lighting and controlled temperature can compensate for the shorter, darker, colder days of

winter and stimulate the birds to go on laying. (In the wild the birds would lay fewer eggs in winter.) Each bird is in its own cage, the cages being arranged in rows and tiers down the sides of the shed. Food and water are constantly provided and in some hen houses there are automatic cleaning and egg-gathering mechanisms.

The reason for keeping hens in battery houses, as they are called, is to keep them under controlled conditions (free from disease, bad weather and other hazards) so that they lay more eggs. It may seem cruel to us because it is clearly unnatural and the hens never get any exercise.

Practice pages *pages 24–25*

a 1 carpet school farm chicken town
2 the name of a game: football
food: potato
bird: eagle
tree: oak
flower: daisy

b 1 They have finished their work.
2 Brian has gone to bed early.
3 It has been fine all morning.
4 Kay and Sandra have collected the books.
5 Sandra has dropped one of the books.
6 I didn't have enough money to buy the shoes.
7 We have won all our matches so far.
8 Everyone in the team has played well.
9 The men have been working hard.
10 One of the men has cut the grass.

c 1 A herd of elephants.
2 A flock of birds.
3 A herd of pigs.
4 A shoal of fish.
5 A brood of chicks.
6 A school of whales.

d 1 classrooms 2 tractors 3 kittens 4 windows 5 gardens
6 books 7 flowers 8 wheels 9 carrots 10 buildings

e 1 The four children were called Jane, Anne, Mark and Steven.
2 The children were running, jumping, climbing and swinging.
3 Two, four, six, eight and ten are even numbers.
4 Cricket, football, hockey, tennis and golf are popular games.
5 Lamb, cub, calf, kitten and pup are names of young animals.
6 We saw lions, tigers, monkeys and giraffes at the zoo.
7 There were blackbirds, thrushes, sparrows and starlings on the lawn.

8 We go to school on Monday, Tuesday, Wednesday, Thursday and Friday.
9 Behind the school they are building houses, flats, bungalows and shops.
10 Mercury, Venus, Mars, Jupiter and Neptune are names of planets.

f birds The Seasons cereals fish Egypt
fruit South America insects musical instruments weather

Tea *pages 26–27*

a 1 Tea is made from the leaves of a small bush.
2 The bushes are grown on the hillsides in India, Sri Lanka and China.
3 The bushes need a hot climate where there is plenty of rain.
4 Tea bushes are usually grown from cuttings.
5 The bushes are cut back so that they do not grow too tall.
6 The young leaves make the best tea.

b 1 bushes 2 wishes 3 brushes 4 crashes 5 thrushes
6 ranches 7 churches 8 matches 9 catches 10 trenches

c 1 Cultivated means grown.
2 Expensive means costly.
3 Pruned means trimmed.
4 Blended means mixed.
5 Beverage means drink.

d First of all, you should warm the tea pot.
Then put the tea leaves in the pot.
Next, boiling water is poured onto the leaves.
Having made the tea, let it stand for a few minutes.
After a few minutes the tea is ready to be poured.

e The name of the drink is coffee and the trees grow (chiefly) in Brazil, Colombia, the Ivory Coast, Angola, Mexico, Uganda and Indonesia.

Cocoa and chocolate *pages 28–29*

a 1 Cocoa is made from the seeds or beans of the cacao tree.
2 Cacao trees grow in tropical countries such as Ghana.
3 The cocoa pods begin to grow when the trees are about four or five years old.
4 The pods grow on the tree trunk as well as on the branches.
5 When the pods are ripe they are cut down and split open.
6 The seed or beans are inside the pods.

b 1 Noun
  2 Verb
  3 Adjective
  4 Adjective
  5 Noun
  6 Verb

c 1 tropical
  2 harvested
  3 ripe
  4 ground
  5 additional

d The Spaniards were the first Europeans to discover a drink made from cocoa beans. This happened over 400 years ago when the Spaniards conquered Mexico. At first they kept their discovery a secret, but at last other countries got to know about it. The first 'cocoa house' was opened in London in 1657. The first cocoa factory was opened in Bristol in 1728.

e cocoa, drinking chocolate, milk chocolate, plain chocolate, chocolate with various fillings and flavours, chocolate liqueurs, Easter eggs, chocolate biscuits, chocolate cake (gateau, roll, log, eclairs, sponge), chocolate sauce, chocolate icing, chocolate-flavoured blancmange, chocolate mousse
(The pupil is asked to name a favourite.)

Cream and butter *pages 30–31*

a 1 The separator separates the cream from the rest of the milk.
  2 Cream is heated and cooled quickly to make it safe to eat.
  3 The cream is churned in big revolving drums.
  4 When the cream is churned small pieces of butter begin to form, floating about in a liquid.
  5 The liquid is called buttermilk.
  6 The buttermilk is drained off.

b 1 The milk arrives at the creamery.
  2 The milk is tested for quality.
  3 The milk is then taken to the separator.
  4 The separator takes the cream from the rest of the milk.
  5 Machines fill cartons or bottles with cream.

c Butter is a very rich food because it contains a lot of fat. This gives us energy and helps to keep us warm. Farmers used to churn butter by hand but the work is now done by machines in factories. Everything that is used is kept very clean.

d 1 separator
2 churned
3 revolving
4 solid
5 mass

e To-day butter is used mainly as a spread on such things as bread, toast, scones, rolls, pikelets, crumpets, muffins and biscuits. It is also used in the making of some cakes and puddings and is sometimes served with or mixed with vegetables. It can also be used for frying.

Margarine *pages 32–33*

a 1 Margarine is made from various edible oils and fats.
2 Most of the oils come from coconuts, ground-nuts and palm kernels.
3 Milk, salt and vitamins are added to the oily mixture.
4 The first margarine was made in France.
5 The first margarine was white.
6 Margarine is coloured so that it looks like butter.

b 1 The sea was calm after the storm.
2 Paul wrote a letter to his uncle.
3 I went to bed at half past nine.
4 A calf is a young cow.
5 Kay fell and hurt her wrist.
6 The driver took the wrong turning.

c 1 substitute
2 edible
3 smooth
4 vitamins
5 sets

d 1 Margarine can be used instead of butter.
2 The oils in margarine come mostly from plants.
3 Ground-nuts are sometimes called pea-nuts.
4 Margarine has been known for over one hundred years.
5 Margarine looks like butter.

e Examples of words (underlined) used in sentences. Other answers are possible.
Sweets and snacks are no <u>substitute</u> for proper meals.
Not all mushrooms are <u>edible</u>.
Most foods <u>contain</u> vitamins.
Pastry is a <u>mixture</u> of flour, fat, salt and water.
<u>Nowadays</u> most people cook by gas or electricity.

Cheese *pages 34–35*

a 1 Cheese is made from the curd of milk.
2 Milk from cows is commonly used.
3 The watery part of milk is called whey.
4 The more solid part of milk is called curd.
5 To make a hard cheese more of the whey is squeezed out.
6 Different cheeses often get their names after the places where they were first made.

b 1 The watery part of the milk is poured off.
2 There are about 400 different kinds of cheeses.
3 Some cheeses have a number of holes in them.
4 I had a piece of cheese and a biscuit.
5 I cut the rind off and threw it away.

c Cheese is a very nourishing food. It contains a lot of vitamin A which we need for growth and general good health. Cheese has been made for thousands of years. It used to be made in the home by anyone who kept a cow or a goat. Nowadays it is made in larger quantities in factories.

d 1 Cheese is made mainly from cows' milk but other kinds of milk can be used.
2 Cottage cheese does not keep well and should be eaten straight away.
3 Cheese is a good food but it is sometimes difficult to digest.
4 There are many different kinds of cheese and each has its own flavour.
5 Cheese 'spread' is easy to spread but may not have as much food value as cheese.

e 1 Cheddar, Cheshire, Double Gloucester, Blue Vinney, Caerphilly, Leicester, Stilton, Wensleydale, Brie, Camembert, Danish Blue, Edam, Gorgonzola, Gruyère, Limburger, Parmesan, Roquefort
2 Welsh rabbit (or, less correctly, Welsh rarebit)

Practice pages *pages 36–37*

a

1 dishes	2 watches	3 guesses	4 benches	5 princesses
6 classes	7 boxes	8 buses	9 dresses	10 branches
11 witches	12 glasses	13 crosses	14 dashes	15 stitches
16 flashes	17 finches	18 foxes	19 passes	20 addresses

b

1 noun	6 verb
2 adjective	7 noun
3 verb	8 adjective

4 verb 9 adjective
5 noun 10 adjective

c 1 Paul goes to school with Sara.
2 Mark sat between Kay and Lyn.
3 George dived into the water.
4 Jam is made from fruit.
5 The cows were taken to the milking parlour.
6 The ball went through the window.
7 I looked closely at the time-table.
8 The cat jumped over the wall.
9 There was a cellar under the kitchen.
10 The audience was quiet during the concert.

d 1 The yellow part of an egg is called the yolk.
2 The wren is a small, brown bird.
3 A list of contents was on the wrapper.
4 She held it in the palm of her hand.
5 The writing was difficult to read.
6 The singer sang a number of folk songs.
7 The teacher took her class for a walk.
8 The wreck was dangerous to other ships.
9 We watched the wrestling on television.
10 We were told to stop talking.

e 1 Mother ordered two bottles of milk.
2 The plane took off at ten o'clock.
3 The young bird fell out of the nest.
4 The notice said KEEP OFF THE GRASS.
5 One of the players was hurt.
6 Another was ordered off by the referee.
7 I enjoy a cup of tea.
8 We sat by the side of the river.
9 The battleship was called 'Duke of York'.
10 Her hat was blown off by the wind.

f 1 The horses are in the stable.
2 John is cleaning his bicycle.
3 'Who is that girl?' asked Simon.
4 There are some fine castles in Wales.
5 The crew returned to their ship.
6 The Queen waved to the crowd.
7 I will write as soon as I get there.
8 The grass has not been cut.
9 He didn't know where to look.
10 We were waiting at the gate.

Fruit *pages 38–39*

a 1 'Cooking' apples need lots of sugar because they may be rather sour.
2 We can't grow all kinds of fruit in Britain because it is often too cold.
3 Oranges and bananas need a hot climate.
4 Unripe bananas are green.
5 Bananas are hung in warm rooms to make them turn ripe.
6 Bananas have been known in Britain since about 1900.

b 1 The grapefruit has a thick skin.
2 Strawberries are soft when ripe.
3 Bananas grow on tall plants.
4 The cherry has a smooth skin.
5 The mandarin is a small orange.

c

Citrus fruits	*Soft fruits*
Orange	Strawberry
Lemon	Raspberry
Lime	Blackcurrant
Tangerine	Gooseberry
Grapefruit	Bilberry

d 1 Apples
2 Strawberries
3 Gooseberries
4 Bananas
5 Dates

e 1 Fruit: eaten raw, eaten cooked, stewed, compot or compote, frozen, dried, fool, mousse, crystallized, purée, in drinks, as flavouring, trifle, tinned, jam, jelly, marmalade, lemon cheese, sauce, tarts, pies, with meat and fish (e.g. pineapple or peach with ham, orange with duck, lemon with fish), in cakes, buns, biscuits, sweets, chocolate etc.
2 currant, damson, tangerine

Vegetables *pages 40–41*

a 1 Vegetables are plants grown for food.
2 The underground stems of the potato plant are called tubers.
3 The darker outside cabbage leaves have the best food value.
4 The inner leaves of cabbages are paler because sunlight has not reached them.
5 Potatoes came from South America.
6 Radishes were first grown in Egypt.

b 1 Cows produce milk to feed their calves.
2 I bought two loaves.
3 The trees had begun to shed their leaves.
4 The books were on the shelves.
5 The cake was divided into halves.

c Yams are vegetables. They are swollen underground stems something like potatoes. Yams are eaten in place of potatoes in many tropical countries. They contain a lot of starch. Before being eaten they have to be boiled.

d 1 We eat the seeds of the broad bean plant.
2 We eat the leaves of cabbages.
3 We eat the root of the carrot.
4 We eat the flower of the cauliflower.
5 We eat the stalk of celery.
6 We eat the root of the parsnip.
7 We eat the seeds of the pea plant.
8 We eat the underground stem of the potato plant.
9 We eat the root of the radish.
10 We eat the buds of the Brussels sprouts.

e 1 leek kale lentil swede yam
2 **Broccoli**
is a variety of cauliflower that produces thick clusters of flower buds. The buds and stems are eaten.

Spinach
is a green vegetable whose juicy leaves can be eaten either raw or cooked. It is rich in vitamins A and C.

Celery
is a plant whose stalks can be eaten raw or cooked. The stalks of common celery are blanched or whitened by being kept away from the light.

Artichoke
The name is used for quite different plants, different parts of which are eaten. The flower buds of the globe artichoke are eaten. In the case of the Jerusalem artichoke it is the underground tubers that are used as food.

Asparagus
The parts that we eat are the young shoots or stems that appear in the spring. These are cut for the table before beginning to branch out.

Sugar *pages 42–43*

a 1 Sugar is made from sugar cane or sugar beet.
2 Sugar cane grows in tropical countries.
3 Sugar cane is a kind of grass with a tall thick stem.
4 The pieces of cane are crushed to get the juice out.
5 Sugar beet grows in colder countries such as Britain.
6 It has a big, white root that contains the sugar.

b 1 The words tall, thick and big are adjectives.
2 The words juice, factory and piece are nouns.
3 The words crushed, heated and sliced are verbs.

c 1 We use sugar to sweeten our food.
2 Sugar cane is grown in Cuba and Jamaica.
3 New sugar cane plants are grown from cuttings.
4 When the cane is ripe it is cut down.
5 The work can be done by hand or by machine.

d 1 In less than a year the cane grows tall.
2 The sugar is made from a juice which is inside the stem.
3 The cane is cut into pieces at the factory.
4 In order to get the juice out the pieces are crushed.
5 In order to get the juice out the roots are sliced and put in water.

e 1 Hundreds of years ago, when there was no sugar in Britain, people used honey as a sweetener.
2 The main producers of cane sugar are Jamaica, Cuba, Brazil, Hawaii, India and Pakistan.
3 The main producers of sugar beet are Russia, U.S.A., France, Poland, West Germany and Italy.

Rice *pages 44–45*

a 1 Rice is grown in flooded fields in warm countries.
2 The flooded fields are called paddy fields.
3 The seeds are usually sown in nursery beds.
4 When the seedlings have grown a little they are planted out in the fields.
5 The paddy fields are drained when the rice is harvested.
6 The plants are threshed to remove the grains.

b 1 India and China grow a lot of rice.
2 Rice grows best in wet fields.
3 The grain ripens fairly quickly.
4 When the plants ripen they are harvested.

5 Rice swells when it is cooked.
6 The grains swell because they soak up moisture.

c 1 nursery
2 seedlings
3 threshed
4 remove
5 starve

d 1 The seedlings are planted out in the fields when they have grown a little.
2 The paddy fields are drained when the rice is harvested.
3 In order to remove the grains the plants are threshed.
4 Rice is the most important crop in some countries of the world.
5 Many people would starve without it.

e First of all wash the rice and put it in a basin.
Add sugar to taste.
Pour milk onto the rice and sugar.
Place in a moderate oven for about 3 hours.

The result would be rice pudding.

Fish *pages 46–47*

a 1 There are over 20,000 different kinds of fish.
2 Cod are found in the North Atlantic and North Pacific oceans.
3 Cod feed on the sea bed.
4 Trawlers catch cod by dragging their nets along the sea bed.
5 The plaice is a flat fish.
6 Herrings feed near the surface.

b 1 Cod is important to us as a food.
2 Mackerel, too, are good to eat.
3 A fish swims by waving its tail from side to side.
4 Some countries catch too many fish.
5 The haddock is similar to the cod.

c 1 Salmon are delicious to eat.
Delicious means tasty.
2 Salmon lay eggs in a depression in the river bed.
Depression means hollow.
3 Young salmon remain in their river for about two years.
Remain means stay.
4 Salmon often make enormous leaps to get up rapids.
Enormous means very large.
5 The salmon are exhausted when they reach the spawning grounds.
Exhausted means tired out.

d 1 In order to lay their eggs salmon swim up rivers.
2 After several weeks the young salmon hatch out.
3 The young salmon swim down to the sea after about two years.
4 The salmon return to their rivers a few years later.
5 While swimming upstream they may have to leap up waterfalls.

e 1 Kippers are herrings that have been split, gutted and smoked.
Bloaters are ungutted herrings that have been salted and partially dried.
2 crab, oyster, whelk
lobster, cockle, periwinkle
prawn, mussel
shrimp

Practice page *page 48*

a 1 full 2 open 3 sharp 4 late 5 strong
6 wet 7 rich 8 old 9 hot 10 thin

b 1 wolves 2 thieves 3 knives 4 wives 5 lives

c 1 adjective
2 adjective
3 verb
4 noun
5 noun

d 1 The man brings the milk at eight o'clock.
2 The men bring the milk at eight o'clock.
3 One of the girls is painting a picture.
4 The cat sits on the rug.
5 The cats sit on the rug.

Book 3

The theme of Book 3 is The Seashore. No one in Britain is much more than about 70 miles from the sea and most people visit some part of our long and varied coastline at some time in their lives. Even the opportunities for worldwide travel have not diminished the appeal of a visit to the beach, while the sea itself has always played an important part in our outlook and history.

Beginning with a brief description of some typical beaches Book 3 goes on to cover many important topics associated with the coast–erosion and deposition, treasure hunting, defence, safety and smuggling. The second half of the book describes many of the forms of life to be found on or near the coast–crustaceans, molluscs, starfish, jellyfish, mammals, birds and fish. The many exercises drawn from this material not only expand the pupils' knowledge of English but also further their awareness and appreciation of the subject matter involved.

The following books cover various aspects of this topic:

The Seashore	Alison Ross	Blackwell
Caves	Frances Wilkins	Blackwell
Lifeboats and Lifeboatmen	E. G. Jerrome	Blackwell
Lighthouses, Lightships and Buoys	E. G. Jerrome	Blackwell
Seashore	Ian Murray	Black
The Seashore	Alfred Leutscher	Watts
I-Spy At the Seaside		
Sea and Shore (Poems and Pictures)	Dennis Saunders and Terry Williams	Evans
Honest Rogues	Harry T. Sutton	Batsford-Heritage
Skeleton Coast	Harry T. Sutton	Batsford-Heritage
Sea and Seashore (The Young Scientist Investigates series)	Terry Jennings	O.U.P.

These provide valuable information for completing some of the assignments and developing the theme further. They include illustrations that show what scope there is for enterprising work in art and craft, some of which could be built up into class friezes or displays on walls and tables.

Beaches *pages 2–3*

a 1 Britain has a long and varied coastline.
2 The rock walls are called cliffs.
3 Wide, level, muddy beaches are called mudflats.
4 Holidaymakers usually like a sandy beach that slopes gently down to the water.
5 Sand is made of tiny grains of hard rock.
6 The rocks have been broken up by the pounding of the sea.
7 Sand is usually reddish-yellow, pale yellow or pale brown.

b 1 cliffs 2 muffs 3 cuffs 4 puffs 5 chiffchaffs
6 ruffs 7 roofs 8 chiefs 9 reefs 10 proofs

c 1 island
2 boulders
3 shingle
4 particles
5 pounding

d On some of our coasts there are piles of sand that are called sand dunes. They consist of various mounds and ridges of sand that has been blown inland by the wind. The soft, dry sand first piles up against small plants or tufts of grass and then each pile gets bigger as more and more sand is blown from the beach. After a time the dunes get higher and higher and move further inland, so that fields, streams and even buildings may be buried by the sand.

e The pupil is asked to write about the kind of beach where he/she would like to spend a holiday. Various answers are possible.

The changing coastline *pages 4–5*

a 1 We hardly notice that the coastline is changing because it happens so slowly.
2 There are many villages now covered by the sea off one stretch of the Yorkshire coast.
3 Lyonnesse is an imaginary land.
4 Lyonnesse was said to be somewhere off the coast of Land's End.
5 It is said that King Arthur fought a battle there.
6 It is said that only the tops of the hills can still be seen.
7 The name of the islands near Land's End is Scilly Isles.

b 1 changing 2 driving 3 hiding 4 living
5 hoping 6 riding 7 baking 8 facing
9 saving 10 loving 11 beating 12 wearing
13 waiting 14 sleeping 15 counting 16 playing
17 drawing 18 raining 19 watching 20 listening

c 1 gradually
2 relics
3 submerged
4 legendary.
5 visible

d The first picture shows the land sloping down to the sea. Waves beat against this and part of the coast breaks off.
This illustration shows the cliff face that has been formed. The dotted line shows the old shape of the land.
Here we can see how the waves then wear away the base of the cliff. In time, part of the cliff face falls down.
This picture shows the new cliff face, further inland than the old one.

e 1 The White Cliffs of Dover. They are made of chalk. Other kinds of rock that cliffs are made of include granite, limestone, sandstone, basalt and shale.
2 The amount of land in the world isn't getting less because, although some of it is being worn away from some parts of the coastline, in others it is being washed ashore, gradually building up the area of land in those parts.
3 Birds that nest on cliffs include cormorant, shag, razorbill, gannet, guillemot, puffin, herring gull and kittiwake. Some (e.g. razorbill and guillemot) hardly make a nest at all; others use mainly grass and seaweed. Puffins nest in holes or burrows. All these birds eat mainly fish, most of them being expert divers and swimmers. Crustaceans, molluscs and worms are also eaten, while herring gulls are fond of scraps, eggs and grubs unearthed by the farmer's plough. Large numbers of these birds nesting together are called colonies.

Caves *pages 6–7*

a 1 Sea caves are formed by the action of the waves pounding against a cliff.
2 The cracks are called faults.
3 As the waves go on beating against the rock the cracks get deeper and wider.
4 The action of the air inside a crack may also help to make it bigger.
5 As the air is trapped it expands.
6 A blowhole is a hole in the roof of a cave.
7 At high tide the floor of a cave may be awash.

b 1 The fishing boats put out to sea.
2 I could see the waves breaking over the rocks.
3 The whole of the treasure was lost.
4 There was a hole in the boat.
5 The ropes were tied together.
6 The beach was covered at high tide.

c Descriptions to fit the four pictures on page 7 of the pupil's book.
The first picture shows a cave on one side of a cliff that juts out into the sea. There is a similar cave at the other side of the cliff that we cannot see.
The second picture shows what happens when the action of the sea has made both caves bigger until they join to make an arch or bridge over the water.
The third picture shows what happens when the top of the bridge falls in, leaving a stack or pillar of rock standing on its own.
The fourth picture shows what happens when the rocky pillar or islet has been worn down almost to the level of the sea. A rocky platform of this kind is sometimes called a stump.

d The men were called smugglers and they tried to bring such things as tea, spirits, silk and tobacco into the country without paying any customs duties on them. The smugglers sometimes used caves for storing contraband (smuggled goods) until they could safely dispose of it. They would be most active at night and at times when the tides were in their favour for landing goods on lonely beaches. Officers of the Customs and Excise service not only had the task of collecting duties but also that of trying to stamp out smuggling. They were supported from time to time by various bodies, such as Riding Officers and a Preventive Water Guard. There were also Revenue cruisers patrolling the coast. The formation of the Coastguard in 1822 did much to cut down smuggling. Nowadays it is carried on in rather different ways and it is unlikely that anyone would use caves for keeping contraband.

e The cave is called Fingal's Cave and it is on the Isle of Staffa in the Inner Hebrides. The overture Fingal's Cave was written by Felix Mendelssohn. The cave is said to take its name from an Irish giant called Fingal. The cave is about 70 metres long and 20 metres high. The floor, walls and roof are made of a black rock called basalt and look as if they had been carved into huge five-sided and six-sided pillars.

Treasure hunting *pages 8–9*

a 1 It is best to look for things at low tide because more of the beach is uncovered then.
2 The sort of treasure that people look for includes bullion, coins and jewellery.
3 Bullion is gold and silver not yet made into coins.
4 Most of the treasure has come from ships that sank near the coast long ago.
5 A good place to look for treasure is near a rocky coast that was dangerous to the old sailing ships.
6 The kind of stones that people look for include jasper, agate and amber.
7 A good time to look for stones and pebbles is after a storm.

b 1 There were several beech trees in the forest.
2 The children were playing on the beach.
3 By mid-day the sun was almost directly overhead.
4 Mr Roberts and his son were on holiday.
5 The plaice is a kind of flat fish.
6 Jane put the money in a safe place.

c Amber is a kind of gum that has become very hard. It is clear enough to let light through but it is not transparent. Amber is brownish-yellow in colour and is often used as an ornament. Pieces of amber are sometimes washed up on the coast and some of them may be valuable. One large piece found on a Norfolk beach was sold for £3000.

d The two reasons why the coin must have been a fake are:
1 There were no Roman Emperors in 55 B.C.
4 In 55 B.C. no one knew that Christ would appear 55 years later.

e 1 Amber is a fossil resin. It was formed from the resin of pine trees that grew millions of years ago.
2 People sometimes use metal detectors to help them detect metal objects buried in the ground.
3 Roman coins are the result of the Roman occupation of Britain A.D. 43–c. A.D. 410.
Spanish coins are from wrecks of Spanish treasure ships or ships of the Armada that were sunk or wrecked near the coast.
4 Treasure Trove means valuables (usually gold and silver in some form) found in the ground or in a building. The word 'trove' simply means found. The Treasure Trove laws are that such apparently ownerless valuables belong to the crown and their discovery should be reported to the police. The finder is usually rewarded in some way, but some or all of a reward may be forfeit if a person fails to report a discovery promptly.

Defending the coast *pages 10–11*

a 1 Dover has been called 'the gateway to England'.
2 The building of Dover castle was begun in Norman times.
3 Deal castle was built in case of invasion by France.
4 Deal castle was built in the shape of a Tudor rose.
5 Henry VIII also built the castles of Pendennis and St Mawes.
6 There was again danger of invasion by France early in the 19th century.
7 Martello towers were built in England as a defence against a possible French invasion.

b

1	shores	2	places
3	castles	4	safes
5	entrances	6	giraffes
7	bees	8	trees
9	knees	10	degrees

c 1 Dover castle was begun in Norman times and strengthened during the reign of Henry II.
2 Henry VIII expected an invasion but it did not take place.
3 In 1804 there was danger of invasion by Napoleon who had become Emperor of France.
4 Martello towers take their name from Cape Mortella which is in Corsica.

d Specimen answer. Slight variations in the wording are possible.
Martello towers are low, round towers measuring about 14 metres across. There is a gun platform on the roof and some are protected by a moat. Martello towers are named after a tower of this kind at Cape Mortella in Corsica. This tower was captured by the British in 1794, but only after great difficulty. This tower became the model for others that were built along the south and east coasts of England in 1804 as a defence against a French invasion that was threatened at that time.

e 1 No. They could be easily picked out and would be vulnerable to modern artillery or rocket attack.
2 Mines. There may be a few left round our coasts. Any found should be left undisturbed and their presence reported as soon as possible.

Practice pages *pages 12–13*

a 1 The white cliffs of Dover are a famous landmark.
2 The reefs were a danger to ships.
3 The chiefs gathered for an important meeting.
4 The sleeves were worn at the cuffs.

5 Both of the safes were locked.
6 The men were sitting with their wives.
7 I put the knives and forks on the table.
8 The music was called The March of the Elves.
9 The corn was bundled into sheaves.
10 Thieves broke into the bank last night.
11 There were two bridges across the river.
12 The pirates buried their treasure.
13 I could hear voices in the next room.
14 Some referees are very strict.
15 Manatees are large sea mammals.

b 1 coastline
2 somewhere
3 overhead
4 limestone
5 classroom
6 livestock
7 countryside
8 football
9 breakfast
10 strawberry

c 1 We were watching television at the time.
2 Stephen was drawing a picture in his book.
3 The passengers were waiting for the fog to lift.
4 I was wearing a new pair of shoes.
5 The rebels were attacking the fort.
6 We are hoping to go on holiday this year.
7 We are saving some of our pocket money.
8 The girls were hiding behind the wall.
9 Jill is inviting her friends to a party.
10 Her mother is icing a birthday cake.
11 The cashier was counting the money.
12 Father was dozing in front of the fire.
13 Mother was writing a letter.
14 Two men were pushing an old car along the road.
15 Mr Robinson is taking his dog for a walk.

d 1 The sea dashed against the rocks.
2 Tom dug a deep hole in the sand.
3 The ribbon was tied in a bow.
4 The beech tree has a smooth grey bark.
5 The sun gives us light and warmth.
6 The book was put in the wrong place.
7 Smoking was not allowed in the factory.
8 Sara got up at eight o'clock.
9 The wind blew the fence down.
10 A boar is a male pig.
11 A beet has a thick, fleshy root.

12 A berry is a fruit.
13 We were asked to be very quiet.
14 The ship set sail in the evening.
15 The rain was beating against the window.

e 1 Mounds of loose sand formed by the wind on or near the coast are called sand dunes.
2 King Arthur is associated with the legendary land of Lyonnesse.
3 A blowhole in the roof of a cave is made by the expansion of trapped air inside the cave.
4 Gold or silver not yet made into coins is called bullion.
5 Amber is a kind of gum that has become very hard.
6 Amber is brownish-yellow.
7 Amber is often used as an ornament.
8 Gold or silver coins, bullion etc. found buried in the ground are called Treasure Trove.
9 Most Martello towers were built in Sussex and Kent.
10 Martello towers got their name from Cape Mortella in Corsica.

f 1 Britain has a long coastline.
2 Dry sand has a paler colour.
3 Lyonnesse was a legendary country.
4 Most caves are not very deep.
5 It is best to look for treasure at low tide.
6 Amber is hard.
7 Amber is not transparent.
8 Deal castle was built by Henry VIII.
9 Martello towers are low and round.
10 Dover castle was built hundreds of years ago.

g 1 Sand consists of particles of rock.
2 Gradually the coastline is changing shape.
3 Large pieces of amber may be valuable.
4 Dover castle was strengthened during the reign of Henry II.
5 Some Martello towers were surrounded by a moat.

Lighthouses *pages 14–15*

a 1 Lighthouses are tall towers with a powerful light at the top.
2 Some lighthouses are built on small rocky islands, while others are built on the coast.
3 The light shines or flashes to warn ships about dangerous waters or to tell them that they are approaching land.

4 Each lighthouse has a different length of flash so that sailors will know which lighthouse it is.
5 In foggy weather most lighthouses give off fog signals as well because the light may not be visible.
6 A fog signal is a loud, booming sound, each lighthouse having a different one.
7 The radio beacon transmits radio signals to help ships find where they are.

b 1 knife
2 kneel
3 knot
4 knuckles
5 knit

c 1 powerful
2 approaching
3 visible
4 booming
5 transmits

d We cannot be sure where the first lighthouse was built, but one of the earliest stood on the island of Pharos which is near the entrance to Alexandria harbour. Built by King Ptolemy of Egypt over two thousand years ago, this lighthouse was made of stone and stood about 122–137 m high. The fire burning at the top was said to be visible over 64 km away. Considered to be one of the Seven Wonders of the ancient world, the Pharos lighthouse was damaged by storm in A.D. 793 and finally destroyed by an earthquake in the 14th century.

e 1 In places where a lighthouse cannot be built a warning light can be carried by a lightship (or light vessel) anchored in the danger area.
2 Buoys.
3 Unmanned, fully automatic lighthouses.
4

Beachy Head	Eddystone	St Catherine's
Berry Head	Hartland	South Foreland
Bishop Rock	Lizard	Start Point
Bull Point	Lowestoft	The Needles
Cromer	Portland Bill	Whitby

Coastguards *pages 16–17*

a 1 The coastguard service was formed in 1822.
2 Spirits, tea, tobacco and silk were being smuggled into the country.
3 The main work of the coastguards to-day is to watch the coast and save lives.
4 The coastguards watch for signs of bad weather and look out for ships in distress.
5 If a ship is in difficulty near the coast coastguards can shoot a rocket carrying a life-line so that people can be hauled to safety.
6 People get into difficulty on cliffs by getting stuck part way up or down.
7 Coastguards have also rescued sheep, cattle, dogs and young birds.

b 1 The coastguard service was set up to stop smuggling.
2 The men were given rewards for capturing smugglers.
3 Some coastguards were killed or wounded on duty.
4 One coastguard was thrown over a cliff by smugglers.
5 Sometimes an old Martello tower was used as a coastguard station.

c 1 prevent
2 spirits
3 haul
4 frequently
5 stranded

d 1 At first the coastguards worked mostly at night, because that was when most smuggling took place.
2 The injured boy was strapped to a stretcher and hauled to the top of the cliff.
3 The coastguards rescued seven crew members, but two others were drowned.
4 A distress signal was picked up from the yacht which had got into difficulties.
5 A helicopter went to the help of a coaster whose engine had broken down.
6 The coastguards rescued a bather who had been swept out to sea.

e 1 Beforehand, tell someone where you are going and when you expect to return.
2 Where possible get expert tuition or advice before setting out.
3 Make sure you are suitably dressed and check your equipment.
4 Don't risk being cut off by the tide.
5 Always be on the lookout for (and obey) warning signs.
6 If you're not used to climbing, begin by tackling an easy climb along a clearly-marked footpath.
7 Don't attempt a difficult climb on your own.
8 Don't risk a difficult descent just to retrieve a ball.
9 Swim within your limits.
10 Don't swim out to sea until you're tired–remember you have to get back again.
11 Don't put out to sea on an inflatable mattress or follow a ball into deep water.

12 Boating:
Go out first with an experienced sailor.
Learn about tides, currents and any local dangers to navigation before setting out.
Find out about weather conditions expected.
Don't overload the boat.
Wear a life-jacket.

Smuggling *pages 18–19*

a 1 Smuggling means bringing goods into a country or taking goods out of a country when it is against the law.
2 Smuggling is usually done to avoid paying the customs duty.
3 A great deal of smuggling went on in Britain between about 1700 and 1840.
4 The smugglers were usually fishermen or sailors.
5 Smugglers knew how to use boats, about tides and currents and the best places to land on the coast.
6 Local people often helped smugglers by unloading a cargo and hiding it quickly.
7 Smuggled goods were often hidden in cellars, farm buildings and even churches.

b 1 The smugglers were busiest in the long, dark, winter nights.
2 The coastguards were not popular with local people.
3 Many houses had cellars where smuggled goods could be hidden.
4 Some buildings had secret rooms and passages where men could hide.
5 Some of the smugglers' boats were heavily armed.

c 1 Duty is a tax on goods entering or leaving a country.
2 Tide means the rise and fall of the sea.
3 Local means living in a certain place.
4 Cellars are underground rooms or basements.
5 Contraband means smuggled goods.

d 1 The smugglers knew all sorts of tricks to help them carry on with their work.
2 Boats were disguised by carrying false names or by changing sails.
3 Some boats that belonged to smugglers had hollow masts for carrying smuggled goods.
4 Other boats had false bottoms and secret hiding places where contraband could be hidden.
5 If a cargo of contraband could not easily be hidden it was made to look like something else.

e 1 Diamonds, gold, narcotics, money, illegal immigrants. Some articles may be smuggled by air.
2 People returning from abroad are asked to say if they are bringing into the country any articles (bought abroad) on which duty should be paid. These usually include such things as watches, cameras, cigarettes, wines and spirits and perfume.

Pollution *pages 20–21*

a 1 Pollution means that things are made dirty.
2 An accident to an oil tanker can cause oil pollution.
3 If the ship is seriously damaged oil from its tanks leaks into the sea and some of it is washed ashore.
4 The biggest tankers are over 365 m long–longer than the longest passenger liner every built.
5 Oil tankers cannot stop quickly because of their great size.
6 Oil leaking from these ships can foul beaches and destroy wild life.
7 Sea-birds, fish and shell-fish have died from oil pollution.

b 1 collision 6 persuasion
2 decision 7 explosion
3 division 8 erosion
4 provision 9 conclusion
5 invasion 10 intrusion

c 1 Oil is transported in oil tankers.
Transported means carried.
2 Bigger and bigger tankers have been constructed.
Constructed means built.
3 Oil tankers have their engines placed aft.
Aft means at the back.
4 This reduces the risk of fire.
Reduces means lessens.
5 Oil in the sea is a menace to wild life.
Menace means threat.

d One of the worst cases of oil pollution happened in March, 1967. The American oil tanker TORREY CANYON was on her way to Milford Haven carrying a cargo of crude oil. Not far from Land's End she ran aground on some rocks. Oil from her damaged tanks spilled into the sea, forming a patch of oil 29 km long. Some of the oil reached the coasts of Cornwall and Devon, polluting the beaches and killing wild life. The ship was later sunk by bombing.

e 1 Detergents can be used to deal with patches of oil in the sea. Another method that has been tried is to place a 'boom' round the oil so that it can be treated before spreading further.

2 Oil has the effect of 'smothering' a bird by matting together the feathers, thus preventing them from trapping a layer of air round the body. The layer of air serves the dual purpose of enabling the bird to float and keeping it warm. Obviously the bird cannot preen itself properly when all its feathers are stuck together.

It is sometimes possible to clean an oil-covered bird but the treatment is not always successful and there may be problems about feeding birds in even temporary captivity. In any case, birds that have been cleaned and seem to have recovered should not be returned to the sea immediately. It is advisable first to place the bird in shallow water to see if it will float. It may take a little time for it to recover its natural buoyancy.

Other affected animals (e.g. seals) may die because they attempt to lick themselves clean and so slowly poison themselves.

3 Oil may reach the shore as a result of ships washing out their tanks at sea. This, of course, is illegal.

Lifeboats *pages 22–23*

a 1 Lifeboats are strong boats specially built for rescuing people at sea.
2 Lifeboats are kept at various lifeboat stations all round our coast.
3 The first real lifeboat was built in 1790.
4 The first real lifeboat was stationed at the mouth of the Tyne.
5 In 1824 an organization was set up to run all lifeboat stations and set up others.
6 The letters R.N.L.I. stand for Royal National Lifeboat Institution.
7 Lifeboats are paid for by voluntary contributions.

b 1 There are over a hundred lifeboat stations round our coast.
2 Lifeboat men depend on the money that we give.
3 It is up to us to help them as much as we can.
4 Mother gave us some money to buy flags.
5 Just beyond the harbour we saw a lifeboat station.
6 It was a great thrill for us to see the lifeboat on the last day of our holiday.

c 1 The first real lifeboat was called the 'Original'.
2 It was built by a man called Henry Greathead.
3 The 'Original' was driven by oars.
4 The boat's bow and stern were filled with cork.
5 The cork helped the boat to keep afloat.

d Lifeboats are often called out in very bad weather to help ships in distress. It is therefore important that they should be as unsinkable as possible. Nowadays lifeboats are made with lots of watertight air spaces in them. The air helps to keep the boat afloat even if the deck is awash. The latest lifeboats are 'self-righting'. This means that if they turn over they roll back upright again.

e 1 Things that lifeboats carrying include:
radar, echo-sounder
searchlight
fire extinguisher
line-throwing pistol
oil spray
loud-hailer
first-aid equipment, food and drink, 'survival bags'

2 Two methods of launching lifeboats are:
(a) down a slipway, in some cases the lifeboat being carried by its own weight;
(b) from a beach, along which it is pulled/pushed on a special carriage by a specially designed tractor.

Practice pages *pages 24–25*

a 1 I couldn't untie the knot.
2 The knife was too blunt to cut the string.
3 She began to knit a jumper.
4 We didn't know which way to go.
5 There was a loud knock on the door.
6 A knight has the title 'Sir' in front of his name.
7 I tried to knock the nail in with a hammer.
8 Lyn was the only one who knew the answer.
9 The child crawled about on its hands and knees.
10 Our knuckles are the joints in our fingers.

b 1 There is a shop at the corner which sells bread and cakes.
2 I rang the bell several times but no one came to the door.
3 I couldn't get into the house because I had forgotten my key.
4 The bridge was closed for repairs and traffic was diverted.
5 James wrote a letter to his auntie who lives in Kent.
6 David went to play with Robert whose mother works in a shop.
7 We tried to move the stone but it was too heavy for us.
8 The little boy was crying because he had lost his way.
9 We saw two girls who were fishing in a pond.
10 Many farmers grow barley which can be used to feed livestock.

c 1 The grass was too wet to cut.
2 Some of the boys were playing football.
3 By ten o'clock they were all in bed.
4 The phone was ringing but nobody answered.
5 One of the girls was climbing a rope.
6 'Where were you going last night?' asked Sandra.

d 1 After a little persuasion he agreed to do it.
2 The referee's decision was accepted by the players.
3 We heard a loud explosion.
4 The Norman invasion took place in 1066.
5 Tea was served at the conclusion of the meeting.
6 There was a collision between the PACIFIC GLORY and the ALLEGRO.

e 1 The heavy rain forced us to take shelter.
2 As soon as we were ready we set off.
3 We have our breakfast at eight o'clock.
4 Mrs Jackson gave us our tickets.
5 After a while we lost our way.
6 It took us hours to find out where we were.

f 1 The map showed where the treasure was hidden.
2 We were waiting at the station.
3 Two cars were stolen during the night.
4 I asked him where he was going.
5 The letters were posted this morning.
6 The hotel where we stayed was near the beach.
7 I didn't know where to look.
8 They were ready in good time.
9 There were mistakes on several pages.
10 No one knew where she lived.

g 1 A tall tower with a warning or guiding light at the top is called a lighthouse.
2 The island of Pharos is near the entrance to Alexandria harbour.
3 The Pharos lighthouse was built by King Ptolemy of Egypt.
4 The Pharos lighthouse was destroyed by earthquake.
5 The coastguard service was formed to prevent smuggling.
6 At first, the coastguards worked mostly at night because that was the time when most smuggling took place.
7 Contraband means smuggled goods.
8 Oil tankers have their engines placed aft (at the back).
9 The TORREY CANYON spilled her oil into the sea because her tanks were damaged when she ran aground.
10 A 'self-righting' lifeboat is one that will roll back upright again after being turned over.

h 1 The light flashes to warn ships.
2 In foggy weather, most lighthouses give off fog signals.
3 Different lighthouses have different lengths of flash.
4 Because of this, sailors know which lighthouse it is.
5 Coastguards watch for signs of bad weather.
6 Oil tankers take a long time to stop.
7 Oil from wrecked tankers leaks into the sea.
8 The oil spoils our beaches and kills wild life.
9 Lifeboats go out in all kinds of weather.
10 Buying flags helps to buy more lifeboats.

Life on the seashore *pages 26–27*

a 1 Crabs are found in rock pools or under stones or seaweed.
2 Limpets and mussels spend much of their time attached to rocks.
3 Sea anemones are animals.
4 Winkles are snails.
5 Creatures of the sandy shore are harder to find because they burrow in the sand.
6 Sandhoppers, cockles and razor shells can bury themselves in the sand.
7 Starfish are usually found on the lower shore.

b 1 The common mussel is often found in estuaries.
2 Mussels can close their shells by using a strong muscle.
3 The razor shell can bury itself very quickly.
4 A berry is a kind of fruit.
5 We walked across the shore when the tide was out.
6 I wasn't sure that I could find the way.

c 1 discovered
2 inhabit
3 attached
4 resemble
5 burrow

d Rock pools are formed when pools of sea water are left behind on the shore every time the tide goes out. They are natural aquariums and may contain many different creatures. Some of these live there all the time but others move about. We may not be able to see all the creatures in a rock pool because some of them hide among seaweed or under stones. Pools with the most hiding places are the ones that most creatures like. On a hot day some of the water will evaporate, but each fresh tide brings more water into the pool.

e 1 The Splash Zone
2 The Upper Shore
3 The Lower Shore
4 The Middle Shore

Crabs *pages 28–29*

a 1 True crabs are protected by a hard shell.
2 The abdomen and tail of the hermit crab are soft.
3 To protect itself the hermit crab looks for the empty shell of a sea snail or whelk.
4 If the shell is suitable the hermit crab reverses into it.
5 As the hermit crab grows bigger it has to find a bigger shell.
6 The hermit crab has five pairs of legs.
7 Two pairs of legs are used for walking.

b 1 Hermit crabs protect themselves by inhabiting an old shell.
2 Some crabs are edible.
3 A crab casts its shell off periodically.
4 Crabs go into hiding when they are moulting.
5 This is the time when they are most vulnerable.

c 1 Crabs have ten legs.
2 Another name for pincers is claws.
3 Crabs lay thousands of eggs.
4 A crab's eyes are on short, movable stalks.
5 Crabs breathe through gills.

d 1 The hermit crab is one of our best-known crabs.
2 The hermit crab lives in a shell in order to protect its soft body.
3 Before moving in the hermit crab examines a shell carefully.
4 Wherever it goes the crab carries the shell with it.
5 By using one of its claws to act as a stopper the crab can close the 'entrance' to the shell.

e 1 Crabs belong to the class Crustacea.
2 Edible crab, Pea crab, Shore crab, Fiddler or velvet swimming crab, Masked crab, Hairy crab, Furrowed crab, Long-clawed porcelain crab, Spider crabs.
3 Crabs act as scavengers by eating dead and decaying flesh. This serves the purpose of helping to keep the sea and shore clean.

Shrimps and prawns *pages 30–31*

a 1 The common shrimp lives in shallow water where the bottom is sandy.
2 The shrimp spends much of the day buried in the sand or sheltering in an empty shell.
3 The shrimp comes out at night.
4 The shrimp eats worms and other small creatures.
5 Prawns are bigger than shrimps.
6 Prawns prefer rocky shores.
7 Prawns are most abundant during autumn.

b 1 The pirates buried the treasure.
2 I emptied the bottle and washed it out.
3 George copied the sentence into his book.
4 We studied the map carefully before setting out.
5 Ann replied to the letter as soon as she got home.

c 1 Acorn barnacles are common on rocky coasts.
2 Young barnacles can swim about.
3 Later they fix themselves to rocks, shells and piers.
4 Under water they open out so that they can feed.
5 When the tide is out they close up again.
6 There may be millions of acorn barnacles along a short stretch of shore.

d 1 The common shrimp comes out at night.
2 Common shrimps are edible.
3 Prawns and shrimps look very much alike.
4 Prawns live in shoals.
5 Prawns are particularly abundant during autumn.

e 1 Lobster.
2 Keeping marine crustaceans is difficult unless they can be kept in well-aerated sea water. Therefore it is best to look at them in their natural surroundings, disturbing these as little as possible. Any stones that are moved or turned over should be replaced as soon as possible.
Freshwater crustaceans may be a little easier to keep, but even these may not survive captivity for very long.

Whelks *pages 32–33*

a 1 The picture shows the common whelk.
2 The common whelk lives among mud and stones on the lower part of the shore.
3 The shell helps to keep it safe from enemies and rough seas.

4 The common whelk may reach a size of about 10 cm, but those found on the shore are usually smaller.
5 The common whelk eats crabs, worms and oysters, but it also eats carrion.
6 As whelks grow bigger they can enlarge their shell by adding further coils.
7 When the first young whelks hatch out they eat the rest of the eggs.

b 1 enemies 2 ladies 3 ponies 4 babies
5 factories 6 fairies 7 parties 8 entries
9 lilies 10 companies 11 gullies 12 stories
13 dairies 14 berries 14 diaries 16 sties
17 spies 18 cries 19 flies 20 injuries

c 1 spiral
2 carrion
3 enlarge
4 survive
5 emerge

d 1 The common whelk is a very familiar animal.
Familiar means well-known.
2 The shell of the common whelk has a pointed apex.
Apex means tip.
3 The whelk converts salts dissolved in the sea into a substance for making its shell.
Converts means changes.
4 The common whelk is a voracious eater.
Voracious means greedy.
5 Enormous quantities of whelks are caught.
Enormous means large.

e Limpets, top shells, periwinkles (winkles), cowries, chitons.

Razor shells *pages 34–35*

a 1 Razor shells are easy to identify because of their oblong shape.
2 The two halves are held together by means of powerful muscles.
3 Razor shells are good at burrowing into deep sand.
4 The razor shell buries itself by means of a special kind of foot which can stretch out, moving downward into the sand. The foot then pulls the shell after it and the move is repeated several times.
5 Razor shells are difficult for us to dig out because they can bury themselves so quickly.
6 Razor shells normally bury themselves when the tide goes out.
7 When the sea covers them again they come to the surface to feed.

b 1 The razor shell has a powerful foot.
2 Some crabs can inflict a painful injury.
3 We found some colourful pebbles on the beach.
4 We were careful to put back the stones.
5 The book, THE SEASHORE, was very useful.

c 1 bivalves
2 identify
3 oblong
4 powerful
5 repeated

d Cockles and mussels are bivalves. Cockles spend much of the time buried in the sand, just below the surface. When feeding they push two short tubes just above the surface. The cockle has a broad foot, using it to move about and to bury itself.
Mussels are more often seen. This is because they do not burrow, but attach themselves in large numbers to rocks or any other surface that is suitable.

e 1 Mussels, cockles, oysters, scallops, Venus shells, carpet shells, razor shells, piddocks, trough shells, gapers.
2 Each of the valves of the razor shell bears a close resemblance to the blade of an old-fashioned 'cut-throat' razor.
3 The pictures show a razor shell burying itself.

Practice pages *pages 36–37*

a 1 The hermit crab is often seen in rock pools.
2 The sea anemone looks like a flower.
3 The common shrimp comes out at night.
4 The hermit crab enters its shell tail first.
5 Crabs have five pairs of legs.
6 The shore crab eats various sea creatures.
7 The shore crab is not good to eat.
8 Sandhoppers bury themselves in the sand.
9 As a mollusc grows bigger its shell grows too.
10 Some shells are shaped like saucers.
11 The limpet's foot holds it firmly in place.
12 Many kinds of periwinkle live on the shore.
13 Cockles feed by means of two short tubes.
14 Mussels are often used as bait.
15 Bivalves have no proper head.

b 1 We hurried along because it was so cold.
2 The boy denied that he had taken the apples.
3 To get the answer I multiplied the numbers together.
4 Mr Davies applied for the post of manager.
5 The pavement dried quickly under the hot sun.
6 Everyone tried to help the unfortunate man.
7 We carried the books into the classroom.
8 The baby cried because it was hungry.
9 Mrs Miller relied on her daughter for help.
10 Sam tidied his room before going out.
11 The thief defied all attempts to capture him.
12 June worried about getting her sums right.
13 A building firm supplied us with the bricks.
14 Peter fried the eggs while Ann made the tea.
15 The king married the princess.

c 1 Some creatures hide among the seaweed.
2 Crabs are protected by their shells.
3 The hermit crab examines a shell carefully.
4 The hermit crab reverses into its shell.
5 Prawns and shrimps are similar in appearance.
6 Prawns have a saw-like 'beak' that projects between the eyes.
7 Not all kinds of periwinkle are edible.
8 The whelk's siphon enables the animal to obtain clean water.
9 Cockles and mussels are bivalves.
10 Some of the water in a rock pool will evaporate.

d 1 crabs 2 shells 3 wings 4 hinges 5 tubes
6 wishes 7 patches 8 ditches 9 torches 10 branches
11 lives 12 wolves 13 calves 14 halves 15 loaves
16 bodies 17 daisies 18 poppies 19 flies 20 hobbies

e 1 The old dog was very faithful.
2 Susan was always a cheerful girl.
3 The girls' dresses were bright and colourful.
4 A dreadful accident happened at the corner.
5 The change in wind direction was a hopeful sign.
6 Tom was successful at the second attempt.
7 The decorations were tasteful and well arranged.
8 They were brought up to be truthful and honest.
9 We were thankful that the child was safe.
10 The new medicine was a wonderful help to people.

f 1 Rock pools contain sea water.
2 Some crabs are edible.
3 Crabs have ten legs.
4 Common shrimps can be eaten.
5 Shrimps are smaller than prawns.
6 Crabs are crustaceans.
7 Whelks eat a lot of food.
8 Whelks are univalves.
9 Razor shells are bivalves.
10 Molluscs have soft bodies.

The starfish *pages 38–39*

a 1 The starfish gets its name from its shape.
2 Most starfish have five arms.
3 Starfish live mostly on the lower part of the shore.
4 The common starfish eats mainly mussels and oysters.
5 The mouth of a starfish is in the middle on the underside.
6 A starfish eats by pushing its stomach through its mouth and putting it round its food.
7 If a starfish loses an arm it can grow another.

b 1 When a mussel is tightly closed it's not possible for a person to open it.
2 The starfish has rows of suckers on its arms.
3 The starfish uses its suckers to open a shell.
4 When it's newly hatched the young starfish doesn't look like its parents.
5 The starfish gets its name from its shape, but it's not really a fish.

c 1 The cushion star is the smallest British starfish.
2 The sun star is a brightly-coloured starfish.
3 Brittle stars have long, thin arms.
4 The long thin arms are easily broken off.
5 The purple sun star is not always purple.

d 1 The starfish feeds on various marine creatures.
Marine means sea.
2 Starfish can be a serious menace to the oyster industry.
Menace means threat.
3 A starfish's eyes are situated at the tip of each arm.
Situated means placed.
4 The loss of an arm is no impediment to a starfish.
Impediment means hindrance.
5 The starfish is appropriately named because of its shape.
Appropriately means suitably.

e 1 **Cushion star or starlet**
A suitable name in as much as this starfish has short, blunt, rounded arms and a comparatively large centre, but this is only a small starfish, rarely measuring more than 25 mm across, and the body is very rough to the touch.

Sun star
The sun star has more than five arms and these may be said to resemble the rays of the sun. The colour varies, but red is predominant.

Brittle star
So-called because the long thin arms are easily shed–deliberately if the creature is trapped or seized by a predator.

Spiny starfish
A suitable name because the body is covered with knobs and spines.

Scarlet starfish or blood star
Quite a suitable name, although the colour varies. Its usual colour is crimson-red or purple-red.

Burrowing starfish or sand star
Common in sandy areas. It uses its feet for burrowing into the sand. A suitable name, therefore.

2 The first picture shows a live sea-urchin, urchin being an old country word for hedgehog. The globe-shaped body is protected by soft spines. The common sea-urchin is about 10 cm across. It lives on the lower shore and eats vegetation and small animals. The mouth is underneath.
After death the spines drop off, as shown in the second picture. The remaining shell, looking rather like delicate basket-work, is made up of numerous tightly-fitting plates. An empty sea-urchin's shell is sometimes called a 'sea-egg'.

Jellyfish *pages 40–41*

a 1 Jellyfish live in the sea.
2 The body of a jellyfish is shaped like a parachute or umbrella.
3 The mouth of a jellyfish is underneath, in the middle.
4 Jellyfish eat tiny sea creatures, shrimps and young fish.
5 Jellyfish catch their prey by stinging it.
6 The four long, trailing tentacles take food to the mouth after it has been stunned.
7 Jellyfish left stranded on the beach soon dry out and die.

b 1 We were stunned by the bad news.
2 I grabbed Tom's arm to stop him falling over.
3 The money dropped through a hole in his pocket.
4 The bread was wrapped in tissue paper.
5 The bus skidded on the icy road.

c Jellyfish lay eggs, each egg becoming a tiny sea creature that swims about for a time. At this stage the young jellyfish doesn't look anything like the jellyfish that we know. Then it settles on a piece of rock or the sea bed. A mouth appears at the top end, surrounded by tentacles. As the creature grows taller, horizontal rings begin to grow round its body until it looks like a pile of tiny saucers. One by one the 'saucers' split off, beginning at the top. Each one turns over and swims away as a small jellyfish.

d 1 In spite of their name jellyfish are not fish.
2 Water is the natural element of a jellyfish.
3 The jellyfish moves gracefully in its natural element.
4 Where there are wide, sandy beaches we often find jellyfish.
5 Jellyfish dry up and die if they are left on the beach.
6 Food is taken to the mouth by means of four long, trailing tentacles.

e 1 Jellyfish move by alternately expanding and contracting their bodies. This squeezes water away from the body, causing the jellyfish to move along.
2 Jellyfish have no bone structure.
3 The Portuguese man-o'-war.
4 The jelly of a jellyfish consists almost entirely of water.

Mammals on the beach *pages 42–43*

a 1 Mammals are animals that suckle their young.
2 Foxes look for crabs and mussels.
3 The fox usually hunts at night.
4 Rabbits make their warrens in sand dunes.
5 Seals come ashore to bask and breed.
6 Seals can stay submerged for more than half an hour.
7 Two kinds of seal are seen round our coast.

b 1 A wild rabbit lives in a warren or burrow.
2 A fox's home is called a lair or an earth.
3 Hares live in a form.
4 An otter's den is called a holt.

c 1 Suckle means give their milk to.
2 Rarely means not very often.
3 Aquatic means living in water.
4 Bask means lie in the sunshine, enjoying the warmth.
5 Breed means produce young.
6 Submerged means under water.

d 1 To protect them from cold seas seals have a thick layer of blubber.
2 With the help of their front flippers seals can wriggle along on land.
3 Compared with that of the grey seal the common seal has a short nose.
4 The common seal is smaller than the grey seal.
5 An alternative name for the grey seal is the Atlantic seal.
6 Before abandoning them grey seal mothers teach their young to swim.

e Rats, hares, stoats, whales, porpoises, dolphins.

Birds *pages 44–45*

a 1 The best-known gull is the herring gull.
2 The herring gull eats worms, molluscs, scraps and other birds' eggs.
3 The herring gull opens the shell of a mollusc by dropping it from a height.
4 Herring gulls usually nest in colonies on cliff tops or ledges.
5 Herring gulls make a tangled, untidy nest.
6 The biggest gull is the great black-backed gull.
7 The great black-backed gull is about 68–76 cm long.

b 1	big	bigger	biggest
2	hot	hotter	hottest
3	fat	fatter	fattest
4	small	smaller	smallest
5	tall	taller	tallest

c 1 Gulls nest in colonies.
2 Gulls often find their way inland.
3 These birds sometimes follow the farmer's plough.
4 Some gulls breed on remote islands and rocks.
5 Black-headed gulls sometimes roost away from the coast.
6 On shore, gulls will eat garbage.
7 The darker plumage of young gulls serves as camouflage.
8 Young gulls may be attacked by predators.
9 Great black-backed gulls are easy to distinguish from other gulls.
10 The front toes of gulls are webbed.

d The knot nests in the arctic and visits Britain in winter. These birds are often seen in big flocks on the shore. They usually keep together, all facing the same way, pushing their beaks into the ground looking for molluscs, worms and crustaceans to eat. In winter these birds are grey above but lighter underneath. Young birds are browner. An adult knot is about 25 cm long.

e The name wader suggests–quite accurately–that these birds spend much of their time wading in shallow water, near the water's edge or in pools, probing the mud and sand with their beaks looking for food. Most waders have long legs and long beaks.

Oystercatcher
The oystercatcher can open oysters, but its food is more likely to be other molluscs, crustaceans, worms and insects.

Turnstone
A more suitable name, as it really does turn over stones in search for food.

Redshank
Another suitable name, as the bird derives this from its red-orange legs.

Fish *pages 46–47*

a 1 The common blenny is often found among the seaweed and stones in shallow rock pools.
2 We can identify the blennies by the long dorsal fin.
3 The word dorsal means on the back.
4 Gobies like to hid at the bottom of a pool.
5 Gobies are difficult to see because their colour often matches the background where they like to hide.
6 The lumpsucker uses its sucker to attach itself to a rock or other object.
7 Lumpsuckers eat small crustaceans, fish and worms.

b 1 The butterfly blenny has a short, blunt head.
2 The dab is commonly found in shallow, sandy bays.
3 The armed bullhead has a long, tapering body.
4 The butterfish gets its name from its slippery, slimy body.
5 Wrasses have strong, sharp teeth for crushing shells.

c Fish are vertebrates. This means that they have a backbone. They have a streamlined body, usually covered with scales. There are a number of fins on the body which are used for steering and balancing. A fish pushes itself through the water by swinging its tail from side to side. Fish breathe by taking in water through the mouth and forcing it out through the gills. When this happens the gills take oxygen from the water and get rid of carbon dioxide, a waste product.

d 1 Pipe fish have long, slim, tapering bodies.
2 The males of some pipefish have a pouch on the underside.
3 The female puts her eggs in the male pipefish's pouch.
4 After the eggs are hatched the young stay close to the male.
5 If danger threatens the young they return to the pouch for safety.

e The only venomous fish in British waters are the weevers. The spines which support the back fin have poison glands. A person stung by a weever fish (by treading on one or by handling one) should be given prompt treatment.

Practice page *page 48*

a 1 The cat was licking its paws.
2 'I think it's going to rain,' said Julie.
3 'I'll let you know when it's ready,' said the lady.
4 The sea scorpion has spines on its body.
5 The starfish gets its name from its appearance.

b 1 The stiff collar rubbed against his neck.
2 We planned to go for a long walk.
3 The blackbird hopped across the lawn.
4 The water dripped onto the step below.
5 The butcher chopped the meat with a cleaver.
6 The cars stopped at the pedestrian crossing.
7 The victim had been stabbed and robbed.
8 The painter propped his ladder against the wall.
9 Two climbers were trapped on a narrow ledge.
10 I begged him not to do it again.

c 1 A wasp lives in a nest.
2 A beaver lives in a lodge.
3 A bee lives in a hive.
4 A badger lives in a sett.
5 A bear lives in a den.

D			
1	thin	thinner	thinnest
2	sad	sadder	saddest
3	long	longer	longest
4	strong	stronger	strongest
5	bright	brighter	brightest
6	smart	smarter	smartest
7	thick	thicker	thickest

e 1 The common starfish is about 10–15 cm across, but some are bigger.
2 A starfish's eyes are situated at the tip of each arm.
3 Seals spend most of their time in the sea.
4 A thick layer of blubber protects seals from the cold.
5 The name 'common gull' is misleading because the bird is not very common.
6 Knots visit Britain in winter.
7 Knots look for food (molluscs, worms, crustaceans) on the shore.
8 Knots and oystercatchers are waders.
9 A dorsal fin is a fin on the back.
10 Fish are vertebrates. This means that they have a backbone.

Book 4

The theme of Homes and Houses provides the basis for the work in Book 4. The book is arranged in five main sections separated by Pratice Pages. The first two sections present a historical survey of houses, from the first home in a tree or cave to houses of the present time. A section on famous homes in different parts of the world is followed by two sections that cover planning and building a house, things we need near our homes and homes in other lands. The pattern and approach laid down in earlier books is followed and developed so that pupils exercise and develop their language as well as working through a carefully-planned topic on one of our most important needs.

As in earlier books the coverage of the subject matter is thorough and sustained, but the opportunity is there for those who wish to pursue the matter further. Among the books that will help pupils and teachers to do this are the following:

The Story of Homes	T. A. Thompson	Blackwell
Houses and Homes	Carolyn Cocke	Macdonald
Houses	R. J. Unstead	Black
The Story of Houses and Homes	Richard Bowood	Ladybird
The Homes We Live In	H. Adams	Cassell
Let's Look at Houses and Homes	Joan Morey	Muller
The Buildings People Lived in	Peter Rice	Dinosaur Publications
Buildings and Building Sites	Eric Jones	Blandford

The first home *pages 2–3*

a
1. The first home was any kind of shelter that a person could easily find.
2. The shelter would serve the purpose of keeping a person warm and dry in bad weather and safe from wild beasts.
3. The first people probably lived in and among trees.
4. A tree would give some shelter from the rain and shade from the sun.
5. A simple 'lean-to' shelter would consist of a few branches propped against a tree.
6. We know that some people lived in caves because we have found caves with paintings on the walls.
7. It would not be possible for everyone to live in caves because in some parts of the world there are few caves to be found.
8. A cave might be cold, dark and damp or it might be the home of a wild animal such as a cave bear or cave lion.

b
1 branches 2 hatches 3 sketches 4 switches 5 punches
6 radishes 7 lashes 8 ambushes 9 rushes 10 clashes

c
1 easily 2 angrily 3 shabbily 4 steadily 5 hastily
6 wearily 7 busily 8 merrily 9 noisily 10 happily
11 She skipped gracefully across the room.
12 They worked steadily all day long.
13 He slept soundly in spite of the noise.
14 Both engines were carefully checked.
15 The jar was accidentally knocked over.

d
After many years people learned to make a kind of shelter. They would first gather some long branches to make a framework. The branches would be fixed in a circle, leaning against each other at the top. Near the top the branches would be tied together. Small branches and twigs were added to the framework. Finally, animal skins and mud were used to cover the twigs and branches.

e
1. Kent's Cavern.
2. Food and clothing.
3. A shelter is mainly a protection against the weather and wild animals. It may just be a resting place for the night or any other short period. A home is a shelter as well but it is likely to be more permanent, more elaborate and more comfortable. It is a place for living in and enjoying life. It is a place that can be used by a family and where friends can be entertained. It is where we keep most of our possessions. A home reflects our personal tastes and way of life as well as our needs.

Tents and huts *pages 4–5*

a 1 A tent has the advantage that it can easily be dismantled and taken elsewhere.
2 People needed a permanent place to live when they learned to grow crops and tame animals.
3 Their choice of building materials was determined by what they could find nearby.
4 Stone is a good building material because it is strong and keeps out the wind and rain.
5 A space was left in the low, circular wall for the entrance.
6 A branch or pole was set up in the middle of the floor to support the roof.
7 Animal skins or pieces of turf were placed on top of the roof framework.
8 Some of the earth inside the hut was taken away to make more headroom.

b 1 The ball was placed in the centre of the circle.
2 A century is a period of one hundred years.
3 The cracks in the wall were filled with cement.
4 Rice and wheat are important cereal crops.
5 The line was ten centimetres long.

c 1 dismantled
2 permanent
3 determined
4 circular
5 entrance
6 support
7 extending
8 removed
9 provide
10 entire

d Another way of building a hut was by a method called wattle and daub. The framework of the hut was made of twigs and branches woven together into a kind of basketwork. This was then smeared or daubed all over with wet clay or mud. The wattle or framework of sticks would help to bind the clay and when the clay hardened it would keep out rain and wind. Wattle and daub was often used if there were no stones to be found for building a wall.

e Settlements built on lakes or marshes are called lake dwellings or lake villages. The houses, made of wattle and daub, thatched with reeds, were raised on wooden platforms supported by piles or posts driven deep into the mud at the bottom of the lake. Sometimes houses were placed on artificial islands made of wood, stones, brushwood and earth and held together and in place by wooden stakes driven into the bottom of the lake. Homes were built over water as a means of defence from enemies and/or wild animals. People reached them by means of a narrow bridge or causeway or by canoe. In England, remains of one of these settlements have been found near the village of Glastonbury in Somerset. This was in use from about 250 B.C. to about A.D. 70. Other examples have been found in Switzerland, Germany, Austria, Italy and Yugoslavia.
A few lake dwellings of this kind are still to be found in parts of New Guinea, Venezuela and the Malay Archipelago.

Roman houses *pages 6–7*

a 1 In Britain the Romans began to build homes similar to those in their own country.
2 The plan shows a large Roman town house.
3 The entrance of a Roman town house was a simple doorway between two shops.
4 The entry hall or lobby led into the atrium or courtyard.
5 In early Roman houses the atrium was the main room.
6 The peristyle was an open courtyard surrounded by pillars or columns.
7 Roman houses were made of stone and concrete.
8 The furniture in a Roman house was simple but elegant.

b 1 The Romans knew how to make concrete.
2 It began to rain at four o'clock.
3 Paul wrote a story and read it to the class.
4 Julie swam confidently and won the race.
5 I drank two cups of tea because I was thirsty.

c 1 The Romans conquered many countries, including England, Wales, France, Spain, Portugal and many other countries round the Mediterranean Sea.
2 We saw all sorts of animals at the zoo, including lions, tigers, elephants and giraffes.
3 At school we play various games, including football, netball, rounders and cricket.
4 Farmers grow different cereal crops, including wheat, maize, barley and oats.
5 We see a number of birds in the garden, including sparrows, blackbirds, thrushes and robins.

d Another kind of Roman house is called a villa. Remains of these can be found in many parts of Europe. The villa was really a country house or large farmhouse. It was built round a central courtyard and may have had an outer fence for protection. The building was usually of two storeys, the lower one made of bricks or concrete, the upper floor being made mainly of wood. The roof was probably tiled and, in colder countries, there would be glass in the windows. The villa would be part of a large country estate and only the wealthiest Romans could afford one.

e 1 The Romans had a system of heating their houses by passing warm air under the floor. The floor was slightly raised for this purpose, being supported on a number of short pillars. Warm air could also be carried upwards, behind the walls. The air was heated in an outside furnance.
(Space under a floor for this kind of heating is sometimes called a hypocaust.)
2 Mosaic is a pattern or picture made by fitting together large numbers of small pieces of coloured stone or glass. The pieces are usually set in cement to hold

them in place. The Romans often used mosaic work to decorate floors and walls in their houses, temples and public buildings.

3 The Romans knew how to make cement and concrete, but (along with many other things) knowledge of this was lost in the confusion that followed the fall of the Roman Empire in the A.D. 400s. Cement was rediscovered by John Smeaton, a British engineer, in 1756.

The Saxons *pages 8–9*

a 1 After the Romans left Britain the country was faced with invasion by a number of overseas tribes.
2 The Saxons came from Germany.
3 Many of the Roman buildings were neglected and fell into ruins.
4 The Saxons made their settlements near the banks of rivers or in a forest clearing.
5 The Saxons began to make the framework for a house by selecting two tree trunks (usually oak) and splitting them down the middle.
6 These pieces were used for the end timbers or crucks.
7 The end timbers were joined at the top by a ridge pole.
8 The walls were filled in with wattle and daub and the roof was covered with such things at bark, turf or rushes.

b 1 The spades were kept in a wooden shed.
2 Mr Brown was careful with his money.
3 We waded across the muddy field.
4 The new chairs are quite comfortable.
5 Some mushrooms are very poisonous.

c 1 tribe
2 permanently
3 neglected
4 clearing
5 selected

d 1 The Saxons lived in small villages.
2 The largest house in the village belonged to the chief.
3 The chief's hut or house is often called a hall.
4 The chief and his warriors ate and slept in the hall.
5 The chief and his family sat at one end of the hall.
6 The warriors sat at tables arranged down each side of the hall.

e 1 The Romans left Britain in order to defend Rome against the barbarian tribes who threatened it.

2 Apart from the Saxons there were raids, and eventually settlements, by the Jutes and the Angles.

3 Essex – the kingdom of the East Saxons
Middlesex – the kingdom of the Middle Saxons
Sussex – the kingdom of the South Saxons
Wessex – the kingdom of the West Saxons
The first three of these have been used as the names of English counties (up to 1965, when Middlesex ceased to have a separate identity).
In the 900s A.D. the kings of Wessex became kings of all England and Wessex ceased to be a separate kingdom. The area finally lost its identity as a result of the Norman conquest and the name has been used since in only a fictional form.

The Normans *pages 10–11*

a 1 To secure his new kingdom William quickly built a number of castles.
2 The mound of earth was called a motte.
3 The adjoining open space was called the bailey.
4 The motte and bailey were surrounded by a palisade and a ditch.
5 The advantage of the early castles was that they could be built quickly.
6 Stone castles replaced the wooden castles.
7 The keep was a stone tower, often built in the bailey. It was usually the strongest part of the castle.
8 The Great Hall was the main living room, used for eating and sleeping.

b 1 The last Saxon king of England was Harold.
2 William of Normandy claimed the English throne.
3 Harold was defeated at the Battle of Hastings.
4 Normandy is part of France.
5 The Normans were descended from the Vikings.
6 They had adopted Christianity and the French language.

c 1 defeated
2 secure
3 palisade
4 connected
5 spiral
6 primitive

d 1 There was local resistance up to about 1071 although William had been crowned.
2 William quickly built a number of castles to secure his new kingdom.
3 The castles were held by Norman barons on behalf of the king.

4 Many of the wooden castles were being replaced by stone structures by the 12th century.
5 A stone tower was often built in the bailey because the motte wouldn't stand much weight.

e 1 A manor was a kind of estate given to a knight in return for services to an overlord. The manor house was where the knight and his family lived. Early manor houses were fortified or had the main living area (the hall) on the first floor where it would be safer in case of attack. The manorial system was introduced into England by the Normans.
2 Some Norman castles and manor houses:

Tower of London	Durham
Colchester	Hedingham
Bamburgh	Ludlow
Berkhamsted	Manorbier
Bramber	Richmond
Carisbrooke	Rochester
Chepstow	Rockingham

Boothby Pagnell
Stokesay Castle

3 **Battlements**
The top of a wall, lower in some places than others, so that men could shoot through the lower part while taking shelter behind the higher part.

Drawbridge
A bridge across a moat, hinged so that it could be raised to prevent an enemy from entering a castle.

Dungeon
An underground prison cell.

Moat
A large, water-filled ditch placed round a castle as an extra line of defence.

Solar
A private upper room at one end of the hall of a manor house. It was for the private use of the lord of the manor.

Practice pages *pages 12–13*

a 1 animals	2 skins	3 twigs	4 sticks
5 houses	6 caves	7 castles	8 races
9 bees	10 settees	11 rupees	12 marquees
13 ditches	14 kisses	15 lashes	16 punches
17 sentences	18 patches	19 soldiers	20 decrees

b 1 The police easily found the missing jewels.
2 We walked slowly up the steep hill.
3 'It's all your fault,' he shouted angrily.
4 Motte and bailey castles could be built quickly.
5 The old man was shabbily dressed.
6 They were severely criticised for their poor workmanship.
7 The gardener proudly displayed his cups and trophies.
8 We narrowly escaped an accident last night.
9 She worked steadily all day long.
10 It was widely believed that the old house was haunted.
11 We hastily retreated when the dog barked.
12 We sadly decided to give up the search.
13 The last man was brilliantly caught.
14 The explorers wearily returned to base.
15 They waited patiently for news of survivors.

c 1 circle 2 safely 3 centre 4 send
5 sun 6 celery 7 sit 8 city
9 simple 10 cycle 11 certain 12 settlement
13 cinder 14 sing 15 side 16 celebrate
17 surprise 18 civil 19 sealing 20 ceiling

d 1 Colin fell and hurt his knee.
2 I rang the bell but no one answered.
3 Ruth drew a picture in her book.
4 Steven woke early but didn't get up.
5 Six or seven people came to the party.
6 Everyone drove carefully round the bend.
7 The wind blew the fence across the garden.
8 The choir sang the first verse.
9 The cheetah sprang at the antelope.
10 Nigel forgot to take his books to school.

e 1 comfortable
2 national
3 triumphant
4 wooden
5 hopeful
6 torrential
7 heroic
8 childish
9 careless
10 friendly
11 sunny
12 mountainous
13 starry
14 quarrelsome
15 lucky

f 1 William built the Tower of London.
2 Treasure Island was written by Robert Louis Stevenson.
3 Crete is an island in the Mediterranean Sea.
4 The capital of Turkey is Ankara.
5 We ordered a turkey for Christmas.
6 The new aircraft landed at New York.

g 1 Cave bears and cave lions used to make their homes in caves.
2 People followed herds of wild animals in order to hunt them.
3 The disadvantage of removing some of the earth inside a hut below ground level was that it might make the floor damp.
4 The method of building consisting of interwoven sticks covered with clay or mud is called wattle and daub.
5 Soon after they had occupied Britain, the Romans set about building roads, forts, towns and houses.
6 A Roman country house is called a villa.
7 The Saxons were mainly farmers.
8 The Saxons lived in small villages.
9 Most of the early castles were made of wood and earth.
10 The last Saxon king of England was Harold.

h 1 Nelson was a famous sailor.
2 The artist was proud of his work.
3 The machinery was defective.
4 The circus clowns were very funny.
5 Trafalgar was an important naval victory.
6 At last he came up with a crafty idea.
7 We were angry at the decision.
8 Adam is writing a romantic story.
9 The newspapers gave horrific details of the accident.
10 Some airlines operate a global network of services.
11 There was a rectangular lawn behind the house.
12 The children's drawings were very colourful.
13 One of the players became aggressive.
14 We were sympathetic towards his appeal.
15 Some fictitious characters are based partly on real people.

The Tudors *pages 14–15*

a 1 The Tudor kings and queens reigned from 1485 to 1603.
2 Some merchants, farmers and shopkeepers became rich enough to build better houses.
3 A Tudor house had a brick or stone foundation.
4 On top of the foundation would be placed the framework of the house.
5 Oak was used for the framework of the house because it was strong and durable.
6 The pieces of timber were held together by wooden pegs.
7 The spaces between the timber were filled with plaster.
8 A house built in this way is called half-timbered.

b 1 Henry VII brought peace and prosperity to the country.
2 Henry fought against Richard III at Bosworth.
3 The fugitives sought in vain for a safe hiding place.
4 Everyone thought that Richard would win.
5 The rich Tudor merchants bought paintings and furniture.

c 1 monarchs
2 prosperity
3 considered
4 durable
5 acquire
6 felled
7 timber
8 protruded
9 extensive
10 patterns

d 1 important 2 rich 3 strong 4 easy
5 narrow 6 large 7 neat 8 regular

e 1

	reigned
Henry VII	1485–1509
Henry VIII	1509–1547
Edward VI	1547–1553
Mary	1553–1558
Elizabeth	1558–1603

From Elizabeth we get the adjective Elizabethan.

2 The Guildhall, Lavenham, Suffolk
Oak House, West Bromwich
Montacute House, Somerset
Compton Wynyates, Warwickshire

Longleat House, Wiltshire
Wollaton Hall, Nottinghamshire
Hardwick Hall, Derbyshire
Burghley House, Cambridgeshire
Levens Hall, Cumbria
Hampton Court, London
Rufford Old Hall, Lancashire
Gilling Castle, North Yorkshire
Little Moreton Hall, Cheshire
Melford Hall, Suffolk
Bramall Hall, Greater Manchester

The Seventeenth Century *pages 16–17*

a
1. An architect is a person who draws the plans of a building and then sees that the work is carried out by the builders.
2. Inigo Jones lived from 1573 to 1652.
3. King James I ordered Jones to design the Queen's house.
4. The Queen's house was to be built for King James I's wife, Anne of Denmark.
5. The Queen's house is now used as a museum of British naval history.
6. Another famous building designed by Jones was the Banqueting Hall in Whitehall.
7. Jones's scheme for the reconstruction of Whitehall never got beyond the planning stage.
8. Craftsmen did their work at home because there were no great factories for people to go and work in.

b
1. Mr Johnson's car is in his garage.
2. David's coat was found on the floor.
3. The little girl's hair was tied with ribbons.
4. The boys were playing with Adam's new football.
5. A crow's nest is usually made of twigs.

c
1. ordered
2. eventually
3. completed
4. famous
5. scheme
6. reconstruction
7. meanest
8. shacks
9. prosperous
10. craftsmen

d

Inigo Jones spent his early years designing sets and costumes for the theatre. After that, in about 1600, he went to Italy to study the work of the Italian architect Andrea Palladio. He paid a second visit in 1613. Palladio, whose style of building was based on that of ancient Rome, wrote a book about architecture which Inigo Jones studied. Palladio's style is sometimes called Palladian. Its influence can be seen on the work that Jones did on his return to England.

e 1 An architect draws the plans of a building and then sees that the work is carried out accordingly. The builder, following the architect's plans, does the actual building.
2 The word maritime means having something to do with the sea or seafaring. Things to be seen in the National Maritime Museum include portraits and seascapes, charts and navigational instruments, models of ships and various articles associated with Nelson, including the uniform that he was wearing at the battle of Trafalgar.

Georgian and Regency Styles *pages 18–19*

a 1 The first four king Georges ruled continuously, one after the other, from 1714 to 1830.
2 There are some fine examples of Georgian buildings in Bath, London and Brighton.
3 Two architects by the name of John Wood (father and son) designed many streets and buildings in Bath.
4 The Royal Crescent in Bath consisted of thirty houses and was the first crescent to be built in England.
5 John Nash worked for the Prinoe Regent (the future George IV).
6 Besides being an architect Nash was a great town planner.
7 Nash planned the new Regent's Park and the surrounding area of streets, terraces and crescents.
8 Only part of Nash's scheme was completed because of the cost.

b 1 An architect is a person who draws plans of buildings.
2 Only part of John Nash's scheme was completed.
3 The continuous noise gave me a headache.
4 The food that we swallow goes into the stomach.
5 Kate plays the clarinet in the school orchestra.

c 1 continuously
2 regent
3 designed
4 replaced
5 medieval
6 continued
7 abandoned

d Another great architect of the Georgian period was Robert Adam, one of four Scottish brothers who were all trained to be architects. Robert studied in Edinburgh and Italy before going to London in 1758 where his brother James worked closely with him. From about 1761 they developed what has been called the Adam style, which applied not only to the actual building but to the things inside it such as fireplaces, staircases, furniture, carpets, wall decorations, lamp standards and even door handles. Adam adapted the Palladian style to suit his own ideas, using motifs from ancient Greek and Roman designs that he had studied. We can see examples of his work in various town and country houses and public buildings in Edinburgh, Derbyshire and Middlesex.

e 1 A terrace is a connected row of houses, of similar style, built in a straight line. A crescent is a connected row of houses, of similar style, built in the form of a curve.
2 A motif is the main idea of distinctive feature of a design or composition.
3 incapacity means inability
absence means being away
minority means being a minor (a person under age–i.e. too young to rule)
The Prince of Wales was appointed regent because of the incapacity (due to a mental derangement) of his father, King George III.

Victorian houses *pages 20–21*

a 1 Queen Victoria reigned from 1837 to 1901.
2 Gothic architecture first developed between about 1200 and 1500.
3 Renewed interest in the Gothic style began about 1750.
4 The Victorians imitated various styles of architecture.
5 The result was that some of their houses seemed to be a mixture of styles, having various porches, gables, towers, turrets, pinnacles and even battlements added on.
6 The interior of a Victorian house was fussy, being filled with lots of furniture, fittings, ornaments, pictures and mirrors.
7 Many poor people lived in small, crowded houses with no proper sanitation and no gardens.
8 People had gone to the big towns and cities to work in the factories that were being established.

b 1 There is a revival of interest in old musical instruments.
2 Concrete is a mixture of cement, sand and water.
3 The singer's appearance was greeted with loud applause.
4 The new firm enjoyed great prosperity.
5 The children were offered a choice of schools.

c 1 revival 4 interior
2 imitated 5 ornate
3 wealth 6 established

d The rapid growth of towns and cities led to all sorts of problems. There were epidemics of diseases such as cholera and typhus. Gradually people began to realize that bad housing conditions were partly responsible. At last, in 1875, an Act of Parliament was passed giving local authorities the power to demolish old houses and build new and better ones. From then on each new house had to have its own water supply, its own lavatory, and its own tap and sink in the kitchen. (Things like bathrooms and a constant hot water supply came later.) The Act of 1875 was an important step forward, but the work of improving houses and knocking down the old ones still goes on.

e 1 An epidemic is the rapid spreading of a disease through a community so that a large number of people have it at about the same time.
2 Sanitation means measures to improve the health of a community, especially the safe drainage and disposal of sewage.
3 The old, overcrowded streets and districts where there are a lot of poor houses close together are sometimes called slums. They are usually found in some of the older and neglected areas of large industrial towns and cities. Most of them have been, or are being, cleared away to make room for better houses.

Houses to-day *pages 22–23*

a 1 A housing estate is a district where there are a lot of houses planned by the local council or a private builder.
2 To avoid monotony in the way houses are built on housing estates different styles of houses are built and grouped in small numbers.
3 Some bedrooms have built-in wardrobes.
4 Kitchens are being made easier to work in by being fitted with kitchen units.
5 Kitchen units include built-in sinks, cupboards, cookers, hobs, refrigerators and freezers.
6 Food is prepared on a long, flat, unbroken surface that runs round the kitchen at a convenient height.
7 We must be more careful about saving fuel because fuel is expensive and because such things as coal, oil and natural gas will not last for ever.
8 We need to insulate our homes so that heat does not escape through the roof, windows or walls.

b 1 external 2 increase 3 interior 4 include 5 outside
6 export 7 upstairs 8 inward 9 outdoor 10 downwards

c 1 monotony
2 identical
3 prepared
4 convenient
5 expensive
6 insulate

d 1 Open coal fires are now forbidden in many parts of the country.
2 Because of this many people have had central heating installed.
3 The whole house is warmed by water from one boiler.
4 At different places round the house there are pipes and radiators.
5 In order to reach the radiators water is pumped along the pipes.
6 The water may be heated by oil, gas or electricity.

e 1 (a) Under-floor heating, hot-water pipes or cables being installed or embedded in the floor.
(b) Warm air heating, the heated air being blown or forced through a system of ducts or pipes from the point where it is heated to each room. The air enters each room through one or more grills.
2 The following methods can be used to stop heat being lost through walls, windows and roofs:
Cavity wall insulation
Double glazing
Loft insulation
3 Solar heating uses the energy of the sun for heating purposes. Black solar panels covered by glass or plastic can be built into the roof or a house. Water circulating over the panel is heated by the sunlight that the panel has absorbed. (Black is used because this colour absorbs sunlight more effectively than any other.)

Practice pages *pages 24–25*

a 1 The players thought that the game was over.
2 Diane brought an extra pair of shoes with her.
3 Mrs Fletcher taught me how to play the piano.
4 Philip caught the ball at the second attempt.
5 I bought a cake and a packet of biscuits.

b 1 The dog's dinner was in the bowl.
2 Mr Black's car is parked next to the trees.
3 The ship's engines stopped and the vessel was stranded.
4 The stamps were in Pauline's purse.
5 The bird's wings were covered in oil and it could not fly.
6 The lady's handbag had been stolen.
7 The ladies were waiting outside the grocer's shop.
8 'Has anyone seen John's socks?' asked Nicholas.
9 None of the girls knew the boy's name.
10 A dragonfly's wings are very fragile.

c 1 The science or art of building is called architecture.
2 Regular visits to the dentist prevent toothache.
3 Kate won a scholarship to the school of music.
4 A monarch is the ruler of a country.
5 An archangel is an angel of the highest rank.
6 A pain in the ear is known as earache.
7 A mechanic is a person who is skilled at mending machinery.
8 The orchid is a beautiful flower.
9 We hear an echo when sound is reflected to us.
10 Paul and Martin sing in the school choir.

d 1 Our arrival had been delayed by fog.
2 The disappearance of the necklace baffled everyone.
3 The injury was not thought to be serious.
4 Everyone praised the professor's invention.
5 I read the introduction before buying the book.
6 Napoleon planned the invasion of Britain.
7 The factory was wrecked by an explosion.
8 The wreckage was scattered over a wide area.
9 He gave me some very good advice.
10 She reported the loss as soon as possible.
11 The rapid growth of towns created many problems.
12 The referee would not change his decision.
13 All the climbers were suffering from exposure.
14 I saw the advertisement in a newspaper.
15 The garments were guaranteed against shrinkage.

e 1 decrease 2 underarm 3 discourage 4 exterior 5 upstream
6 import 7 downhill 8 exhale 9 inflate 10 minimum

f 1 farmhouse
2 bedroom
3 elsewhere
4 framework
5 drawbridge
6 craftsmen
7 necklace
8 downstream
9 nearby
10 whereabouts

g 1 The family name given to the kings and queens who ruled England from 1485 to 1603 is Tudor.
2 There was sometimes a shortage of oak for building houses because many trees had been felled to build ships.
3 The building known as 'the Queen's house' is at Greenwich.
4 Inigo Jones went to Italy to study the work of the Italian architect Andrea Palladio.
5 Regent's Park was called after the future King George IV.
6 Robert Adam was a Scottish architect.
7 Gothic architecture was often used in cathedrals, churches, palaces, town halls and university buildings.
8 Cholera and typhus are diseases.
9 The interior of a building is the inside.
10 Open coal fires are now forbidden in many parts of the country.

h 1 She grabbed Tom's arm to steady herself.
2 The bread was wrapped in tissue paper.
3 The shoe rubbed against my heel.
4 We were stunned by the distressing news.
5 We passed the lorry as soon as possible.
6 Mother wrote a note to explain my absence.
7 Joanne swam well in the relay race.
8 Some men dug a deep hole in the road.
9 Peter sang a solo at the festival.
10 After dinner I drank a cup of tea.
11 We hurried because we were late.
12 I tried in vain to reach the top shelf.
13 They carried their books upstairs.

The White House *pages 26–27*

a 1 The President of the United States of America lives at the White House.
2 There are 132 rooms in the White House.
3 The original building was begun in 1792.
4 The first White House was built of sandstone.
5 The first President to live at the White House was John Adams.
6 British troops set fire to the White House in 1814.
7 President Theodore Roosevelt authorized 'White House' as the building's official title.
8 Much of the interior of the White House is now furnished as it would have been in the late 1700s and early 1800s.

b 1 British 5 Nigerian 9 Canadian
2 American 6 Australian 10 German
3 European 7 Chinese 11 Indian
4 African 8 Japanese 12 Russian

c 1 British troops occupied Washington for a short time.
2 After the fire, the White House was restored.
3 The White House has been enlarged several times.
4 The square portico is the main entrance to the building.
5 The White House is visited by over one million people annually.

d 1 The White House was completed in 1799.
Completed means finished.
2 The two wings of the White House have been added subsequently.
Subsequently means later.
3 The Lincoln bedroom is named after a former president.
Former means earlier.
4 The state dining room can accommodate 140 guests.
Accommodate means hold.
5 Extensive repairs were carried out between 1945 and 1953.
Extensive means far-reaching.
6 Concrete and steel were used to reinforce the foundations.
Reinforce means strengthen.
7 The White House is the official reisdence of the President of the United States.
Residence means home.

e 1 Kings and queens, emperors and empresses, heads of governments, ambassadors, consuls, high commissioners, governors, governors-general.
2 The chief ministers who govern a country.
3 A portico is a porch consisting of a roof supported by a series of columns or colonnade. It is an Italian word, coming from the Latin porticus meaning a porch.

Number 10, Downing Street *pages 28–29*

a 1 The Prime Minister of Great Britain lives at number 10, Downing Street.
2 The chancellor of the Exchequer lives at number 11, Downing Street.
3 Downing Street is in London--between Whitehall and St James's Park.
4 Downing Street is named after Sir George Downing who bought some land and built some houses there.
5 Robert Walpole is generally regarded as Britain's first prime minister.
6 George II offered number 10 to Robert Walpole.
7 Members of the government meet in the cabinet room which is on the ground floor.
8 The double doors are so that nothing can be heard outside the room.

b 1 residence 4 ensure
2 declined 5 concluded
3 discussed 6 sworn

c 1 Sir Robert Walpole, who is reckoned to be the first Prime Minister of Britain, accepted number 10 as an official residence.
2 Sir George Downing, who lived from 1623 to 1684, built some houses in Downing Street.
3 David Lloyd George, who became Prime Minister in 1916, had a bathroom installed at number ten.
4 Downing Street, which is situated just off Whitehall, is one of the best known streets in London.
5 The cabinet room, which is on the ground floor, is used by government ministers.

d Between 1960 and 1964 numbers 10 and 11 Downing Street were rebuilt behind the old frontages and number 12 was entirely rebuilt. As parts of the buildings were knocked down the workmen came across remains of the old Tudor Palace of Whitehall. This had been built in about 1530 by Henry VIII and destroyed by fire in 1697. Parts of the wooden structure of an old Saxon hall were also discovered. A considerable amount of Tudor and Roman pottery was found as well.

e 1 The Chancellor of the Exchequer is the minister in charge of financial (money) matters in the British government.
2 Any confidential information written in ink might appear on any blotting paper used to dry it. The imprint would be the wrong way round, but it might be possible to read it if the blotting paper were held up to a mirror.
3 Chequers. This is the official country home used by Prime Ministers of Great Britain. It is a Tudor mansion that was given to the nation in 1917 and the first Prime Minister to use it was David Lloyd George. Originally a 13th-century manor house, it was later rebuilt. The house is well away from the road in hundreds of acres of private parkland and so offers a private and secure retreat.

Buckingham Palace *pages 30–31*

a 1 Buckingham Palace was originally built for the duke of Buckingham.
2 George III purchased Buckingham Palace for £21,000.
3 George IV engaged John Nash to enlarge and reconstruct the building.
4 Queen Victoria adopted Buckingham Palace as her official London home.
5 Sir Aston Webb designed the new front.
6 The royal family's private apartments are in the north wing.
7 The private garden is behind the palace.
8 The Queen's Gallery is sometimes open to the public.

b 1 The palace was slightly damaged during the war.
2 The players proudly displayed the cup they had won.
3 We waited patiently for the rain to stop.
4 James slept peacefully throughout the storm.
5 They left hurriedly and made straight for the station.

c 1 monarch 6 reconstruct
2 originally 7 succeeded
3 purchased 8 familiar
4 engaged 9 apartments
5 enlarge 10 exhibited

d 1 Buckingham Palace, one of London's most famous buildings, has been the chief royal residence since 1837.
2 A new front, designed by Sir Aston Webb, was built in 1913.
3 The private garden, situated behind the palace, covers about 40 acres.
4 The Queen's Gallery, the only part of the palace open to the public, is used for exhibitions of pictures.
5 The Brigade of Guards, famous for its bright red coats, carries out guard duty at the palace.

e 1 Monarchy
2 Balmoral
Hampton Court Palace
Holyroodhouse Palace
Kensington Palace
Sandringham
St James's Palace
Windsor Castle

The Palace of Versailles *pages 32–33*

a 1 The palace of Versailles is situated about 19 km south west of Paris.
2 The first royal building at Versailles was a modest hunting lodge, built by Louis XIII in 1623.
3 Louis XIV decided to build a palace at Versailles.
4 Much of the work was done between 1665 and 1683.
5 The palace was built to house the royal family and court.
6 There are 483 mirrors in the Hall of Mirrors.
7 The front of the palace overlooks carefully laid-out gardens, complete with lawns, paths, ponds, fountains and statues.
8 The palace of Versailles is now used as a national museum.

b 1 The hotel was enlarged to accommodate more guests.
2 The new motorway enabled us to reach the coast in two hours.
3 I enclosed a cheque with my order.
4 Their lives were endangered by the rising waters.
5 The soldiers were encircled by a ring of hostile tribes.

c 1 To do the work he engaged some of the best architects, builders, sculptors and landscape gardeners.
2 The building is considered to be something of a masterpiece.
3 The French royal family and nobles enjoyed a life of luxury and ease at Versailles, but most ordinary people in France were then very poor indeed.
4 This was one of the reasons why the French people eventually turned against their kings.
5 It has been restored to something like its former splendour.

d 1 In the grounds of Versailles there are two smaller palaces.
2 In various parts of the gardens there were marble and bronze statues.
3 Louis hired the best craftsmen to carry out the work.
4 The Hall of Mirrors connected the apartments of the king and queen.
5 The royal family were removed from Versailles in 1789.

e 1 (a) republic
(b) court
2 (a) Landscape gardeners plan the layout of gardens so as to produce an overall effect that is harmonious and pleasing to the eye.
(b) Sculptors carve things, especially in stone, wood, ivory or marble. They also model things in clay or wax.
3 In 1789, during the early stages of the French Revolution, the deputies of the Third Estate (the common people) met in the royal tennis court at Versailles to demand a proper constitution for France.
Versailles was used as the German army headquarters at the time of the siege of Paris 1870–1871 during the Franco-Prussian war.
At the end of the Franco-Prussian war, in the Hall of Mirrors, the German Empire was proclaimed and the king of Prussia was proclaimed Emperor of Germany.
After the end of World War One the Treaty of Versailles was signed (June, 1919) in the Hall of Mirrors.

Blenheim Palace *pages 34–35*

a 1 The palace of Blenheim is situated near Woodstock in Oxfordshire.
2 Blenheim Palace was built for John Churchill, 1st Duke of Marlborough, as a reward for his brilliant victory against the French and Bavarians at the Battle of Blenheim.

3 The Battle of Blenheim took place in August, 1704 near the Bavarian village of Blenheim.
4 The estate at Blenheim extends to some 2500 acres.
5 Sir John Vanbrugh designed Blenheim Palace.
6 The grounds at Blenheim were planned by Henry Wise, Queen Anne's gardener, and by the outstanding landscape gardener 'Capability' Brown.
7 'Capability' Brown got his nickname because, when he was asked to remodel an estate, he would often say that he could see capabilities of improvement.
8 The lake was made by damming the river Glyme.

b 1 a collection of pictures
2 a suite of furniture
3 a suit of clothes
4 a bundle of rags
5 a flight of steps
6 a fleet of ships
7 a set of tools
8 a bunch of grapes
9 a chest of drawers
10 a group of islands

c

Ordinary private house	*Mansion or palace*
humble	palatial
modest	magnificent
small	splendid
usual	vast
undistinguished	grand
common	massive
little	impressive
lowly	notable
plain	stately
unpretentious	spacious

d 1 A bridge spans the river.
Spans means extends over.
2 Beautiful vistas can be seen from the bridge.
Vistas means views.
3 From here can be seen the enormous column of victory.
Enormous means huge.
4 A statue of the Duke surmounts the column.
Surmounts means is on top of.
5 The Duke is attired in a Roman cloak.
Attired means dressed.
6 Round the base of the column is a record of the Duke's battles.
Base means bottom.

e 1 Queen Anne.
2 It means that parts of the gardens at Blenheim remind us of those at Versailles.

3 The Battle of Blenheim.
The Battle of Blenheim took place on 13 August 1704 near the village of Blenheim in Bavaria (now part of West Germany). It was the decisive battle of the War of the Spanish Succession, so called because of a dispute as to who should succeed the childless Charles II as king of Spain. When Charles died Louis XIV of France claimed the throne for his own grandson, so England, Holland and Austria formed an alliance and declared war on France. In 1704 the French and their Bavarian allies were threatening Vienna and it was to deal with this situation that the Duke of Marlborough led his Anglo-Dutch army in an invasion of Bavaria. There he was joined by an Austrian army under Prince Eugene. Marlborough decided to force a battle and after fierce fighting his men broke through the French centre. This split the French force in two and eventually they were all killed, scattered or forced to surrender. Vienna was saved, Bavaria withdrew from the war and the French survivors were forced back to their own country.

Practice pages *pages 36–37*

a 1 sandstone
2 outstanding
3 bedroom
4 motorway
5 overseas
6 masterpiece
7 courtyard
8 anything
9 throughout
10 himself

b 1 A special messenger was entrusted with the secret documents.
2 All the ropes were entangled with each other.
3 An otherwise dull concert was enlivened by an amusing sketch.
4 The new king was enthroned with great ceremony.
5 Our lives can be enriched by the books that we read.
6 The wild beast was enraged by the hunters' attempts to trap it.
7 The small boat was soon engulfed by the waves.

c 1 Egyptian
2 Irish
3 French
4 Polish
5 Welsh
6 Mexican
7 Turkish
8 Libyan
9 Greek
10 Belgian
11 Peruvian
12 Burmese
13 Dutch
14 Chilean
15 Swiss
16 Danish
17 Norwegian
18 Portuguese

d 1 The king's bodyguard served him loyally.
2 Our French host spoke English fluently.
3 We approached quietly so as not to disturb anyone.
4 I dressed hurriedly and rushed downstairs.
5 All gifts were gratefully acknowledged.
6 They wandered aimlessly as if they were lost.
7 I estimated correctly what the cost would be.
8 He explained clearly how the machine worked.
9 The soldiers charged bravely at the enemy position.
10 The stars shone brightly in the clear night sky.

e 1 Buckingham Palace was built orginally for the Duke of Buckingham.
2 There is a large private garden behind the palace.
3 Works of art are sometimes exhibited in the Queen's Gallery.
4 The entrance to the Queen's Gallery is from Buckingham Palace Road.
5 The British monarch is head of state.

f 1 In 1799 the White House was completed.
2 Between 1945 and 1953 extensive repairs were carried out.
3 On certain days some rooms are open to the public.
4 British troops occupied Washington during a war with the United States.
5 The official residence of the Prime Minister of Great Britain is number 10 Downing Street.
6 In 1940 Buckingham Palace was damaged by bombs.
7 Since 1837 the Palace has been the main royal residence.
8 One of the most splendid of all palaces is the palace of Versailles.
9 The grounds at Blenheim Palace were planned by Capability Brown.
10 The river is spanned by a bridge.

g 1 The White House is the home and official residence of the President of the United States of America.
2 The Lincoln bedroom gets it name from a former president.
3 Members of staff who do this work are sworn to secrecy.
4 David Lloyd George became Prime Minister of Britain in 1916.
5 The picture on page 30 shows (an aerial view of) Buckingham Palace.
6 The Hall of Mirrors is in the palace of Versailles.
7 The French royal family were taken away from Versailles in 1789.
8 Pictures, china, furniture, carvings and tapestries are to be found in Blenheim Palace.
9 Sir Winston Churchill was born at Blenheim Palace in 1874.
10 A statue of the Duke of Marlborough surmounts the victory column at Blenheim Palace.

h 1 There are 132 rooms in the White House.
2 The total number of rooms in the White House is 132.
3 The president and his family live in the White House.
4 Members of the government meet at number 10, Downing Street.
5 The private apartments at the palace are on the north side.
6 The Brigade of Guards carries out guard duty.
7 The guards wear colourful uniforms.
8 The Hall of Mirrors is in the palace of Versailles.
9 There are 483 mirrors in the Hall.
10 A record of the Duke's battles surrounds the base of the column.

Surveyors and Architects *pages 38–39*

a 1 Surveyors measure the land.
2 Surveyors use instruments such as theodolites and dumpy-levels.
3 A dumpy-level is a kind of spirit-level.
4 Architects design houses.
5 A plan shows one floor of a house as seen from above.
6 A section is what you would see if the house were cut through from top to bottom and opened up to show the inside.
7 An elevation shows an outside view of the house, often the front.
8 An elevation shows what the house will look like when it is completed.

b 1 Through rhymes with true.
2 Rough rhymes with gruff.
3 Bough rhymes with cow.
4 Cough rhymes with off.
5 Though rhymes with blow.
6 Bought rhymes with sort.
7 Drought rhymes with trout.

c 1 suitable
2 obtain
3 permission
4 regulate
5 designing
6 inside
7 outside
8 accuracy
9 representation
10 completed

d 1 top 2 ruler 3 spring 4 plot 5 spirit

e 1 Ground floor; first floor.
2 Architects show the real size of a house on a small drawing by using scale.
3 Quantity surveyors work out how much material (bricks, tiles, timber etc.) will be needed to build a house or other building.

Preparing to build *pages 40–41*

a 1 A right angle is an angle at the corner of a square.
2 To measure a right angle the builder uses a big set square, one corner of which is a right angle.
3 Concrete is poured into the foundation trenches so that each wall can be built on a firm foundation.
4 Concrete is made from gravel, sand, cement and water.
5 To make sure that each row of bricks is level bricklayers use a spirit level or builder's level.
6 To make sure that a wall is upright bricklayers use a plumb-line or plum-bob.
7 Mortar is used to hold the bricks together.
8 Mortar is made from lime, sand and water or cement, sand and water.

b 1 A surveyor measures the land.
2 An architect draws the plans.
3 A bricklayer builds with bricks.
4 A stonemason builds in stone.
5 A plumber puts in the water pipes.
6 An electrician installs the electric wiring.
7 A carpenter fits the doors and windows.
8 A glazier puts glass in the windows.
9 A plasterer covers the inside walls with plaster.
10 A decorator papers the walls.

c 1 Bricks are made from clay.
2 The clay is dug out of the ground.
3 Any stones or lumps are removed.
4 The clay is mixed by machine.
5 The clay comes out of the machine as a long strip.
6 The long strip of clay is then cut into pieces.
7 Each piece of clay is the size and shape of a brick.
8 The pieces of clay are then dried.
9 This takes out most of the water.
10 The raw bricks are put in an oven to be baked.
11 The ovens are called kilns.

d 1 surveyor
2 architect/builder
3 bricklayer
4 bricklayer
5 bricklayer
6 painter/decorator
7 carpenter
8 glazier
9 painter/decorator

e 1 Gravel is a mixture of small stones, pebbles and fragments of rock.
2 The concrete container on the back of the lorry rotates slowly as the lorry is driven along. This prevents the concrete from setting during delivery.
3 The earliest bricks, used in Babylonia, Assyria and Egypt, were made from a mixture of such things as clay, mud, straw and sand. They were shaped in moulds and left to dry in the sun. Straw was used in sun-baked bricks because it helped the bricks to hold together. Later, it was found that burning the clay with fire was a better way of baking the bricks because it made them stronger and more resistant to damp. Fire-burnt bricks do not need straw to bind them together.
Well-burnt bricks at least 6,000 years old have been found in the ruins of ancient Babylon.

Bricklaying and bonding *pages 42–43*

a 1 A bricklayer must interlock the bricks so that the vertical joint between two bricks is always covered by a brick above and a brick below.
2 The way in which bricks are arranged in a wall (to overlap each other) is called bonding.
3 Besides giving strength to the wall bonding helps to make it attractive by giving it a pattern.
4 The picture shows a man building the outside wall of a house.
5 The bricklayer is using a bond called stretcher bond.
6 A stretcher is the long, oblong surface of a brick.
7 The man is building a cavity wall (two walls close together).
8 The gap prevents cold and damp from getting into the house and helps to keep warmth inside the house.

b 1 Each brick is arranged to overlap a joint in the row below.
2 The police car tried to overtake the lorry.
3 In time the settlers were able to overcome all difficulties.
4 We saw the car overturn and land on its roof.
5 Mr West would never overcharge his customers.

c 1 endeavours
2 durable
3 attractive
4 verticle
5 unbroken
6 topple
7 pattern
8 lengthwise
9 occurs
10 prevents

d The foundations of a house are below ground level. Because of this, damp from the ground can pass upwards through the bricks. This can happen because bricks are slightly porous. To stop this, a layer of waterproof material is put between two rows of bricks. This is called the damp-proof course. It is usually possible to see it a little way above ground level.

e 1 The damp-proof course is usually made of bituminous felt, but slate, copper or lead can be used.
2 A builder calls a row of bricks in a wall a course.
3 The pieces of metal are called wall ties or metal ties. They keep the two walls of a cavity wall the right distance apart.
4 Stretcher bond.
Flemish bond.
English bond.
Dutch bond.
5 Porous means having many pores or tiny holes in it that allow liquid to pass through.

Floors and doors *pages 44–45*

a 1 Carpenters put in such things as floors, window-frames and doors.
2 The wall plates rest on small brick supports inside the walls a little way above ground level.
3 The wall plates support the joists.
4 Joists are parallel pieces of timber that stretch from wall to wall.
5 The joists are placed on edge for greater strength.
6 Floor boards (or sheets of strong plywood) are nailed to the joists.
7 Door and window frames may be temporarily supported by leaning planks against them.
8 Scaffolding is a framework of poles or metal tubes on which planks can be placed at different levels.

b 1 The men erected some scaffolding.
2 The fire was extinguished before any serious damage was done.
3 The game was postponed because of heavy rain.
4 I couldn't tolerate the noise any longer.
5 The money had been saved in case of need.

c 1 The bricklayer had a trowel in one hand and a brick in the other.
2 Bricklaying looks easy but it is difficult to do well.
3 The carpenter was fixing the joists while the bricklayer went on building a wall.
4 Wood must be properly dried or it will shrink later on.
5 Britain has to import timber because we do not grow enough of our own.

d The framework of a roof is made of sloping beams called rafters. The rafters are covered with felt. The felt is fastened down by thin strips of wood. The thin strips of wood are called battens. Most roofs are covered with tiles. The tiles are fastened to the battens. The tiles overlap to keep out the rain. The builders begin tiling a roof at the bottom and then work their way up.

e 1 Tiles can be made of clay or concrete.
Other materials used to cover roofs are stone slabs, straw or reed thatch and corrugated iron.
2 Different styles and shapes of roofs:
Flat, plain pitch, mansard, hipped, butterfly.

Services to the home *pages 46–47*

a 1 Water is brought to our houses along water mains.
2 The water that comes into a house is cold.
3 In many homes gas is used for cooking and heating.
4 Since 1967 we have been using natural gas.
5 Our natural gas comes from deposits under the North Sea.
6 It was necessary to convert existing gas appliances in order to burn natural gas.
7 In most homes electricity is used for lighting and for running such things as television, vacuum cleaners, irons, hair dryers, washing machines and food mixers.
8 Electricity is made by generators in power stations.

b

1	important	more important	most important
2	careful	more careful	most careful
3	beautiful	more beautiful	most beautiful
4	comfortable	more comfortable	most comfortable
5	dangerous	more dangerous	most dangerous

c 1 The first gas used in Britain was manufactured from coal.
2 Deposits of natural gas have been found under the North Sea.
3 Most homes use a variety of electrical appliances.
4 The old gas cooker was converted to burn natural gas.
5 Letters about conversion were distributed to all households.
6 Petroleum, coal, natural gas and water power are our chief sources of energy.

d A fuel of some sort is used to fire the boilers.
The fuel used is usually coal or oil.
The boilers raise steam to drive the turbines.
The turbines drive the generators.
The generators make the electricity.

e 1 The amount of gas and electricity that we use in our homes is recorded by meters.
2 Nuclear power stations use uranium.
3 The world's first large-scale nuclear power plant was built at Calder Hall in England.
4 The largest hydro-electric plants in Britain are in Scotland.

Practice pages *pages 48–49*

a 1 Plough rhymes with allow.
2 Tough rhymes with bluff.
3 Dough rhymes with go.
4 Thought rhymes with short.
5 Head rhymes with bed.
6 Heed rhymes with bead.
7 Fare rhymes with hair.
8 Are rhymes with far.
9 Front rhymes with hunt.
10 Font rhymes with want.

b 1 bat
2 bank
3 knot
4 chest
5 vessel

c 1 A jockey rides in a horse race.
2 A detective investigates crimes.
3 A florist grows or sells flowers.
4 An engineer builds and looks after engines and machines.
5 An artist paints pictures.
6 A librarian is in charge of a library.
7 A reporter writes accounts of the news.
8 A surgeon carries out operations.

d 1 The car was taken to the garage to be overhauled.
2 The aircraft overran the runway.
3 I overslept because I was so tired.
4 The garden was overgrown with weeds.
5 I overheard everything that was said.
6 We were overjoyed to hear the good news.
7 Some boxes were taken off the overloaded lorry.
8 The government was overthrown by the rebels.
9 Long before the storm broke the sky was overcast.
10 The peasants complained that they were overworked and underpaid.

e 1 The dog that worried the sheep had to be destroyed.
2 Mr Williams has gained a lot of weight lately.
3 One of the players made an appearance later on.
4 The police arrived and stopped the trouble.
5 He fell awkwardly and dislocated an elbow.
6 The price of milk was increased last week.
7 We were rather inconvenienced when they arrived unexpectedly.
8 New carpets were fitted before we moved in.
9 Too much sugar had been added to the pudding.
10 The rebellion was suppressed with great cruelty.

f 1 We stayed indoors because it was raining so hard.
2 The clock must be wound daily or it will soon stop.
3 One group made a model while the others painted a frieze.
4 She bought a loaf of bread and four cakes.
5 The wind had dropped but it was still very cold.

g 1 A site is a plot of ground used for building.
2 Houses should not be built too close together.
3 Each corner of a house is usually a right angle.
4 The damp-proof course keeps out any moisture that rises from the ground.
5 Carpenters put in such things as floors and doors.
6 Battens are thin strips of wood.
7 Water comes to our houses along water mains.
8 There are deposits of gas under the North Sea.
9 Electricity is made by generators.
10 Boilers raise steam to drive turbines.

h 1 A new housing estate must be carefully planned.
2 The trenches were filled with concrete.
3 The men tiled the roof with concrete tiles.
4 Water is piped to our houses from the mains.
5 The site sloped gently towards the road.
6 The plans were scrapped and new ones prepared.
7 The zebra has a striped coat.
8 The thrush hopped along the path.
9 The campers were robbed during the night.
10 The dog pined for its absent owner.
11 A vigorous campaign against the terrorists was waged.
12 He tapped me lightly on the shoulder.

Finishing off the house *pages 50–51*

a 1 The plaster makes the walls look more attractive and also helps to make the walls more airtight.
2 Plaster is made from a mixture of such things as lime, sand and water.
3 Hair or fibre is sometimes added to the plaster to strengthen it.
4 The first part of the picture shows a plasterer at work.
5 A hawk is a square board with a short handle fastened on the bottom. It is used for holding mortar.
6 A float is used for putting on and smoothing the plaster.
7 Plasterboards are used to cover ceilings (and sometimes walls).
8 The woodwork has to be painted to preserve the wood. This also makes the wood look better.

b (Specimen answers; the words on the left can also be used in sentences to show the alternative meaning.)

1	even	(adjective) smooth and level
2	can	(noun) a tin or metal container.
3	just	(adjective) fair, right, proper
4	like	(verb) to be fond of or find agreeable
5	lime	(noun) a citrous fruit
6	hawk	(noun) a bird of prey
7	board	(noun) a group of people managing something
8	right	(adjective) correct, just, true
9	float	(verb) to lie or rest on top of a liquid
10	apply	(verb) to put in for (a job)
11	stick	(noun) a small, thin piece of wood
12	well	(noun) a hole or pit, usually round, dug in the ground to obtain water, oil, gas etc.

c 1 A trowel is used for spreading mortar.
2 Sometimes an outside wall is covered with plaster.
3 Scaffolding is put up to provide a platform for workmen.
4 Concrete is made from gravel, sand and cement.
5 Water is added to the mixture.

d 1 butcher
2 brick
3 measure
4 trowel
5 house
6 wall
7 door
8 kitchen
9 sampan
10 mansion

e 1 The origin of the word, as used in this sense, is unknown but it may have something to do with a comparison between the way the plasterer holds his board and the way in which a falcon or hawk is held on the outstretched (gloved) hand.
2 'Float' may suggest the action of the plasterer as he uses his float to make the plaster smooth.

Inside the house *pages 52–53*

a 1 Carpets can be made of a natural material, such as wool, but man-made fibres, such as nylon, are also used.
2 Carpets can be made by hand, but are usually manufactured in factories on power-driven looms.
3 Axminster and Wilton carpets get their names from the towns in Devon and Wiltshire where they were first made.
4 Fitted carpets are carpets that extend from wall to wall.
5 It is usual to have a layer of foam rubber or felt under the carpet. This makes the carpet feel softer and helps it to last longer.
6 Curtains can be made out of man-made fibres or natural materials such as silk or cotton.
7 Net curtain is a kind of curtain that lets in the light but stops people outside from seeing inside.
8 A Venetian blind is a type of window covering (sometimes used in a kitchen or bathroom) made of a number of horizontal slats that can be opened or closed.

b 1 Wool, silk, hair and cotton are examples of natural fibres.
2 Persian carpets show remarkable craftsmanship.
3 Hand-made carpets are very expensive.
4 Oriental rugs are noted for their beautiful patterns.
5 Chinese carpets often have floral designs on them.

c 1 In ancient times people used to spread animal skins on the floor.
2 People were able to make carpets when they had learned to weave.
3 The Moors brought the craft of carpet weaving into Europe.
4 In the making of carpets both natural and artificial fibres are used.
5 Persian, Turkish, Chinese and Indian are examples of Oriental rugs.

d We cannot be sure when the first carpets were made, but it seems likely that the art of weaving began in Egypt or Mesopotamia. Crusaders returning from the east no doubt brought back rugs and carpets, although it was many years before such things were widely used in Western Europe. Before then people were content to cover their floors with rushes. Knowledge of carpet weaving seems to have come through Spain and France and was established in England by about the sixteenth century. At first only a few people could afford carpets, but now it would be difficult to find a home without them.

e 1 Reasons for having carpets in the home:
appearance
warmth
comfort
as a sound-deadening material
to protect floors
can be tastefully used as part of general colour scheme and decor of a room

2 A carpet is usually larger than a rug, probably covering a whole room or staircase. A carpet is often shaped to fit a particular room and may be fastened down in some way–often at the edges. A rug (e.g. a hearthrug) may be used in one particular part of a room.

3 The Venetian blind is so called because this type of window covering was widely used in Venice in the 1600s. This kind of blind had, however, been used somewhat earlier by the Japanese.

4 Mesopotamia corresponds to parts of modern Iraq, Syria and Turkey. The name means 'between the rivers' because it lies between the rivers Tigris and Euphrates.

Different types of houses *pages 54–55*

a 1 Semi-detached houses are houses that are built in pairs.
2 Terraced houses are rows of houses built in one block.
3 Terraced houses are usually cheaper to build because there are fewer outside walls.
4 Large numbers of cheap terraced houses were built to accommodate the factory workers at the time of the Industrial Revolution.
5 Bungalows are one-storeyed houses.
6 A dormer bungalow is a bungalow with an extra room made inside the roof space.
7 Bungalows may be more expensive than ordinary houses because they need more land and more roof.
8 Bungalows are very suitable for people who cannot easily climb stairs.

b 1 The old lady could not climb the stairs.
2 The thumb is set apart from our other fingers.
3 A lamb is a young sheep.
4 The boy was told to comb his hair.
5 My fingers were numb with cold.

c 1 They live in a semi-detached house.
2 After winning the semi-final the team looked forward to playing at Wembley.
3 A semi-circle is half of a circle.
4 After a second blow to the chin the boxer was semi-conscious.

5 Amethyst is a semi-precious stone used in the making of rings, brooches and necklaces.
6 The semi-colon is a punctuation mark; it is sometimes used between sentences.
7 The semi-breve is the longest musical note in general use.

d 1 We went through a number of stiles on our walk across the fields.
2 Two pairs of shoes were left in the cloakroom.
3 The desks were arranged in rows.
4 Diane was reading a story about pirates.
5 Sometimes a person stares in surprise and wonder.
(Nos. 6–10 are specimen answers; others are possible)
6 There was a great contrast of styles between the two teams.
7 I opened a tin of pears at tea-time.
8 The gardener was pruning the rose tree.
9 His office was on the fourth storey.
10 She waited for me at the top of the stairs.

e 1 Rough cast is a wall covering consisting of a layer of plaster or cement against which (while it is still wet) pebbles are flung so that they become embedded in the surface. Rough cast is often used on the outside of brick walls.
2 The main advantage of building tall blocks of flats is that they do not need much land. The disadvantages of living in them are numerous. People do not have a garden and cannot just step outside. They must rely on lifts, and if these break down face perhaps a long climb up or down stairs. Elderly people tend to become 'trapped' in tall towers because it requires such an effort to get out and back again. Parents with young children find extra problems such as where to dry the washing and where to let the children play. There is also the hazard of carrying a pram or a baby in and out of lifts or up and down stairs. Older children may look upon lifts and corridors as play areas and this can annoy some of the residents.
3 An advantage with living in terraced houses is that they are generally warmer. The chief disadvantage is that most of the occupants do not have private access to the rear of the house. There may also be the problem of where to put cars, since there can be no parking or garage spaces at the side of each house.
4 A detached house is a house that is not joined to any other house.

Things we need near our homes *pages 56–57*

a 1 Shops–especially those that sell food–are perhaps the most important of the facilities that we need close to our homes.
2 Good general stores are useful because they sell so many different things.
3 Families with young children like to be near a school.

4 It isn't as important for older children to be near their school because they can more easily travel by themselves.
5 It is a good idea to be near some form of public transport because it would take too long to walk everywhere we want to go.
6 Using public transport avoids the problem of parking the car.
7 It is an advantage to be fairly near a doctor because people who are ill don't feel like taking a long journey.
8 A clinic nearby is a useful service for parents with young children.

b 1 'Is this seat taken?' she asked.
2 'I don't think so,' the man replied.
3 'Jane has won the first prize,' announced the judge.
4 'I'll call for you tomorrow,' said Martin.
5 'I am the owner of this land,' the man explained.

c 1 Sarah isn't in school today.
2 I couldn't understand what he was talking about.
3 Arthur didn't explain where he was going.
4 Simon doesn't seem to care much for swimming.
5 We weren't able to help very much.

d 1 Post office
2 Hospital
3 Library
4 Church, chapel, synagogue or mosque
5 Park
6 Supermarket
7 Theatre
8 Cinema

e 1 In remote country areas people sometimes buy their food from mobile shops. These may be specially built or (more likely) converted vans or buses that visit outlying areas.
2 The two most important shops in the list are the grocer's shop and the chemist's shop because these supply us with many of our most important daily needs. The least essential are probably the betting shop and the antique shop as they do not provide any of our most vital requirements.

Homes in other lands *pages 58–59*

a 1 Things that determine the style of a house include climate, materials available, technical knowledge, tradition, religion, how much land can be used and how much money a person can afford.
2 The Bedouin tribes wander across the desert in search of pasture and water.

3 They live in tents because they lead a nomadic existence and tents can easily be carried about.
4 The yurt or ger is a kind of Mongolian portable home.
5 People who are settled in towns also live in yurts.
6 The yurt is more like a round hut than a tent. It has a trellis framework covered with layers of felt, canvas and hide. A decorative door is another feature.
7 Most Eskimos now live in wooden homes.
8 Both snowhouses and sod houses are called igloos.

b 1 a tribe of natives
2 a gang of thieves
3 a crowd of spectators
4 a team of footballers
5 a crew of sailors
6 a troupe of dancers
7 a choir of singers
8 a company of actors
9 a class (or group) of pupils
10 a board of directors

c 1 determine
2 climate
3 tradition
4 pasture
5 nomadic
6 portable
7 trellis
8 hide
9 associate
10 compact

d The Dyaks, a tribe of people living in Borneo, live in unusual houses called long houses. They get this name because they may be as much as 274 m long, with enough room inside for 50 families. The houses are made of bamboo and are raised off the ground on poles—an arrangement that helps to keep them cool in hot weather and dry in wet. The Dyaks get into their houses by means of short ladders that can be pulled up at night.

e 1 **Junk**
Junks are wooden sailing vessels used in China and the Far East for carrying goods on rivers or across the open sea. Some are used as houseboats.

Sampan
Sampans are similar to junks, but smaller. They are used mostly on rivers and in coastal waters. They, too, are often used as floating homes.

Mud hut
In some parts of Africa the soil is particularly suitable for making mud houses. These dry in the hot sun and are remarkably durable, being especially suitable for those areas where there is little heavy rainfall.

Log cabin
These are particularly associated with some of the early settlers in North America, particularly those who emigrated from forest areas of Scandinavia, Switzerland and Germany. Log cabins look very picturesque, but they are not easy to build. Most early log cabins had one storey, with perhaps an extra 'room' in the loft reached by a ladder.

Tepee
A kind of tent, commonly used by the Plains Indians of North America. The tepee was made of buffalo skins stretched over a framework of poles meeting at the top in the shape of a cone. Tepee (or teepee) comes from a Sioux word meaning dwelling.

Caves
Caves have been used–and still are in a few parts of the world–as homes. The most suitable are shallow caves where light can get in. Deep caves are usually too dark and damp to make suitable homes.

Chalet
A chalet is a summer house or country house made mostly of wood. They are found in Switzerland, but the style has been copied in other parts of the world.

Barge
Barges are sturdy, flat-bottomed freight boats used mostly for transporting bulk cargoes on canals and rivers, though there are larger, ocean-going barges in use as well. Some of the barges that used to be common on British canals are called narrow boats because they had to be narrow enough to pass through some of the locks.

Caravan
The caravans that we are familiar with are those that are either towed by a car or taken by lorry or transporter to a site and left there permanently. Some of the latter type are now fitted out with power, mains water supply, flush toilets, showers, fitted carpets, and fully-equipped kitchens. Caravans are sometimes called trailers or mobile homes.
A motor caravan or motor home has its own engine and therefore does not have to be towed into position. Motor caravans are usually commercial vans that have been specially converted. Like ordinary caravans, many of them offer high standards of comfort and an ingenious layout that makes the most of limited space.

2 Homes in cold climates can be made more comfortable to live in by being provided with central heating and extra insulation against heat loss. The latter point is now receiving increasing attention, especially in countries that have a cold climate but not much in the way of coal, oil or natural gas.
Homes in hot climates need to be as cool as possible. Thick walls keep out the sunlight, while houses built 'on stilts' will have air circulating underneath to help keep them cool. Flat roofs are suitable for hot countries where there is

little rainfall as the area can be used as extra living space in the cool of the evening.

3 Eskimos live in the arctic regions of Greenland, Canada, Alaska and Russia.

Why we need homes *pages 60–61*

a 1 The two main reaons why we need homes are that they give us shelter and protection.
2 There are few places in the world where people could continue to exist without shelter.
3 People have been making shelter for themselves since earliest times.
4 Two of the great problems of the modern world are how to house the homeless and how to provide better homes for those in sub-standard dwellings.
5 Besides shelter and protection we need privacy and solitude at some time or other.
6 We also use our homes as a place where we keep our possessions and entertain friends.
7 Children may reveal our need for a home when they play at 'house' or with a doll's house.
8 We should perhaps interpret children's play as the expression of a very basic instinct that we all have.

b 1 zoo — zoological gardens
2 pram — perambulator
3 exam — examination
4 taxi — taxi-cab
5 phone — telephone

c 1 provide
2 survive
3 advantages
4 privacy
5 solitude
6 possessions
7 entertain
8 trivial
9 expression
10 instinct

d A doll's house or dollhouse is a miniature house fitted out with small pieces of furniture and fittings. It may surprise us to learn that the first dollhouses were made for adults and it was some time before they became popular for children. Some of the early dollhouses, called cabinet dollhouses, were in the form of cabinets, with small-scale rooms in place of shelves. Later dollhouses were made to look like real houses from the outside by having a front resembling the wall of a house. This was usually hinged at one side so that it could be opened.

e 1 Eating, sleeping, working, studying, convalescing after illness, carrying out a hobby or special interest.
2 Abode, domicile, habitation, dwelling, place, residence, seat.
3 Charity begins at home.
There's no place like home.
Home is where the heart is.
An Englishman's home is his castle.

Practice pages *pages 62–64*

a 1 page
2 mint
3 arms
4 model
5 lap

b 1 There was a festive air about the town.
2 Everyone was enthusiastic about the idea.
3 Mr Cross was very proud of his chrysanthemums.
4 It is customary to give presents at Christmas.
5 We were fortunate not to run into any trouble.
6 The smoky atmosphere made rescue difficult.
7 The Huns were a race of warlike people.
8 The victory was an occasion for national rejoicing.
9 The old chairs were not very comfortable.
10 We were warned not to be too adventurous.
11 A fishy smell came from the direction of the harbour.
12 A palatial residence was built for the Duke.
13 An angry dog stood at the gate.
14 He greeted us with a boyish grin.
15 The carpenter was using a circular saw.

c 1 dumb
2 bomb
3 limb
4 tomb
5 honeycomb

d 1 'What is your name?' the man asked.
2 'Stop!' I shouted as loudly as I could.
3 'I think it's time to go home,' said Barbara.
4 'I think you're right,' agreed Terry.
5 'I'm sorry about that,' the lady apologised.
6 'Be quiet,' whispered Tom. 'We want to surprise them.'

7 'Oh do stop!' exclaimed Sam. 'I can't stand any more.'
8 'Let's walk home,' suggested Denise. 'It won't take long.'
9 'Please help us,' begged Arthur. 'We're lost.'
10 'We were the better team,' he boasted. 'I knew we would win.'
11 'That wasn't fair,' protested Peter, 'You started before I did.'
12 'It's ten o'clock,' she reminded me. 'You mustn't be late.'

e 1 'What's the time?' asked Amanda.
2 'It's three o'clock,' replied Jeremy.
3 'We're not ready yet,' said Philip.
4 'You'll have to hurry,' said Ann. 'We aren't waiting much longer.'
5 'We won't go without you,' said Mother.
6 'Where's my ball?' said Frank. 'I shan't go without it.'
7 'We haven't got it,' said Ann. 'It'll be in the house.'

f 1 congregation
2 audience
3 orchestra, band, group, trio, quartet etc.
4 mob, rabble
5 platoon, squad
6 panel
7 posse
8 jury
9 choir
10 field

g

1	flu	influenza
2	cello	violoncello
3	gym	gymnasium
4	photo	photograph
5	fridge	refrigerator
6	plane	aeroplane or airplane
7	lab	laboratory
8	quad	quadrangle
9	sub	substitute
10	vet	veterinary surgeon

h

Positive	*Comparative*	*Superlative*
cold	colder	coldest
good	better	best
bad	worse	worst
easy	easier	easiest
sad	sadder	saddest
plentiful	more plentiful	most plentiful

1 Last night's storm was the worst on record.
2 I carried the heavier of the two parcels.
3 It was the happiest day of her life.
4 George is the taller of the twins.
5 The goalkeeper is the youngest player in the team.

i 1 typist
2 mechanic
3 policeman
4 jockey
5 farmer
6 miner
7 butcher
8 conductor
9 artist
10 surgeon

j 1 The advantages in using plasterboards to cover ceilings and walls are that they can be put up quite quickly and require only a thin coat of plaster over them.
2 Wool is a natural material.
3 Nylon is an artificial material.
4 Long before they had carpets and rugs people used such things as animal skins and rushes as floor coverings.
5 Houses that are built in pairs and joined together on one side only are called semi-detached.
6 Good general stores are the most useful kind of shops to have near our homes.
7 People who wander from place to place in search of pasture for their animals are called nomads.
8 The Dyaks live in Borneo.
9 The Dyak houses are called 'long houses'.
10 The first dollhouses were made for adults.

k 1 bricklayer
2 plasterboard
3 airtight
4 goalkeeper
5 stronghold
6 sometimes
7 honeycomb
8 lengthwise
9 staircase
10 plywood

Book 5

Language and Communication, the theme of Book 5, is treated in much the same way as earlier topics, but there are some variations. The greater length of the book allows plenty of room for the more traditional type of exercise, together with a number of other approaches as well. Many of these involve the use of illustrations–photographs as well as line drawings–and emphasise the importance of the visual element in communication.

Book 5 traces the origin of language in general and the English language in particular, following the latter from being a relatively unimportant tongue outside the mainstream of mediaeval European civilisation to an importance that continues to grow. This may be quite fortuitous, but it is perhaps appropriate that a language that has drawn so much on others should itself have become the means by which so many people of the world communicate with each other.

The importance of English as a living, changing and growing language should be emphasised and pupils and teachers should be alert to its development and use in many situations. Some are illustrated and discussed in Book 5, while more recent examples of the use of English include a pop festival in Japan, a chess tournament in the Philippines and a conference of non-aligned countries in Yugoslavia. A survey of the many forms of verbal and non-verbal communication, both ancient and modern, concludes with a brief reference to the various forms of literature that children will be likely to meet.

Books that would give useful support to the work of Book 5 include

What's in a Word?	Denis and Helen Ballance	E. J. Arnold
Signs and Signals	Philippa Harverson	Penguin
Communications: Signs to Satellites	Eric Jones	Blandford
Sending Messages	B. Knight	Blackwell
Symbols and Signs	Frances Wilkins	Blackwell
Heraldry	J. Brooke-Little	Blackwell
A Ladybird book of Flags	David Carey	Ladybird
Oxford Junior Encyclopaedia		
Children's Britannica		

Using Language *pages 2–3*

a 1 A candidate is making a political speech as part of his campaign to persuade people to vote for him at a forthcoming election.
2 The men appear to be sharing a joke or humorous anecdote.
3 The swimming coach or teacher is explaining something to the children in the water.
4 The boy could be asking the policeman for directions or it may be a general conversation between a boy and the village policeman.
5 The man on the left is showing his produce to the lady and no doubt trying to persuade her to buy. The lady seems quite pleased and the other man is poised ready with a bag as though expecting a quick sale.
6 The picture shows a television news reader.
7 The girls are probably encouraging each other with a whispered confidence as they cautiously take their first steps in what (it would seem) has hitherto been a boys' school.
8 An army sergeant or sergeant-major is giving out brisk words of command to a squad of (possibly) new recruits.
9 The picture shows two people involved in an argument.

b 1 The phrase 'first and foremost' means above all else.
2 Simon cut his forehead just above the left eye.
3 A heavy fall of snow was forecast.
4 The gypsy claimed she could fortell the future.
5 The artist painted a few flowers in the foreground.

c 1 dogs bark (growl)
2 frogs croak
3 lions roar
4 bears growl
5 owls hoot
6 snakes hiss
7 horses neigh (whinney)
8 donkeys bray
9 oxen low
10 hounds bay

d 1 Another word for language is tongue.
2 The black death was a form of bubonic plague.
3 The Football League was formed in 1888.
4 A catalogue is a list of books or other items.
5 The climbers suffered from extreme fatigue.

e 1 The materials could be used to draw a message by means of pictures and signs. However, unless the meanings of these were clearly understood by both parties it is likely that the message would not be altogether clear. Quite a lot might depend on the skill with which the pictures were drawn in the first place.
Picture writing has the advantage that it might be understood by someone who spoke a different language, but a disadvantage is that it could be interpreted incorrectly and might even give rise to a serious misunderstanding.

2 The essential difference between the sounds made by animals and the language that human beings use is that animal sounds are merely general cries and calls and not properly formed words with specific meanings. Human language also has greater range, flexibility and capacity for development as well as offering greater scope for individual use.

The beginning of language *pages 4–5*

a 1 We cannot be sure how language began.
2 We cannot be sure when language began, though it would seem to have developed during the stone age.
3 Natural sounds that could be imitated by people include such things as the cries of animals, the sound of wind and rain and the breaking of a twig.
4 Another idea about the origin of language is that the earliest words were sounds that would accompany certain gestures, especially those made by hands and arms.
5 A person working with the hands would not be able to signal with them.
6 The mouth, lips and tongue might be used to try to copy hand movements.
7 It seems likely that language began because of need.
8 Perhaps when people cooperated in certain ways (in hunting, for example) they would need something more than signs and cries.
9 Early language was likely to be about the things people did and the tools they used.
10 Stone age people would have no word for money because they had none.

b 1 the tick of a clock
2 the beat of a drum
3 the blare of a trumpet
4 the boom of a cannon
5 the wail of a siren
6 the rustle of leaves
7 the popping of corks
8 the thunder of hoofs
9 the creak of hinges
10 the tinkle of bells

c 1 theory
2 origin
3 imitation
4 accompany
5 gestures
6 gesticulate
7 arose
8 cooperated

d 1 Having neither cars nor buses the stone age people had no words for them.
2 Thinking that everyone had left I switched off the lights.
3 Hoping to catch a glimpse of the procession Jill stood on tiptoe.

4 Knowing that the shops would be crowded I set out in good time.
5 Clinging to the upturned boat the crew managed to avoid drowning.

e 1

Stone Age	Palaeolithic	(Old)	30,000 BC–8,000 BC
	Mesolithic	(Middle)	8,000 BC–4,000 BC
	Neolithic	(New)	4,000 BC–1,800 BC
Bronze Age			1,800 BC–1,400 BC

These dates are only approximate; Neolithic culture continued in some areas (especially the north) till later.

2 We are not likely to find anything that will help us find out how language began, because its earliest form–oral–would leave nothing behind.
3 People cannot communicate by gesture or sign language (a) when it is dark, and (b) when they are out of sight of each other or not looking at each other.

The beginning of writing *pages 6–7*

a 1 The beginning of writing came about through pictures.
2 Pictures can be used to tell a story or to illustrate a particular event or a single object.
3 Pictures that stand for words are sometimes called pictograms.
4 The beginning of real writing happened when a picture was used to show an idea and not merely an actual object.
5 A picture of the sun could mean heat or daylight.
6 The drawing of the sun would become simplified by being replaced by a circle.
7 Symbols or signs that represent ideas are called ideograms.
8 Picture writing has the advantage that it may enable people who do not know each other's languages to communicate.
9 The disadvantages in setting down a complicated message in pictures are that it could take a long time to draw and could be misunderstood by somebody else.
10 Pictograms and ideograms tend to become cumbersome because large numbers of them are required to convey a message.

b 1 A circle is a simplified drawing of the sun.
2 We were perfectly satisfied with the new arrangements.
3 The water was purified before being used again.
4 The villagers were terrified by the appearance of the lion.
5 The outlaw defied all attempts to catch him.

c 1 As picture writing developed the drawings were simplified.
2 A symbol would eventually replace a more detailed drawing.
3 A triangle might represent a tent.
4 People of different races might communicate by means of pictures.
5 A disadvantage with pictures is that they can be misunderstood by other people.

d 1 Headland are points of land that project into the sea.
The children were working on a project.
2 A picture can be used to illustrate an object.
Two players began to object to the referee.
3 The farmer was proud of his produce.
I was asked to produce my passport.
4 A baton is used to conduct an orchestra.
They were praised for their good conduct.
5 A hot piece of metal will contract if it is cooled.
The player signed a new contract.

e 1

mouth	hunger, speech
whip	punishment
drums	preparations for battle
fire	warmth, an encampment
lion	strength, leadership
canoe	travel, war party

2

The first true writing *pages 8–9*

a 1 The first true writing was probably developed by the Sumerians who lived in southern Mesopotamia thousands of years ago.
2 The Sumerians drew their ideograms on tablets of wet clay.
3 When pictures were 'scratched' into the clay the stylus picked up a small mound of clay as it went along, so blurring the picture.
4 A better method was to press the end of the stylus into the clay.
5 Each mark was about 8–9 mm long.
6 The word cuneiform means wedge shaped.
7 Straight lines were the easier shape to make.
8 Cuneiform writing is difficult to translate because a character may stand for a word or part of a word.
9 Cuneiform was deciphered between about 1800 and 1850.
10 Our understanding of cuneiform has provided historians with information that they would not otherwise have had.

b 1 wedge
2 sledge
3 bridge
4 edge
5 porridge

c 1 stylus
2 blurring
3 translate
4 character
5 gradually
6 deciphered
7 otherwise

d 1 A system of writing called cuneiform was used by the Sumerians.
2 It is difficult to translate cuneiform writing.
3 Other people of the ancient world used cuneiform writing.
4 The oldest and the most complicated cuneiform is Sumerian.
5 There were about 600 characters in the Sumerian system.

e 1 After the clay tablets had been marked they were dried–either in the sun or in an oven.
2 An inscription is a word or series of words or characters marked or engraved on such things as coins, monuments, buildings, stone or rock.
3 A stylus would not be suitable for our kind of writing on paper because there are too many curves in our lettering and because the stylus could not make an impression on the paper.
4 Pencils and ball pens are more suitable for a cursive style of writing.

Ancient Egyptian writing *pages 10–11*

a 1 The ancient Egyptians developed a system of writing called hieroglyphics.
2 Ancient Egyptian writing consisted of a number of pictures which represented objects, ideas and sounds.
3 Hieroglyphics are usually read from right to left.
4 Hieroglyphics came into use about 3500–3000 B.C.
5 Hieroglyphics were first used mainly for inscriptions on temples, monuments and tombs.
6 The Egyptians developed a kind of paper made from layers of the stem of a water plant called papyrus.
7 The scribes wrote with a kind of pen made from a sharpened reed.
8 The ink was made from soot and water.
9 The first kind of simplified writing was called hieratic.
10 The later kind of simplified writing was called demotic.

b 1 Noun
2 Verb
3 Adjective
4 Noun
5 Noun
6 Verb

c 1 The Egyptian way of writing lasted for thousands of years.
2 Hieroglyphics are an early stage in the development of writing.
3 Hieroglyphic inscriptions were carved on temple walls.
4 By about A.D. 500 knowledge of hieroglyphics had been lost.
5 People thought that hieroglyphics were a secret code.
6 Hieroglyphics were not deciphered until about 1820.

d The Rosetta Stone was the key to our understanding of hieroglyphics. It was a piece of stone measuring 114 × 72 cm found near the town of Rosetta on the Nile delta. The stone carried an inscription in three languages–hieroglyphics, demotic and Greek. A Frenchman called Champollion used his knowledge of Greek to translate the other two parts. Champollion's work enabled scholars to understand other ancient Egyptian writings.

e 1 Napoleon was campaigning in Egypt 1798–9. It was an officer of his engineering corps who found the stone.
2 The Rosetta Stone is now in the British Museum.
3 Our word paper is derived from the word papyrus.
4 Dead languages include Hittite, Lydian, Akkadian, Manx and Cornish. Latin may be regarded as a dead language but it is still used in some church services.

Practice pages *pages 12–13*

a 1 The foreman supervised the other workpeople.
2 The crew's quarters were in the forecastle.
3 The tennis champion had a strong forehand stroke.
4 Our forefathers are our ancestors.
5 He pointed out the route with his forefinger.

b 1 ducks quack
2 wolves howl
3 cats mew (purr)
4 cockerels crow
5 doves coo
6 lambs bleat
7 pigs grunt (squeal)
8 turkeys gobble
9 mice squeak
10 bulls bellow

c 1 A brogue is a type of strong shoe.
2 The rogue absconded with most of the money.
3 A meringue is made from sugar and the white of an egg.
4 The professor and his colleague were working on an experiment.
5 The message was so vague that nobody knew what it meant.

d 1 the crack of a whip
2 the call of a bugle
3 the twang of a bow
4 the swish of a cane
5 the boom of a gun
6 the patter of raindrops
7 the screech of brakes
8 the rustle of silk
9 the rattle of chains
10 the shuffle of feet

E 1 The lens magnified the seeds, and we could see the detail clearly.
2 Sound that is amplified is made louder.
3 The parents pacified the distressed children.
4 Some of our railways have been electrified.
5 The police were mystified by the man's disappearance.

f 1 It was impossible to convict the man on such slender evidence.
The convict climbed over the prison wall.
2 She tried to console the bereaved relatives.
The organist sat at the console.
3 The subject of his talk was 'Prehistoric Animals'.
Genghis Khan was able to subject much of central Asia to his rule.
4 Equipment was set up to record the concert.
The athlete set up a new record for the high jump.

5 The lid was a perfect fit.
The inventor was able to perfect his design.

g 1 Adjective
2 Verb
3 Noun
4 Noun
5 Verb
6 Adjective
7 Adjective
8 Noun
9 Verb

h 1 Bursting into the room Amanda told us that she had won.
2 Apologising for the delay the chairman opened the meeting.
3 Leaving his car by the roadside the driver set out to find help.
4 Pretending that I hadn't seen him I walked away in the opposite direction.
5 Arriving late for the concert we found that all the tickets had been sold.

i 1 It seems certain that spoken language came before written language.
2 Another word for language is tongue.
3 Apart from eye a picture of an eye could mean sight or looking.
4 The Sumerians lived in southern Mesopotamia.
5 Sumerian wedge-shaped writing was called cuneiform.
6 There were about 600 characters in the Sumerian system of writing.
7 The ancient Egyptians developed a kind of paper made from layers of the stem of a water plant called papyrus.
8 The Rosetta Stone was found near the town of Rosetta on the Nile delta.
9 The Rosetta Stone carried an inscription in three languages–hieroglyphics, demotic and Greek.
10 A Frenchman called Champollion deciphered the Rosetta Stone.

j 1 The wreck (wreckage) was a danger to other ships.
2 The ball struck him on the wrist and broke his watch.
3 The wren is a small, brown bird.
4 I couldn't see anything wrong with it.
5 The miserable wretch was found sheltering under a hedge.
6 A wreath was placed on the war memorial.
7 The books were wrapped in thick brown paper.
8 A wrench is a kind of spanner and is used for turning nuts and bolts.
9 The hand rail was made of wrought iron.
10 The old woman's face was wrinkled and careworn.

The alphabet *pages 14–15*

a
1. An alphabet is a set of symbols called letters that we use when writing.
2. Each letter stands for a given sound or sounds.
3. We get the word alphabet from alpha and beta–the names of the first two letters of the Greek alphabet.
4. There are 26 letters in our alphabet.
5. The Semites lived in the Middle East.
6. The Phoenicians produced an alphabetical system consisting of 22 signs for the consonants only.
7. The Greeks got to know about Phoenician writing through trading with the Phoenicians.
8. The Etruscans lived in Italy.
9. The later Roman alphabet had 23 letters.
10. J, U and W were added later.

b
1. The Greeks used Phoenician symbols in their alphabet.
2. The elephant is the largest land animal in the world.
3. The doctor examined the graph of the patient's temperature.
4. We read about other countries in our geography books.
5. Alexander Graham Bell invented the telephone.

c

1 answer	6 jaguar	11 sandal
2 clarinet	7 laundry	12 thermometer
3 dolphin	8 mosque	13 violin
4 frigate	9 nomad	14 woodpecker
5 harness	10 quadrant	15 yacht

d *First stage*
(Early Greek inscriptions were written like this.)
At first, the direction of Greek writing was from right to left.
Second stage
(This shows the second stage in the direction of Greek writing. It is sometimes called ploughwise. The word ploughwise may perhaps give you a clue.)
In this stage of Greek writing one line went from right to left, the next line going from left to right, then right to left, and so on.
This form is called boustrophedon, meaning ox turning, to suggest the way in which the direction of the writing followed that of an ox when pulling a plough.
Third stage
(This arrangement was used after about 500 B.C.)
This shows a later development in the way in which words were set down. Spaces between words, punctuation and the use of lower-case (small) letters came later.

e 1 Before they had any kind of writing, people preserved such things as stories, poems, traditions etc. by word of mouth.
2 The Phoenicians were noted sailors and explorers, travelling throughout much of the Mediterranean area and even beyond. They were also great traders, while the cities of Tyre and Sidon were famous for their purple-dyeing industry. The Phoenicians were also skilled at weaving cloth.

Development of the alphabet *pages 16–17*

a We can trace the letter M back to an Egyptian symbol which was not much more than a wavy line. The Semites borrowed this, calling it mem which was their word for water. The third picture in the line shows how the Phoenicians altered the Semitic symbol, making it more like one of our letters, but still keeping the wavy line. The Greek letter M, which they called mu, is almost the same as ours. The elegant Roman M is shown in the fifth picture.
Similarly, the letter R can be traced back to an Egyptian symbol, this time showing a human head. The Semites borrowed and adapted this, calling the letter resh which was their word for head. In the third picture we can see how the Phoenicians simplified the Semitic symbol into something like a triangle with one of its lines extended. The Greek letter rho is a reversal of the Phoenician and with the triangle now rounded to give a P-shape. The last picture in the line shows the Roman capital R derived from the Greek.

b 1 Wednesday
2 February
3 a
4 WREN
5 first ghost chops

c 1 Bible, the sacred writings of the Christian faith, means 'the books' because the Bible is really a collection of books, not just one book.
2 bibliography–usually a list of books on a particular subject.
3 paternal–fatherly or related through one's father.
4 patriotic–loving one's native country or fatherland.
5 monopoly–having sole control over something.
6 monoplane–an aircraft with one set of wings.
7 geology–the science of the earth's crust.
8 geography–the science of the earth, its features, climate and people.
9 polygon–a figure with many sides (usually more than four).
10 polygamy–having several wives or husbands (or more than one wife or husband).

d Our alphabet has 26 letters, but some languages have a different number. Russian has 33. Arabic has 28. Gaelic has 18. Some alphabets are very complicated and attempts have been made to simplify them. In 1928 the Turks changed their alphabet from the Arabic to the Roman style, while the Japanese have more recently tried to simplify their system of writing.

e 1 We use the expression 'alpha and omega' to mean the beginning and the end of something.
Alpha is also used in astronomy (alpha centauri) and in physics (alpha rays).
Gamma is used in physics (gamma rays).
Delta appears in geography (a river delta), in aeronautics (delta wing) and in physics (delta rays).
Iota is used to mean a jot or very small quantity of something.
Pi is used in geometry to express the ratio of the circumference of a circle to its diameter. It is usually written π and equals 3.14159.
Some of the names of Greek letters are also used as trade names.
2 A feature of Roman inscriptions was that 'U' was written as 'V', the Romans using the letter V for both U and V sounds.

The Roman alphabet *pages 18–19*

a 1 The Romans took their alphabet from the Etruscans (who got it from the Greeks).
2 Roman lettering was graceful, clear and easy to read from a distance.
3 It was especially important for the lettering to be clear when it was some way above ground, as in inscriptions on buildings, arches and memorial columns.
4 The unconnected ends of letters caused the carvers most problems.
5 The unconnected ends of letters were finished off with a short cross-line.
6 The short cross-lines are called serifs.
7 Roman children learned their letters by writing them on wooden tablets coated with wax.
8 The children used a pointed instrument called a stylus to write with.
9 The wax tablets could be used more than once because, when a piece of work was finished with, the wax could be made smooth again so that more writing could be done.
10 The Romans also wrote on papyrus or (more commonly) parchment.

b 1 He walked carefully across the icy road.
2 We were successful at the second attempt.
3 The mural was beautifully painted.
4 She danced gracefully round the stage.
5 The crew were respectful to their captain.
6 I was thankful to see him safe and well.

c 1 centurion–an officer in the (ancient) Roman army in command of 100 men.
2 century–a period of 100 years or 100 runs in cricket.
3 supervise–to look over or superintend the work or activity of other people.
4 superior–better or higher in rank or quality.
5 manuscript–a piece of work written by hand.
6 manual–a handbook, e.g. of instructions (noun); done with the hands (adjective).
7 multitude–a large crowd.
8 multiple–having many parts (adjective)
a number that divides exactly by another number (noun)
9 union–a joining of separate things (or people) into one.
10 unison–agreement; voices or instruments singing or playing at the same pitch.

d Papyrus was the monopoly of the Egyptians and they either charged other people dearly for it or prohibited its export altogether. So other people began to look for an alternative, and this led to the discovery of parchment. This took place in Pergamum, a Greek city in Asia Minor in about 190 B.C. Parchment is made from the skins of animals such as sheep or goats. A fine quality parchment called vellum is made from the skins of young animals such as calves, lambs or kids.

e 1 A.D. Anno Domini = in the year of our Lord.
a.m. ante meridiem = before noon.
p.m. post meridiem = after noon.
etc. et cetera = and the rest.
N.B. nota bene = note well.
Some other abbreviations that stand for Latin words:
e.g. exempli gratia = for example
i.e. id est = that is
Q.E.D. quod erat demonstrandum = which was to be shown
R.I.P. requiescat in pace = rest in peace.
2 Writing was sometimes scraped off parchment so that it could be used again. Valuable information might be lost in this way, although, by using infra-red photography, it is sometimes possible to read the very faint traces of the original writing.
(Twice-used parchments are called palimpsests.)

The English language *pages 20–21*

a 1 Before about A.D. 450 the people of Britain spoke a Celtic dialect.
2 The Roman occupation of Britain had little effect on the language.
3 The Anglo-Saxon occupation of Britain began soon after the Romans left.
4 Anglo-Saxon became the dominant language in England.
5 In about 750–1050 new words were brought into English as a result of Viking raids and influence.

6 The Normans invaded Britain in 1066.
7 The conquerors spoke French.
8 English had become widely used in Britain by about 1400.
9 Many French words are of Latin origin.
10 The English used about 500 years ago is sometimes called Middle English.

b
1 conqueror
2 competitor
3 explorer
4 jeweller
5 inventor
6 writer (author)
7 actor
8 employer
9 manufacturer
10 collector

c
1 Many foreign words have passed into our language.
2 It has been very wet during the past week.
3 Mandy passed her driving test yesterday.
4 The programme began at half past two.
5 The week's holiday passed quickly.
6 Mark passed the ball to his goalkeeper.
7 He talked a lot about his past life.
8 The dog wouldn't let us get past.

d
1 Our Father, which art in heaven, hallowed be Thy name.
(The opening of the Lord's Prayer.)
2 (In truth) when Jesus had come down from the hill, many people followed him.
(Matthew, Chapter 8 verse 1)

e
1 The words England and English come from the word Angles.
2 The word Norman comes from Northman because they came originally from Scandinavia in northern Europe. Normandy was named after the Northmen or Norsemen who conquered it in the 800's.
3 The Vikings came from present-day Sweden, Denmark and Norway. (The Vikings were also called Northmen, Norsemen or–rather loosely–Danes.)

Printing *pages 22–23*

a
1 The first printing was done from wood blocks, the shapes of the letters being carved by hand.
2 The disadvantages of printing from wood blocks were that it was a slow process and every page of every book had to be carved separately.
3 The Chinese discovered the use of movable type.
4 The use of movable type was known in Europe by about 1440.
5 In the method of printing by movable type individual letters were made from

separate pieces of metal. These letters could be assembled to make words and sentences. If the letters were inked over and pressed on to paper they would print the words.

6 Johann Gutenberg printed the 42-line Bible.
7 The 42-line Bible got its name because it had 42 lines on each page.
8 The first book printed in English was about the history of Troy.
9 Caxton set up a printing press in England at Westminster.
10 Caxton printed nearly 80 books.

b 1 television
2 telephone
3 telescope
4 telegram
5 telepathy

c 1 diminished 3 separately 5 recounted
2 requiring 4 assembled 6 established

d Most historians consider Johann Gutenberg to be the inventor of movable type in Europe, although a Dutch printer called Laurens Coster had been working on the same idea. At first Gutenberg worked in secret. This may have been to keep the idea to himself, or he may have felt that some people would mistrust his invention. Even when printing had been established some people regarded it as a kind of magic or 'black art'. They could not understand why all printed copies of a book looked alike and how they could be made so quickly.

e 1 Before any kind of printing had been invented books had to be written out by hand.
2 Flanders is mainly in Belgium and France, plus a small area in the Netherlands.
3 Books, newspapers, catalogues, magazines, comics, diaries, calendars, programmes, tickets, brochures, leaflets, posters, wrappers, bags, labels, games, charts, maps, time-tables, forms, stamps, postal orders, cheques, licences, money, money orders, invitations, instructions, handbooks, notices, circulars, pamphlets, guides, letterheads, menus, Christmas cards, birthday cards, other greetings cards, membership cards, race-cards etc. etc.
4 Paper.

Practice pages *pages 24–25*

a 1 judge
2 badge
3 hedge
4 dodge
5 nudge

b

1 aircraft	6 equator	11 kitchen
2 alligator	7 gnome	12 knight
3 biscuit	8 guard	13 professional
4 bottle	9 illustration	14 puppet
5 elephant	10 imitation	15 pyramid

c 1 pentathlon–an athletics contest consisting of five parts.
2 pentagon–a five-sided figure.
3 astronomy–the study of the heavenly bodies.
4 astronaut–a space traveller.
5 megaphone–a device for magnifying the sound of the voice.
6 megatherium–a large prehistoric mammal sometimes called the giant sloth.
7 hydrofoil–a boat whose hull is raised just above the water when the vessel travels at speed.
8 hydrant–a connection (often in the street) to which a hose may be connected for the purpose of drawing water, usually for fire-fighting purposes.
9 microfilm–film on which a very small copy of something (e.g. a document) may be photographed.
10 microbe–a very small organism, usually one that causes disease.

d 1 The old dog was faithful to its master.
2 I was painfully aware that my ankle was sore.
3 The man was wrongfully accused of fraud.
4 The acrobats gave a wonderful display of their skills.
5 They waited cheerfully for the match to begin.
6 We were hopeful that the weather would improve.
7 The art exhibition was very colourful.
8 Everything was tastefully arranged.
9 News of the victory was joyfully received.
10 Overeating can be harmful.

e 1 A phrase is a short group of words.
2 The pheasant is a game bird with a long tail.
3 A photograph is a picture produced by a camera.
4 To prophesy means to foretell what will happen.
5 For years no one knew how to decipher hieroglyphics.

f 1 aquarium–a tank in which water plants and animals are kept.
2 aqueduct–an elevated bridge-like structure for carrying a pipe or channel along which water is conveyed from a distance.
3 bicycle–a two-wheeled riding machine.
4 biplane–a flying machine with two sets of wings.
5 omnibus–a bus; a public passenger vehicle (for all).
6 omnipotent–all powerful; having great power.
7 pedal–a kind of lever worked by the foot.
8 pedestrian–a person who goes on foot (i.e. walking).
9 contraband–smuggled goods; goods against which there is a ban.
10 contradict–to speak against someone by opposing or denying something.

g 1 commander
2 inspector
3 director
4 defender
5 sailor
6 governor
7 lecturer
8 announcer
9 donor
10 astronomer

h 1 S
2 LACES; SCALE
3 I
4 B
5 G
6 EMU
7 N
8 U
9 L
10 S

English as a world language *pages 26–27*

a The four illustrations show English in use in a number of ways:
(i) It is widely used in football coaching in many parts of the world. A number of British coaches and managers have been engaged in introducing and developing our national game abroad and English is now the official language of F.I.F.A.
(ii) It is the official language by means of which pilots communicate with air traffic controllers.
(iv) The world's popular music is now on a much more international scale as groups and individuals appear–and sometimes compete–all over the world. The influence of the United States and Britain in this field has tended to make English the dominant language, many titles and lyrics being in English to give them perhaps a wider appeal.
(iv) English is widely used in diplomacy and many of the world's political leaders and heads of state speak English fluently.

b 1 air hostess, steward, flight attendant
2 referee, umpire
3 guide, courier

4 merchant, trader, dealer
5 receptionist
6 diplomat, envoy
The pupil is asked to explain how it could be helpful to each of these people if there were such a thing as a world language.

c Over the years several artificial languages have been created. The first one, called Volapuk, was created in 1879. Unfortunately, Volapuk was very complicated and soon died out. It was followed a few years later by Esperanto. This has become the most successful artificial language.

d Another attempt to devise a world language was called Basic English. It was devised by C. K. Ogden and I. A. Richards between 1925 and 1932. The idea was to produce a kind of simplified English that would be easy for everyone to learn. Altogether there are about 600,000 English words, but Basic English used only about 800 of these. A number of books were translated into Basic English, but in recent years the idea has not been widely used.

e 1 The reason why English is used in so many parts of the world can be traced back to about the 16th century, when England became an important sea power and her ships sailed all over the world. Explorers and missionaries travelled extensively and they were soon followed by colonists and settlers who, of course, took their language with them.
Nevertheless, the English arrived rather late on the exploration and discovery scene. In many cases English–or British–explorers were not the first Europeans to discover some of the far-away places where English is now spoken. The Portuguese were probably the first to reach Australia, while the Dutch were the first to sail in New Zealand waters. A Norwegian explorer was perhaps the first to land in North America. Very often, however, little or nothing was done to follow up an early visit and this gave others the opportunity to establish themselves–and their language.
One of the most important reasons for the subsequent spread of English is the fact that it became *the* language of North America. In 1788 the population of the United States was less than 4 million people. Now it is something like 220 million. Only China, India and Russia have more people but none of the languages they speak is used in any other country. Many Americans are descendants of people who came from such countries as Germany, Italy, Austria, Hungary and Russia, but most of the early settlers were English and so that became the language of the United States. The increasing importance and influence of the United States in world affairs, especially in the fields of science, diplomacy and communications, has meant greater use of English by the nations of the world in conducting their affairs and exchanging information.

2 The language is Chinese. It is not really suitable as a world language because hardly anybody outside China can understand it. It is also difficult to learn as it uses a series of characters instead of a western-style alphabet.

How we get new words *pages 28–29*

a 1 Language changes because it needs new words for new inventions, discoveries, instruments and ideas.
2 Words sometimes drop out of use because they are names of things that people no longer use.
3 Inventions are sometimes named after the people who invented them.
4 Materials are sometimes named after the places where they were first made.
5 Many new words come from Latin or Greek.
6 The word multinational comes from two Latin words.
7 The word protoplasm comes from two Greek words.
8 The Greek word automobile comes from a mixture of Latin and Greek.
9 The word television comes from a mixture of Latin and Greek.
10 Words such as fabulous and chronic have taken on a new and popular meaning that has almost obliterated the old.

b 1 runway
2 underpass
3 sunspot
4 spacecraft
5 blackout
6–10 Specimen answers; others are possible.
6 The runway was extended so that larger planes could use the airport.
7 Traffic congestion was eased by the new underpass.
8 A large sunspot may be almost 160,000 km across.
9 Unmanned spacecraft are used to explore the planets.
10 The blackout was caused by a power failure.

c 1 NATO
2 DORA
3 RADAR
4 NALGO
5 ERNIE
6 LASER

d 1 Balaclava: a close-fitting woollen cap or 'helmet' covering head, ears and back of neck. (After Balaclava in the Crimea).
2 Jersey: a close-fitting upper garment made of wool. (From Jersey, largest of the Channel Islands.)
3 Bikini: A brief, two-piece bathing costume worn by women. (After Bikini, an atoll or group of small islands in the Pacific.)
4 Fez: A red, brimless hat made of wood or felt and having a small, black tassel. (From Fez in Morocco.)
5 Duffel: A coarse, heavy woollen cloth. (From Duffel, near Antwerp.)
6 Cashmere: A fabric made from goats' hair. (From Kashmir in Asia.)

7 Denim: A twilled cotton fabric used in overalls and other garments. (From the French 'de Nimes'–from Nimes in southern France.)
8 Calico: A plain (usually white) cotton cloth. (First obtained from Calicut in India.)
9 Suede: The skin of a kid. (Swedish-made gloves of this material were called 'gants de Suede'–Suede being the French word for Sweden.)
10 Muslin: A fine, soft cotton fabric with a gauzy appearance. (Originally from Mosul in present-day Iraq.)

e 1 Astronaut
2 Pandemonium: a tumultuous and disorderly uproar. (Milton)
Chortle: to chuckle (Lewis Carroll)
Runcible: An adjective applied to a spoon in a poem by Edward Lear.
3 QANTAS: The Australian national airline.
(Queensland and Northern Territory Aerial Service Ltd.)
SABENA: Belgian world airlines.
(Societe Anonyme Belge d'Exploitation et Navigation Aerienne.)
FIAT: A make of Italian motor vehicle.
(Fabbricca Italiana Automobili Torino.)
SAAB: A Swedish firm that makes cars and aircraft.
(Svenska Aeroplan Aktiebolaget.)

Borrowed words *pages 30–31*

a
1	Yacht	Holland
2	Matador	Spain
3	Gong	Malaya
4	Bungalow	India
5	Piano	Italy
6	Kangaroo	Australia
7	Robot	Czechoslavakia
8	Zebra	Africa
9	Caravan	Persia

b (1) These words are French and they are all concerned with food or cooking.
(2) These words are Italian and they are all concerned with music, particularly the way in which music should be played.

c
1 kangaroos	5 igloos	9 tattoos
2 pianos	6 casinos	10 salvoes or salvos
3 chefs	7 scarves or scarfs	11 potatoes
4 bureaux	8 plateaux	12 tomatoes

d

	A	B
1	fiord	Norway
2	chimpanzee	Africa
3	boomerang	Australia
4	cafe	France
5	waltz	Germany
6	piccolo	Italy
7	judo	Japan
8	kiwi	New Zealand (Maori word)
9	tomahawk	North America (Indian word)
10	vanilla	Spain

e 1 The Maoris were the people who lived in New Zealand before the arrival of settlers from Europe. Originally they had migrated from the Polynesian islands of Tahiti and Raratonga. There are about a quarter of a million Maoris now living in New Zealand.

2 cobalt, quartz, poodle

3

algebra	Arabic	oasis	Egypt
broccoli	Italy	ukulele	Hawaii
tattoo	Tahiti	geyser	Iceland
mosquito	Spain	shampoo	India
skipper	Holland	umbrella	Italy
balsa	Spain	sauna	Finland
kiosk	Turkey	kimono	Japan
toboggan	North American Indian		

Spelling *pages 32–33*

a 1 The chief cause of spelling difficulty is that spelling and pronunciation don't always match very well.

2 Pronunciation means the way we say words.

3 We can spell fish as 'ghoti' by taking the 'gh' from cough to give the f sound, the 'o' from women to give the i sound and the 'ti' from nation to give the sh sound.

4 The remarkable thing about the pronunciation of the letter 'e' in defender is that each time it makes a different sound.

5 The distinction that used to be made between the pronunciation of father and farther is probably that the first 'r' in farther used to be given a distinctive trill.

6 The letter 'b' is silent in subtle.

7 The letter 'p' is silent in receipt.

8 Subtle comes from the Latin sub tela.

9 Receipt comes from the Latin recipere.

10 The word debt comes from the Latin debitum.

b
1 address
2 currant
3 answer
4 chocolate
5 squirrel
6 carriage
7 excitement
8 February
9 parliament
10 guide
11 immediately
12 foreman
13 guarantee
14 medicine
15 appetite

c
1 daffodil
2 traffic
3 rabbit
4 forty
5 gorilla
6 tragedy
7 luggage
8 annual
9 walnut
10 until
11 quarrel
12 amount
13 icicle
14 privilege
15 asphalt

d
1 said
2 friend
3 school
4 wrong
5 cough
6 plough
7 doctor
8 who
9 ghost
10 ache
11 centre
12 bomb
13 knock
14 laugh
15 bought

e
1 (a) We bought some stationery from the newsagent.
(b) She used to practise the piano every day.
(c) If you have a television set you have to have a licence.
(d) He wouldn't accept advice from anyone.
(e) The shoes were not quite what I wanted.

2 At first sight there would seem to be some advantages, especially for learners, if words were spelt as they are pronounced. Difficulties could arise, however, if there were further changes in pronunciation. Would spelling have to be revised again, to keep up with new trends? And what about dialect? What influence would this be allowed to have on a spelling system geared to pronunciation?

In any case, a serious problem that spelling reform would come up against is that all existing books would have the 'old' spelling and this would pose a special problem for schools and libraries. They would simply not be able to afford to throw away all their old books and buy new ones.

For this and other reasons there would have to be a lengthy transition period, but this itself could lead to problems and prolong any resistance to change. Meanwhile, the mixture of 'old' and 'new' spelling in different books in use could be very puzzling for most of us and particularly daunting for just those people whom change was perhaps meant to help most. Changes in money systems and in weights and measures are comparatively simple and straightforward since these involve only a few new words and ideas.

Widespread spelling reform could affect some part of everything we read or write. Perhaps the best thing to do would be to change a small number of specially difficult words.

Overworked words *pages 34–35*

a
1 We boarded the train at Manchester.
2 The continual noise irritated my nerves.
3 They have prospered since they enlarged the shop.
4 The battalion withdrew while there was still the chance to do so.
5 The bus company issued a new time table.
6 Eventually we recovered from the shock.
7 For a time the patient's condition deteriorated.
8 After a few days his health improved.
9 Jane scored full marks for her work.
10 He passed his final examination without difficulty.
11 The prisoners escaped by climbing a high wall.
12 I persuaded Father to take me to the match.

b
Specimen answers; others are possible.
1 a fine day
2 a warm fire
3 a fragrant smell
4 an attractive garden
5 a refreshing drink
6 a stimulating argument
7 a lovely girl
8 a terrible mess
9 a kind thought
10 a juicy orange
11 a friendly dog
12 a welcome present

c
1 He decided to apply for the job.
2 The ship altered course because of bad weather.
3 I poured the milk into the jug.
4 The old lady had some difficulty in paying the rent.
5 The property was offered for sale.
6 We were able to accommodate them for the night.
7 The author was upset by the bad reviews of his book.
8 All the mistakes were corrected (rectified).
9 We planted the bulbs in the front garden.
10 Although Tim was small he would not let the bigger boys bully him.
11 The programme was broadcast (televised) at eight o'clock.
12 The lights were turned (switched) off at ten o'clock each evening.

d
Specimen answers; others are possible.
1 a well-behaved boy
2 a careful look
3 an interesting book
4 an amusing joke
5 a bright light
6 a hard worker
7 an enjoyable holiday
8 a satisfying dinner
9 a clever idea
10 a skilful driver
11 a graceful dancer
12 an entertaining match

e 1 (a) I try to save a little (a certain amount of) money each week.
(b) We saw a platoon (company etc.) of soldiers marching along the road.
(c) There was a drop of milk left in the jug.
(d) There were several (a number of) cars in the car park.
(e) In spite of the cool breeze, a few people were bathing in the sea.
(f) We were kept waiting for quite a long time.

2

extensive	enormous
vast	gigantic
huge	colossal
bulky	immense
massive	tremendous

considerable
great
spacious
commodious
gargantuan
prodigious
monstrous etc. etc.

Practice pages *pages 36–37*

a

	A	B
1	budgerigar	Australia
2	ballet	France
3	kindergarten	Germany
4	gondola	Italy
5	orang-utan	Malaya
6	squaw	North America (Indian word)
7	igloo	Eskimo
8	armada	Spain
9	tea	China
10	vodka	Russia

b

1	undercarriage	10	manpower
2	skateboard	11	splashdown
3	airlift	12	stockpile
4	soapflakes	13	flashback
5	layby	14	newsprint
6	taskforce	15	output
7	moonscape	16	cutback
8	hatchback	17	scoreboard
9	motorway	18	windtunnel

c 1 acquaintance
2 handsome
3 muscle
4 lettuce
5 arctic
6 pneumonia
7 juice
8 column
9 rhyme
10 possess
11 necessary
12 miniature
13 schedule
14 leopard
15 rheumatism
16 quickly

d 1 unnnecessary
2 accurate
3 cocoa
4 vigorous
5 professor
6 trespassers
7 longitude
8 paraffin
9 harass
10 omitted
11 occasion
12 garrison
13 plague
14 blissful
15 fulfil
16 aggregate

e 1 biscuit
2 echo
3 build
4 nation
5 debt
6 parachute
7 scheme
8 daughter
9 sausage
10 opaque
11 persuade
12 xylophone
13 photograph
14 cylinder
15 psalm
16 enough

f 1 Sightseers were kept away from the scene of the crash.
2 I had seen the programme before.
3 Vegetarians do not eat meat.
4 We arranged to meet again on the following Wednesday.
5 Some of the brake fluid had leaked.
6 There was a break for coffee at half past ten.
7 The ice floe was drifting towards the ship.
8 We could do nothing to stem the flow of water.
9 The umpire replaced the dislodged bails.
10 The straw was arranged in neat bales.

g

infinitesimal	diminutive
limited	trivial
puny	microscopic
trifling	brief
paltry	fine

tiny
minute
slight
slender
Lilliputian
scanty
mean etc. etc.

h 1 Letters that are not vowels are called consonants.
2 The Russian alphabet has 33 letters.
3 The Gaelic alphabet has 18 letters.
4 In 1928 the Turks changed their alphabet from the Arabic to the Roman style.
5 The discovery of parchment took place in Pergamum, a Greek city in Asia Minor.
6 Parchment is made from the skins of animals such as sheep or goats.
7 Vellum is a fine quality parchment made from the skins of young animals such as calves, lambs or kids.
8 Johann Gutenberg is generally considered to be the inventor of movable type in Europe.
9 At first Gutenberg worked in secret either to keep the idea to himself or perhaps because he felt that some people would mistrust his invention.
10 Volapuk and Esperanto are artificial languages.

i 1 Adjective
2 Noun
3 Noun
4 Adjective
5 Verb
6 Noun
7 Verb
8 Noun
9 Adjective
10 Noun
11 Noun
12 Verb
13 Verb
14 Noun
15 Adjective
16 Noun

Days of the week *pages 38–39*

a 1 Sunday is the first day of the week among Christian peoples.
2 We get the word Sunday from two Old English words sunnan daeg, meaning sun's day.
3 We get the word Monday from the Old English monan daeg, meaning moon's day.
4 We get the name Tuesday from Tyr, the old Norse god of war. His name is sometimes spelt Tiu or Tiw, giving the Old English Tiwes daeg, from which we get our Tuesday.
5 Wednesday gets its name from Wodnes daeg, which is Old English for Woden's day.
6 The Norse name for Woden or Wotan is Odin.
7 We get the word Thursday from Thor, son of Odin.
8 Frigga's day is Friday, the sixth day of the week.
9 Frigga's husband was Odin.
10 We get the word Saturday from Saturn (Old English Saeter-daeg), the Roman god of Agriculture.

b 1 The Norse gods' home was called Asgard.
2 Odin's spear was made by the dwarfs.
3 Odin made plans to meet the giants' threat.
4 The warriors' hall was called Valhalla.
5 The warriors' wounds were made whole.
6 One of the giants stole Thor's hammer.

c 1 reserved 3 regarded 5 akin
2 pagan 4 acknowledged 6 agriculture

d 1 A jovial person is merry and full of fun.
2 The floral decorations were very colourful.
3 The weight lifter was a man of herculean strength.
4 The regimental band played a selection of martial music.
5 A mercurial person is quick and sprightly.

e 1 The Romans didn't use the names of the planets Uranus, Neptune and Pluto because they didn't know about them. (Uranus was discovered in 1781, Neptune in 1846 and Pluto in 1930).
2 Sabbath comes from a Hebrew word meaning to rest. The Hebrew Sabbath comes on Saturday–the seventh day of the week. Christians sometimes use the word Sabbath for their day of rest, which is Sunday.
3 Shrove Tuesday–the day before Ash Wednesday. It was a time for confession, the old word shrove being the past tense of shrive, meaning to hear the confession of. Shrove Tuesday is sometimes called Pancake Tuesday, pancake eating being a survival of the old custom of eating well in anticipation of Lent.

Ash Wednesday–the first day of Lent, traditionally a period of fasting and penitence. Ashes are used as a symbol of penance, some churches using ashes to mark people's foreheads.
Good Friday–the Friday before Easter and the anniversary of Christ's crucifixion. 'Good' in this sense means 'holy'.

Months of the year *pages 40–41*

a 1 All our names for the months of the year are based on the Roman.
2 There were ten months in the earliest known Roman calendar.
3 By 46 B.C. the Roman calendar was about three months ahead of where it should have been.
4 Julius Caesar consulted an Alexandrian astronomer called Sosigenes. The result was a calendar of 12 months, beginning with January.
5 Quintilis was later renamed July, in honour of Julius Caesar.
6 Sextilus was later renamed August, after the Emperor Augustus.
7 The Julian calendar was a big improvement, but each year was about 11 minutes too long.
8 By 1580 the discrepancy amounted to 10 days.
9 Pope Gregory decreed that 10 days be removed from the calendar and that, from then on, only the century years that could be divided exactly by 400 would be leap years.
10 Britain adopted the Gregorian calendar in 1752.

b 1 January is named after the Roman god Janus. Janus had two faces looking in opposite directions, one to the past and the other to the future.
2 February takes its name from the Latin word februa. This was the name of a Roman festival of purification held in this month.
3 Our third month, and the first in the old Roman calendar, takes its name from Mars, the Roman god of war.
4 The Latin word Aprilis, meaning to open, gives us the name for the fourth month of the year.
5 There are various theories as to how we get the word May, but one is that it comes from Maia, the Roman goddess of spring and growth.
6 The month of June may take its name from Juno, the chief Roman goddess, but another explanation is that the word comes from juniores (which is Latin for young men) to whom the month was dedicated.

c 1 Our names for the months come from the Roman.
2 The earliest Roman calendar that we know of consisted of ten months.
3 January and February were later additions.
4 The old Roman calendar was rather inaccurate.
5 The Romans added extra days in alternate years.
6 The Julian calendar was much better than the old one.

d Arthurian, Edwardian, Elizabethan, Jacobean (Jacobite), Georgian, Victorian, Napoleonic, Mosaic, Franciscan, Cyrillic.

e 1 Thirty days hath September,
April, June and November.
All the rest have thirty-one,
Excepting February alone,
Which has but twenty-eight days clear
And twenty-nine in each leap year.
Note: There are some minor variations in this rhyme, particularly in the last line or two, for example:
And leap year coming once in four
Gives to February one day more.
2 1600, 2000
3 14 September 1752
4 Day: The time that the Earth takes to spin once on its axis.
Month: A month is roughly the time it takes for the moon to go round the earth.
Year: The time it takes the Earth to go once round the sun.
The week is the odd one out. The Romans (and certain other people before them) may have opted for a seven-day week after the seven heavenly bodies (Sun, Moon, Mercury, Venus, Mars, Jupiter and Saturn) that they knew and generally lumped together.

Using words *pages 42–43*

a 1 The doctor examined the patient.
2 Nigel peeped through the keyhole.
3 A number of men surveyed the proposed building site.
4 Karen glanced briefly at her watch.
5 We watched the programme with great interest.
6 The rescue team searched for survivors.
7 Colonel Fanshaw inspected the regiment.
8 The man at the turnstile scrutinised our tickets.
9 I stared in amazement at what I saw.

b 1 The rich people despised their poorer neighbours.
2 Mrs White took care of our cat when we went on holiday.
3 The detectives investigated the robbery.
4 The recruits were told to be quick.
5 All the parishioners respected the vicar.
6 'Watch out!' he shouted. 'There's a car coming.'
7 The grocer said that trade was improving.
8 We didn't like the appearance of the food.

9 Julie doesn't seem well this morning.
10 'I shall expect an improvement in our next game,' said the trainer.

c Specimen answers; others are possible.

1	heavy	10	fertile
2	dark	11	sharp
3	refreshing	12	deep
4	warm	13	friendly
5	thrilling	14	playful
6	delicious	15	winding
7	difficult	16	steep
8	stiff	17	attractive
9	comfortable	18	long

d 1 After some time the fire was put out.
2 They were tired by the time they reached the top.
3 We found a narrow passage hidden behind the panel.
4 She opened the book at the right page.
5 We bought enough food to last for a week.
6 He tried to overcome all obstacles.
7 We met stormy weather when we reached the hills.
8 The two cars left at the same time.
9 The lecturer showed how the chemical was made.
10 The patient took up a sitting position.

e round, wrong, drunk, old, kind, fat, rich, poor, calm, greedy.

Place names travel *pages 44–45*

a 1 Many American place names are taken from Britain, France, Spain, Portugal and Holland.
2 The previous name of New York was New Amsterdam.
3 New York was named after the Duke of York, later James II.
4 Louisiana got its name from King Louis XIV of France.
5 North and South Carolina are named after Charles I.
6 Lake Louise gets its name from the first name of a daughter of Queen Victoria.
7 The province of Alberta gets its name from the third name of a daughter of Queen Victoria.
8 The words Los Angeles mean the angels.
9 The words Las Vegas mean the meadows.
10 The names Ontario, Toronto, Missouri and Wichita are of Indian origin.

b 1 Maryland is named after Queen Henrietta Maria, the wife of Charles I.
2 The state of Vermont derives its name from the French words for green (vert) and mountain (mont).
3 George Washington, the first president of the U.S.A., is the man after whom the state of Washington gets its name.
4 The name Maine probably comes from mainland and may have been first used to distinguish the mainland from certain offshore islands.
5 Iowa gets its name from an Indian word of obscure meaning.
6 An Aleutian word meaning mainland is how Alaska gets its name.
7 It is thought that the state of Oregon may derive its name from ouragan, a French word meaning hurricane.
8 The origin of the name Illinois is the French form of an Indian tribal name.
9 Another Indian tribal name–that of the Ute Indians–is the origin of the name of the state of Utah.
10 Montana takes its name from a Spanish word meaning mountainous.

c 1 Hudson Bay is called after an English explorer.
2 The name Montreal is French for Mount Royal.
3 The port of San Diego is named after a Spanish saint.
4 The city of Ottawa takes its name from an Indian word.
5 The state of Virginia is named after Elizabeth I of England.

d 1 Texas
2 Washington
3 Maryland
4 Iowa
5 Illinois
6 Maine

e 1 New Hampshire: One of the early settlers (John Mason) gave it this name after his native county–Hampshire in England.
San Jose: The name is Spanish for Saint Joseph in whose honour the town was named.
Chattanooga: The name is taken from some Creek Indian words that referred to a mountain in the area.
Baton Rouge: This is the capital of Louisiana so it is not surprising to find that the name is of French origin. The name means 'red stick'. The 'stick' was a red-strained pole originally used to separate the territories of two Indian tribes.
Pittsburgh: Fort Pitt, a British post set up in 1758, was named after William Pitt who was British Prime Minister at the time. A settlement outside the fort then took on the name of Pittsburgh.

2 Ayr: Australia
Boston: U.S.A.
Cambridge: U.S.A.
Halifax: Canada
Hamilton: Australia, New Zealand
Hastings: U.S.A., New Zealand
Ipswich: Australia
Kingston: Canada, Jamaica, U.S.A.
Launceston: Australia
London: Canada
Nelson: Canada, New Zealand
Newcastle: Australia
Perth: Australia
Richmond: U.S.A., Australia, New Zealand
Roxburgh: New Zealand
Stratford: Canada, New Zealand
Tamworth: Australia
Warwick: Australia
Wellington: Australia, New Zealand
Windsor: Canada

Names of countries *pages 46–47*

a 1 The name Italy comes from the Roman word Italia, though this was first applied only to the southern part of the Italian peninsula.
2 The word Romania simply means land of the Romans.
3 We get the word Spain from Hispania–the Roman name for that province.
4 The Romans called Portugal Lusitania.
5 Portugal got its present name from Portus Cale–the Roman name for the town of Porto.
6 Colombia is named after Christopher Columbus.
7 America got its name from Amerigo Vespucci, an explorer who claimed he had discovered the New World.
8 Czechoslovakia got its name when the Czechs and the Slovaks joined to form a new independent country.
9 Tanzania was formed from the union of Tanganyika and Zanzibar.
10 The name Pakistan was formed by combining parts of the names Punjab, Afghan frontier, Kashmir, Sind and Baluchistan.

b 1 There are various ways in which the countries of the world have acquired their names.
2 The Roman name Italia gives us the word Italy.
3 Our word Spain comes from the name of the Roman province Hispania.
4 Amerigo Vespucci gave his name to the American continent.
5 The discovery of the New World was claimed by Amerigo Vespucci.

c 1 The word Ecuador comes from the Spanish for equator. The country is so called because the equator passes through it.
2 Bolivia is called after Simon Bolivar, a Venezuelan general who helped Spanish colonies in South America to gain their independence.
3 The Indian word chilli, meaning 'place where the land ends', is the origin of the name Chile.
4 Canada gets its name from an Indian word Kanata or Kanada that means a village or a group of huts.
5 The name France is derived from that of the Franks who were a group of tribes who attacked the Roman province of Gaul in 486 and set up a kingdom there.

d 1 Ireland
2 Ethiopia
3 Holland
4 Russia (Soviet Union)
5 Iran
6 Egypt
7 Botswana
8 Thailand
9 Sri Lanka
10 Taiwan

e 1 Switzerland
2 Belgium
3 Germany
4 Austria
5 Spain
6 Denmark
7 Iceland
8 Sweden
9 Norway
10 Netherlands (Holland)

Practice pages *pages 48–49*

a 1 The lady's coats were in her wardrobe.
2 The ladies' coats were in their cloakroom.
3 The children's playground has been resurfaced.
4 The doors of the men's changing room were locked.
5 The woman's car was parked outside her house.
6 The women's clothes are on the first floor.
7 The play was performed in the Infants' hall.
8 There were boxes of apples and oranges outside the greengrocer's shop.
9 We heard the sound of horses' hoofs in the distance.
10 Simon's dog has hurt its paw.

b 1 July is named in honour of Julius Caesar who was born in this month. Its previous name was Quintilis, meaning fifth, because it was the fifth month of the old Roman calendar.

2 Augustus, the first Roman Emperor, gave his name to August. It was formerly known as Sextilis, meaning sixth, because it was the sixth month of the old Roman calendar.

3 September was the seventh month of the old Roman calendar, taking its name from septem, meaning seven.

4 The eighth month of the old Roman calendar, and our tenth, derives its name from octo, which is Latin for eight.

5 From novem, meaning nine, we get the name November. It was so called because it was the ninth month of the old Roman calendar.

6 In the old Roman calendar the tenth month was called December, from decem meaning ten. It is now the twelfth month, but the old name has survived.

c 1 At the conclusion of the meeting everyone left the hall.
Conclusion means end.

2 The mob dispersed when the mounted police arrived.
Dispersed means scattered.

3 The game of golf originated in Scotland in about 1100.
Originated means began.

4 The customers complained about the exorbitant prices.
Exorbitant means high.

5 One member expressed dissent, but everyone else was in favour.
Dissent means disagreement.

d 1 stories
2 storeys
3 radii
4 cacti or cactuses
5 mottoes
6 solos
7 shelves
8 dwarfs
9 handkerchiefs
10 branches
11 taxes
12 sheep

e 1 The name Texas is derived from the Spanish pronunciation of Tejas, an Indian word meaning friends or allies.

2 The probable origin of the name Missouri–both the state and the river–is an Indian word meaning 'town of the big canoes'.

3 The state of Delaware takes its name from that of Lord de la Warr, a governor of Virginia.

4 Georgia is named after King George II of England, from whom the early settlers received their charter in 1732.

5 The meaning of Pennsylvania is 'Penn's Wood' and combines the name of William Penn, who founded the colony in 1681, with sylvanus, which is Latin for wood.

f 1 Alaska
2 Missouri
3 Vermont
4 Oregon
5 Louisiana

g 1 Many borrowed words are now widely used in ordinary speech.
2 Several New World place names are connected with kings and queens.
3 New York used to be called New Amsterdam.
4 Many place names in America have come from Indian words.
5 The countries of the world have come by their names in several ways.

h 1 Canaries (birds)
2 Jaffa oranges
3 The game of rugby
4 The game of badminton
5 Madeira wine
6 Champagne–a white wine
7 Gorgonzola–a kind of cheese
8 Stilton–another kind of cheese
9 Wine made near Oporto (port)
10 Panama hat

i 1 Tyr was the old Norse god of war.
2 Saturn was the Roman god of agriculture.
3 The Romans named the days after the sun, the moon and five planets–Mars, Mercury, Jupiter, Venus and Saturn.
4 The early Roman calendar did not keep in step with the seasons.
5 The Roman god Janus was unusual in having two faces looking opposite ways.
6 Mars was the Roman god of war.
7 The name Vermont comes from the French words vert (meaning green) and mont (meaning mountain).
8 The word Spain comes from Hispania, the Roman name for that province.
9 Amerigo Vespucci gave his name to the New World.
10 The country of Bolivia is named after Simon Bolivar.

j 1 meaning
2 using
3 running
4 making
5 putting
6 shopping
7 having
8 writing
9 keeping
10 replacing
11 beginning
12 explaining
13 indicating
14 trying
15 choosing
16 arranging
17 waiting
18 hitting
19 hunting
20 hopping
21 hoping

Signs and notices *pages 50–51*

a 1 Signs and notices help us to find our way along roads, round towns and in buildings.
2 Signs and notices are used in shops and places of entertainment.
3 Signs and notices should be clear, not too long, informative and placed where people can easily read them.
4 There shouldn't be too many signs and notices or people will be bewildered rather than helped.
5 An outsize department sells items of clothing that are larger than the usual sizes required.
6 The connection between 'outsize' and 'larger' is that they both mean roughly the same thing, the play on words arising from the way they are used here.
7 SMOKING CAN CAUSE FIRES–PLEASE USE ASHTRAYS FOR CIGARETTE ENDS
8 The double meaning in the butcher's notice is that the word killed clearly refers to the meat, but the way it is put here makes it look as though it refers to the farmers.
9 The double meaning in the driving school notice is (i) don't stop your wife from learning to drive, and (ii) don't stand in front of her car while she is doing this.
10 The dogs are not likely to see the point of the notice on the dog bowl.

b		
	1 informative	5 interpreted
	2 bewildered	6 deliberate
	3 convey	7 displayed
	4 ambiguous	8 intention

c 1 The notice suggests that we should knock gently in order not to cause an explosion.
2 Remains can mean relics or what is left. The expression 'That remains to be seen' means something like 'We will have to see about that' or 'We will see how things turn out'.
3 The play on words is on 'service'. In the first place it means assistance. In the second place it refers to a meeting at the church for purposes of worship and prayer.
4 The play on words is on 'prints' which also sounds very much like 'prince'–charming prints or prince charming.
5 The implication is that the cut-price paperweights will not run you into great expense in the first place. They will then help you to keep your papers in a tidy pile.

d 1 The newsagent wants boys and girls to take the papers round, but it sounds as though he wants boys and girls made of paper.

2 The heavy plant is likely to be a large piece of construction or engineering equipment, but it sounds as though possibly an outsize geranium may be making its way across the road.

3 The notice means that the closure will take place next week and will then last for a fortnight. It sounds as though a week's closure will last for a fortnight.

4 Presumably the notice means 'Open seven days a week'. As it is, it means that the restaurant will be open for just seven days and then close. A certain lack of ambition or confidence is suggested.

5 The notice means to say that the chemist prepares his medicines with great accuracy. Unfortunately, it can also mean that he does away with or does without accuracy.

e 1 (a) The notice means that there is one sausage roll and that it is for sale. It is intended to say that there are a number of them for sale and so should be:
SAUSAGE ROLLS FOR SALE
(b) It reads as though it is addressed to child-drivers whereas it is really meant for adults to read. It would be better put like this:
PLEASE DRIVE SLOWLY–CHILDREN

2 The purpose of this notice is to discourage people from driving too close to the vehicle in front. (In long, slow traffic queues this may be unavoidable, but generally the notice is giving sound advice.)

Word puzzles *pages 52–53*

a

1 C	Y	2 P	H	3 E	R		4 H	5 I	S	6 S
O		U		N		7 Y		N		P
8 P	E	N		9 T	H	E	A	T	R	E
Y		C		E		L		E		E
	10 S	T	A	R		11 L	Y	R	I	C
12 S		U						P		H
13 C	R	A	S	14 H		15 W	O	R	D	
R		T		A		E		E		16 M
17 I	N	I	T	I	A	L		18 T	O	Y
P		O		L		S		E		T
19 T	U	N	E		20 C	H	U	R	C	H

Note: 'cypher' may also be spelt 'cipher'

b
1. bib
2. did
3. deed
4. ewe
5. kayak
6. dad
7. solos
8. gag
9. toot
10. rotor

c
1. Was it a cat I saw?
2. Rise to vote, sir.
3. A man, a plan, a canal: Panama.
4. Step on no pets.
5. Never odd or even.
6. Madam, I'm Adam.
7. Draw pupil's lip upward.
8. Live on, time, emit no evil.
9. Able was I ere I saw Elba.
10. Now stop Major-General, are negro jam pots won?

d 1 stew
2 lamb
3 plea
4 vase
5 wrote
6 steak
7 these
8 neigh
9 crocus
10 recipe

e

S	A	T	O	R
A	R	E	P	O
T	E	N	E	T
O	P	E	R	A
R	O	T	A	S

The words can be read in four different ways.

Words that may be confused *pages 54–55*

a 1 The doctor put the thermometer in my mouth.
2 The python is one of the world's largest snakes.
3 A surgeon is a doctor who performs operations.
4 A party of sailors boarded the Spanish galleon.
5 There were two taxis waiting outside the station.
6 Another name for caterpillar is larva.
7–12 Specimen answers; others are possible.
7 A barometer is an instrument for measuring atmospheric pressure.
8 Overhead electricity cables are usually supported by pylons.
9 The sturgeon is a large fish that can be eaten.
10 A gallon equals just over four and a half litres.
11 The government collects taxes from us to pay for such things as education, roads and defence.
12 Molten rock that flows out of volcanoes is called lava.

b 1 The neglected wound had turned septic.
2 I waited outside the telephone kiosk.
3 The patient was suffering from a rare malady.
4 Mrs Moore bought a carton of ice-cream.
5 A glazier is a person who puts glass in windows.

c 1 I decided to accept the invitation.
2 The boy's handwriting was illegible.
3 A sheik is an Arab chief.
4 We saw a short excerpt from the play.
5 The cabbage was strained through a colander.

d 1 'May I try on that dress that is in the window?' she asked.
2 Mrs Ward and her husband stuffed the turkey.
3 Mr and Mrs Scott had lived in their house for ten years.
4 Yesterday Auntie Jane had dinner with us.
5 Mr Jackson teaches people to play the piano.
6 There was no one to cook for us so we had to cook for ourselves.
7 Mr Brown and his wife are both teachers.
8 We sat round the table and ate the breakfast that Father had cooked.
9 The batsman wore a cap to keep off the sunlight.
10 'I'm not very hungry,' said Simon. 'I don't feel like having a dinner.'
11 He was unable to play on account of his injured knee.
12 The soldiers at the front wore Balaclava helmets to keep themselves warm.

e Specimen answers; others are possible.
I ignored the irrelevant details in the report.
It would be considered irreverent to hold a loud conversation in a church.
The guide spoke both languages fluently and was able to interpret our request.
Someone in the crowd tried to interrupt the speaker.
The driver was prosecuted for not having a licence.
Some religious groups have been persecuted for their beliefs.
An alligator is a reptile related to the crocodile.
An allegory is a story that has more than one meaning.
An epitaph is something that is inscribed on a gravestone or tomb.
An epithet is an adjective used to express some quality or attribute that a person has.

Names *pages 56–57*

a 1 First names are sometimes called Christian names.
2 Another name for surname is family name.
3 In the first place names were formed from ordinary words.
4 Some names that were introduced by the Normans are William, Robert, Charles, Richard and Geoffrey.
5 Some Biblical names that we use are Mary, Elizabeth, Hannah, John and David.
6 Some Greek and Latin names are Margaret, Patricia, Barbara, Helen, Alexander and George.

7 The feminine forms of Paul, Julian and Stephen are Pauline, Julie and Stephanie.
8 Linda and Tina are shortened forms of Belinda and Christina.
9 Second names came into use during the Middle Ages.
10 Second names were useful to distinguish between people of the same name.

b

Common nouns	*Proper nouns*
uncle	Sarah
president	Everest
composer	Wednesday
title	Macbeth
saint	Queensland
university	Nigeria
mountain	Jeremy
prayer	February
river	Auckland
planet	Mississippi

c 1 Ampere–unit for measuring the flow of an electric current.
2 Beaufort–the Beaufort scale measures wind velocity.
3 Braille–a method of representing words by raised dots on paper that blind people can read by touch.
4 Bunsen–the Bunsen burner is a gas burner that has a hot, smokeless flame.
5 Cardigan–a knitted woollen jacket.
6 Colt–the first really successful repeating pistol.
7 Derby–a horse race run annually at Epsom in Surrey.
8 Diesel–a type of internal combustion engine used mainly in larger commercial vehicles but also in some cars.
9 Guillotine–a machine for beheading people.
10 Macadam–a road covering consisting of small broken stones pressed into a smooth surface.

D 1 Walter Wall–the carpet salesman.
(From wall-to-wall carpeting.)
2 Albert Ross–the authority on sea birds.
(From albatross, a kind of large sea bird.)
3 Horace Cope–the astrologer.
(From horoscope, a chart of stars and planets used by astrologers in preparing their forecasts, or an observation of these bodies at the time of a person's birth and an interpretation of their supposed influence on his/her life.)
4 Ida Downes–the bedding saleswoman.
(From eiderdowns, the kind of bed coverings that she might sell.)
5 Roland Butter–the continental waiter.
(From roll and butter, a simple kind of breakfast often favoured on the Continent.)

e Baker: probably came from the name of a person's occupation.
Forest: may have come from a description of where someone lived.
York: its first use may have referred to a person who lived there or came from there.
Armstrong: may have originated as a nickname.
Johnson: in the first place this probably meant 'son of John'.

The language of headlines *pages 58–59*

a 1 There are headlines in books, spoken headlines on radio or television and headlines that appear in newspapers or on placards.
2 They have to be brief.
3 Headlines are made to sound interesting so that we are enticed to read on.
4 Headlines on placards are a form of advertising and are no doubt used to whet our appetites in the hope that we buy a copy of the newspaper.
5 Short, forcible words and abbreviations are used in headlines to save space and arouse interest.
6 Demonstration, earthquake, helicopter, operation.
7 The headline word for 'something that is prohibited' is 'ban'.
8 A 'mercy dash' is a journey undertaken to rescue someone.
9 Words used in place of manager are boss, chief or top boss.
10 A business transaction is a deal and an inquiry is a probe.

b 1 NEW MOVE TO BAN DEMO
2 COPTER MAKES MERCY DASH or COPTER IN MERCY DASH
3 RAIL CHIEF IN PEACE TALKS
4 ARMS DEAL PROBE
5 LEAK HITS SHARE PRICES

c 1 The police are interviewing a number of football supporters.
2 A man has been detained in connection with the discovery (or recovery) of a quantity of drugs.
3 Discussions have been badly affected by a new argument.
4 A trade union has complained about an inquiry into jobs.
5 A manager has resigned because of a surprise report that has been issued.

d 1 The meaning is that the M P is in favour of the bridge, but it sounds as though he, personally, is holding it up.
2 It means that a minister does something to stop a theatre being closed or knocked down, but it sounds as though he/she is performing for the same purpose.
3 It means that the police are taking some action to promote good race relations, but it sounds as though a number of police, taking part in an athletics event, have got under way.

4 The headline means that a man has stolen a report that was issued by, or is the property of, the government. However, it sounds as though the man has stolen all the ministers who run the country.

5 The intended meaning is that a number of Japanese are involved in discussions about cars (buying and selling each other's cars) but it sounds as though an individual person from Japan, occupying a motor vehicle, has started to talk.

e (a) The 'jabs' for the boys are the inoculations they are being given. However, the headline is a play on words for 'jobs for the boys', as it is sometimes suggested that ex-public school pupils are adept, in later life, at helping each other find suitable employment.
(b) Business people sometimes talk about 'net losses', meaning losses that remain after other things have been taken into consideration. The play on words comes about because the ball landed in the goalkeeper's net three times.

Practice pages *pages 60–61*

a 1 When the volcano erupted hot lava poured out of the crater.
2 The archaeologists excavated a neolithic site.
3 A century is a period of one hundred years.
4 The singer had a large repertoire of songs.
5 The choir sang a descant to the second verse.

b 1 SLOW. OLD PEOPLE CROSSING ROAD.
2 NOKOFF RELIEVES COUGHS. FROM YOUR CHEMIST.
3 ANTIQUES. PLEASE DRIVE IN.
4 GUARD DOGS. KEEP AWAY.
5 POLICE NOTICE. NO PARKING.
6 The notice means that the people crossing the road are slow and old.
7 The notice means that 'Nokoff' relieves those coughs that you catch from your chemist.
8 The notice seems to be inviting the antiques to drive in.
9 The notice means that guard dogs keep away from the premises. Alternatively it could be addressed to guard dogs, advising them to keep away.
10 The notice implies that what the police notice is no parking.

c 1. level
2 noon
3 peep
4 poop
5 radar

d 1 face
2 heir
3 tale
4 knee
5 cider
6 maple
7 ocean
8 seldom
9 insect
10 organist

e

Common nouns	*Proper nouns*
lake	Panama
sea	Arabic
explorer	Tasmania
language	Baltic
poet	Michigan
inventor	Sydney
island	Sahara
desert	Edison
canal	Tennyson
city	Livingstone

(This list could also be arranged so that each common noun was placed opposite the appropriate proper noun: lake/Michigan sea/Baltic explorer/Livingstone etc.)

f 1 Macintosh (or Mackintosh)–A raincoat or waterproof coat.
2 Morse–A code consisting of dots and dashes in various combinations. Messages can be sent by telegraph or lamp.
3 Pullman–A luxury railway coach with very comfortable individual seats.
4 Plimsoll–A line (or series of lines) marked on the side of a ship to show how much cargo the ship can carry. (A ship will settle lower in the water as it is loaded, but should not go down beyond the appropriate mark.)
5 Sandwich–Two slices of bread with meat, cheese, egg, tomato etc. between.
6 Saxophone–A musical instrument. It is made of brass but has a reed like that of a clarinet.
7 Shrapnel–A shell filled with explosive and bullets. The bullets are scattered over a wide area on explosion.
8 Volt–The unit that is used to measure the force of an electric current.
9 Watt–A unit of power, usually electric power.
10 Wellington–A waterproof rubber boot covering the leg up to the knee as well as the foot.

g 1 Ann Cuff–the policewoman.
(From handcuff.)
2 Noah Drinkwater–the Scottish innkeeper.
(From the implication that he doesn't (no) drink water.)
3 Claire Round–the successful horsewoman.
(From 'clear round'.)
4 Matt Black–the painter.
(From matt or mat meaning a kind of paint finish which is dull or without a shine.)
5 Nesta Robins–the ornithologist.
(From 'nest of robins', an ornithologist being a person who studies birds.)

h 1 The headline means that the police issue a warning because of the danger of flooding. It sounds as though the police are watchful while the water is rising.
2 This means that the doctors have issued a warning that they will leave (the country), but it sounds as though they are saying that they will leave a warning.
3 The point of this headline is to remind us that things that appear to be free, such as education, have to be paid for somehow by somebody. The wording seems to be contradictory, but in this case that may have been the intention.
4 This means that a number of soccer fans have been accused of certain offences. but it sounds as though they have attacked something by rushing at it. (This headline could make sense either way.)
5 The headline means that the Prime Minister intervenes in some dispute or discussion concerning the docks, but it sounds as though he actually walks into the area where ships are loaded and unloaded.

i 1 A word, sentence or verse that reads the same backwards as well as forwards is called a palindrome.
2 The words minim and deified are palindromes.
3 A word or phrase whose letters can be re-arranged to make another word or words is called an anagram.
4 Many of the clues in crossword puzzles are in the form of anagrams and puns.
5 The names William, Robert, Charles, Richard and Geoffrey were introduced by the Normans.
6 The names Mary, Elizabeth, Hannah, John and David came from the Bible.
7 A common noun refers to a class of things and not to an individual object or person.
8 A proper noun is the name of a particular thing or person and should be written with a capital letter.
9 The names of Louis Braille, Rudolf Diesel and John McAdam are unusual or special because the surnames became the names of things that the people concerned discovered or invented.
10 Surnames originated from such things as place names, names or descriptions of a locality or district, names of occupations, names of parents and nicknames.

j 1 The notice means that the price of the suits has been reduced, but it sounds as though the suits themselves have been cut.
2 We are asked to draw the bath curtain before using the bath, but it sounds as though we should draw the curtain before using the curtain.
3 We are asked to give the food to the keepers, presumably so that they can hand it on to the animals, but it sounds as we should give it to the keepers so that they themselves can eat it.
4 The notice suggests that even people who have no rubbish to put in the bins will be prosecuted, whereas that is presumably intended for those who dispose of their rubbish in some unauthorised manner.
5 An improved version of the notice would be:
FOR SALE: FRESHLY-CUT FLOWERS
As it is, it sounds as though a new wound is being offered for sale.

k 1 Confusion between some pairs of words can produce absurd results.
Absurd means ridiculous.
2 We are accustomed to people having at least two names.
Accustomed means used.
3 Headlines may give brief summaries of the news.
Summaries means outlines.
4 An interesting headline may entice us to read further.
Entice means tempt.
5 An interesting headline may whet our appetite for more.
Whet means sharpen.

Letter writing *pages 62–63*

a 1 Brian Matthews has written to Mrs Parker.
2 Ann Parker (Mrs Parker) has written to Mr Matthews.
3 Brian Matthews lives at 123 Thornfield Crescent.
4 The Matthews family are going to Minehead for their holiday.
5 Mr Matthews wrote to Mrs Parker asking her to reserve two rooms on 15th May 1978.
6 Mr Matthews sent a deposit with his letter.
7 Mrs Parker sent a receipt with her reply.
8 We can tell that Mr Matthews and Mrs Parker had exchanged letters previously because Mr Matthews begins his letter by saying 'Thank you for sending the illustrated brochure'.
9 Mrs Parker forgot to say if pets were allowed at the hotel.
10 Mrs Parker has asked Mr Matthews to let her know what time he expects to arrive.

b 1 Mrs Pool writes with feeling but uses a rather rambling and inefficient style that won't help the supplier of the washing machine to help her. She forgets to give her full address, the make and type of machine she is using and such things as when and where she bought it. Instead she goes on about the extent of the mess and the age and cost of the carpet and what her husband thinks of it all. (It might have been better if he'd tried to do something about it instead of leaving everything to her.)

2

191 Townend Road
Ashbury
AS14 5LA
8 1 79

Dear Sir

On October 28 last year I bought a new POWERHOUSE 'Luxitub' washing machine from your discount warehouse in Castle Street, Westford.
A week ago the machine sprang a serious leak, causing a great deal of damage and inconvenience. I would be grateful if you would arrange to look at the machine with a view to repairing it as soon as possible. I can arrange to be at home any day after 2 p.m.

Yours sincerely
Susan Pool.

c 1 The style of this letter is brisk and efficient, but somehow it is all very cold and unfriendly. It sounds more like an impersonal business letter rather than a note from a friend about a holiday.

2 Dear James

Thanks a lot for your letter telling me the time of our flight to Majorca. That sounds fine. If we get to the airport about an hour or so before kick-off that should give plenty of time to sort things out and make sure that everything is O.K. As soon as I've parked the car I'll come along to the main terminal and look forward very much to seeing you there.

All the best
Yours etc.
Peter.

d The pupil is asked to write a letter to the local electricity board suggesting that he/she has been overcharged for electricity and giving reasons why he/she thinks this is so.

e The pupil is asked to draw a rectangle about 5½″ × 3¾″ (about 14 cm × 9½ cm) and write a name and address on it as though it were an envelope to be posted.

Communication for the handicapped *pages 64–65*

a 1 Children who are blind or deaf are taught in special schools where they are given extra help with their problems.
2 Braille is a special kind of alphabet that enables the blind to read by touch.
3 Braille gets its name from Louis Braille who invented the system in about 1829.
4 Raised dots are used to enable the reader to feel them.
5 The various arrangements of dots represent different symbols.
6 Sixty-three different arrangements of dots are possible.
7 Besides letters of the alphabet the dots stand for numerals, punctuation, common words (such as the, of, and) and the commoner parts of words (such as ch, ed, ing).
8 A blind person reads by running the fingertips lightly over the dots.
9 An experienced braille reader can read at about 200 words a minute.
10 A blind person can write by means of a braillewriter–a machine resembling a typewriter.

b 1 conventional 4 represent
2 universal 5 symbols
3 utilizes 6 resembling

c 1 The children were taught how to play the recorder.
2 An old proverb tells us that practice makes perfect.
3 I asked David if I could borrow his ruler.
4 'I think it's going to rain,' said Mother.
5 Because of the rain there were fewer people at the match.

d People who are deaf can communicate by such means as lip reading, sign language and the manual alphabet. Lip reading is difficult because there are instances when different words produce the same lip movements. Sign language consists of gestures, some of which are in the form of a simple mime. The manual alphabet is made by positioning the fingers and hands to stand for different letters so that words can be spelt out. For those who are both deaf and blind the method of communication is by touch, the speaker using his right hand to make signs on the left hand of the listener.

e 1 Books printed in braille are bigger and more cumbersome than ordinary books because the arrangement of dots takes up more space than ordinary letters and because the paper used has to be thicker than usual so that the patterns of dots will stand out.
2 Touch typing means typing without actually looking at the typewriter keys. It is obviously useful for blind people to know how to do this because they cannot see the keys anyway. (The value to a sighted person is that, while typing by touch, they can look elsewhere–for example at a letter or memo that has been written for them to type.)

3 (a) Helen Keller (1880–1968) was an American woman who, as a result of a serious illness, lost her sight and hearing before she was two years old. A dedicated teacher, Anne Sullivan, eventually got through to her by spelling out words on the girl's hand. Once she grasped the idea that everything had a name Helen made good progress, eventually learning braille, how to use a typewriter and how to 'listen' to other people by putting her fingers on their lips as they spoke. In spite of her great affliction she learned to speak and was able to go to College.
Helen Keller wrote books and was very active in the cause of helping the blind, including soldiers who had been blinded in battle.
(b) Joseph Hatton (1928–), an Englishman, became blind and deaf when he was four, but he has learned no fewer than four ways of communicating with other people,–by the deaf/blind manual alphabet, by the deaf manual alphabet, by placing his fingers on the lips of someone speaking to him and by putting a thumb against a speaker's throat. The last method, relying only on vibrations, is by far the most difficult one to master.

Heraldry *pages 66–67*

a 1 The idea of using coats of arms probably began with the Crusades.
2 The first English king to have a coat of arms was Richard I.
3 The lion of Scotland appeared as a heraldic symbol in 1222.
4 Rules about coats of arms came into being by 1245.
5 A coat of arms and the surrounding parts is called an achievement of arms.
6 The helmet rests on top of the shield.
7 The wreath fits round the top of the helmet and just below the crest.
8 The mantling is an array of ornamental drapery around the shield.
9 The motto, written on a scroll, is usually found below the shield.
10 We get the word heraldry from 'heralds' who were the king's officers in charge of the rules about the design and use of coats of arms.

b 1 A dragon is a large, imaginary creature with a generally reptilian kind of shape. It was very fierce and much given to breathing out fire. It had massive claws, wings and a long tail.
2 In Greek mythology Pegasus was a winged horse. For a time it was ridden by Bellerophon.
3 With the head and trunk of a woman and the tail of a fish a mermaid was a cross between a person and a fish.
4 The phoenix was a unique bird, which means that at any time there was only one in existence. After living for some 500–600 years the phoenix burned itself on a funeral pyre. After the flames had died down a new phoenix arose from the ashes of the old.

5 The unicorn was a legendary creature with the body of a horse and the tail of a lion. Its special distinguishing feature was one straight horn that projected from its forehead.

c 1 Oxford
2 Maidenhead
3 Gateshead
4 Barrow
5 Arundel

d 1 Penzance: The supporters remind us of 'the pirates of Penzance' and the fact that Penzance is a fishing port.
2 Stoke: The potter of ancient Egypt on the crest symbolises Stoke as the centre of the pottery industry in the U.K.
3 Newmarket: There is a running horse on the shield because Newmarket is the headquarters of horse-racing in Britain and the site of a famous race-course. It is also the home of the jockey club and the National Stud.
4 Banbury: The lady on a horse on the crest evokes the 'fine lady' of the old nursery rhyme associated with Banbury.
5 Lambeth: Lambeth Palace is the London home of the Archbishop of Canterbury, hence the archibishop's cross-staff and mitre on the Lambeth coat of arms.

e 1 The tournament was a contest and display in which knights in full armour and carrying shields and weapons took part in various combats or jousts. These served the purpose of exercising and developing skills while at the same time providing an exciting and colourful spectacle for those who were watching. A knight would often display a 'favour' (such as a glove) that had been given to him by a lady and he would try to do well in order to justify her interest and support. The winner of a joust would be permitted to name his lady as queen of the tournament for a day or two and she would preside over events for that time and award prizes.
The tournament seems to have originated in France, where the fighting was often very realistic. One French king was killed in a tournament. In England, after an early period when it was little more than a disorganised free for all, the tournament became more of a sporting occasion, with the use of blunted lances or swords to minimise the risk of serious injury. Strict rules of conduct came to be applied, with a system of points for correct blows and disqualification for serious fouls.
2 Latin and French.
3 The crusades were a series of military expeditions carried out by various Christian nations and groups of people from western Europe to drive the Muslim Turks out of the Holy Land.
There were several Crusades between 1096 and 1254, but they had no lasting success and gradually the Europeans began to lose interest.

Signs and symbols *pages 68–69*

a 1 Organisations such as companies, societies, industries, clubs, trades and crafts use signs and symbols.
2 The origin of many of our signs and symbols goes back to the days when few people could read.
3 When few people could read, traders and innkeepers would advertise their goods and services by means of pictures.
4 The sort of pictures then used were often straightforward illustrations of what was for sale or else of something connected with it.
5 A tobacconist's shop might be identified by a model or a picture of a pipe.
6 A tailor would display a picture of a pair of scissors.
7 As more people learned to read, the original purpose of many signs and symbols was lost.
8 Signs and symbols are used on the road, on buildings, on forms of transport, in books and on maps, on coins, pottery, silver ware and on school and club badges.
9 Signs and symbols on clothes convey instructions about washing, bleaching, drying and ironing.
10 Words, letters and figures are sometimes added to signs to give further information or to give a message that cannot easily be conveyed by a picture.

b 1 government 6 recognize
2 people 7 design
3 scissors 8 wreath
4 building 9 island
5 school 10 guard

c 1 On the sleeve of a sergeant in the army, air force or police. (Sometimes they are used to indicate years of service.)
2 The site and date of a battle. Used on ordnance survey maps.
3 The badge of the Red Cross–an international organisation for the care of war wounded and to bring relief to those suffering from the effects of floods, earthquakes, famine and other disasters.
4 The Olympic flag, the five interlocking circles representing the five continents joined together in a common purpose.
5 A system used by the Automobile Association to grade the quality of hotels and restaurants by awarding one or more stars.

d We see these signs on our roads. They mean:
Roundabout
Double bend
Slippery road
Road narrows on both sides
Dual carriageway ends

Steep hill downwards
Steep hill upwards
Hump bridge
Uneven road
Road works
Level crossing with barrier or gate
Level crossing without barrier or gate
No right turn
No left turn
No U turns

e 1 Canada
2 India
3 Japan
4 Russia or U.S.S.R.
5 Wales

Communication without words *pages 70–71*

a 1 Here, a cricket umpire is giving hand signals to indicate that the batsman has just scored a 'six'. Although such signals are a useful guide for players, spectators and commentators, they are primarily for the benefit of the scorer who is probably quite a long way from the wicket.

2 This illustration shows a conductor conducting an orchestra. He not only beats time but also conveys his ideas of how the music should be played. If effective, such gestures can be seen and followed at once without in any way spoiling the flow of the music.

3 A flag at half mast on a public building is usually a mark of respect for someone–usually a well-known public figure–who has recently died. This simple but effective device can easily be seen by a large number of people over a wide area.

4 The picture shows a policeman directing traffic. The type of signals used can be clearly seen and promptly understood by all road users.

5 The illustration shows a set of traffic lights as seen at crossroads and road junctions. Easy to see and understand at a glance, they tell drivers when to stop and when to go. A similar device may be used on very narrow bridges and where there are restrictions due to road works.

6 The man in the picture is signalling to a pilot so as to help him park his aircraft. Words could hardly be used on account of the noise of the aircraft's engines. It is because of this that the man wears protective pads over his ears.

7 These signs are seen on our motorways. They convey essential information about services to motorists who can 'read' them at a glance, without losing concentration on their driving.

8 The picture shows a buoy. Buoys are used to mark safe channels (especially near the entrance to a port) and to warn ships of such things as shallow water, sandbanks and wrecks. Buoys of different shapes and colours are used to mean different things.

9 The referee is holding up a card, giving a warning or order to one of the players. Cards of different colour are used. A red card, for example, means that the player concerned is being sent off. The system has the advantage that it can easily be seen and understood by players and spectators.

b 1 They communicated by means of sign language.

2 The linesman waved his flag to indicate that the ball was out of play.

3 He didn't respond to any of our signals.

4 The onlookers gesticulated by waving their arms.

5 She reacted by looking surprised.

c 1 This means 'yes' or is a way of expressing agreement, approval or support.

2 This means something like 'be quiet' or 'don't say anything' or 'keep it to yourself'.

3 This indicates anger or resentment or is intended as a threat or warning.

4 This sign has come to mean disapproval or rejection or is an indication of failure.

5 This can indicate doubt or questioning or mild surprise.

6 This is a way of showing indifference, unconcern, disinterest or doubt.

d 1 Waving the hand and arm outwards and towards the person who is leaving (or vice versa).

2 Placing the cupped hand, or one or two finger tips, behind the external ear.

3 Beckoning by means of several quick movements of the outstreched hand, often with the forefinger prominent.

4 Holding the outstretched hand, fingers straight and closed, outwards and slightly upwards so that the palm faces the person or thing to be stopped.

5 Raising the outstretched arms above the head.

6 Making a rapid circular movement–clockwise or anti-clockwise as the case may be–with the outstretched forefinger of one hand.

7 Shaking the head from side to side.

8 Closing the eyes and/or slumping backwards into a chair or resting the inclined head on the hands that have been placed together, palm to palm, and held as a headrest above one shoulder.

e 1 Mime

2 Flashing lights (e.g. Morse), flags, semaphore, smoke, heliograph, bonfire, rocket, drums, tomtom (bush telegraph), whistle, siren, pipes, horn, bugle, gong, trumpet, bells (e.g. on sheep), churchbells, starting pistol, yodelling.

Practice pages *pages 72–73*

a
1 typewriter
2 innkeeper
3 straightforward
4 headline
5 sometimes
6 outspoken
7 fingertips
8 newspaper
9 playwright
10 earthquake

b
1 I am pleased to reply to your letter of the 14th June.
2 We are sending a copy of our catalogue that you have asked for.
3 Thank you for your order.
4 We are writing to remind you that your account is overdue and we would be glad if you would settle it.
5 Please tell us if you are not satisfied with our goods.

c
1 We were quite satisfied with the arrangements.
2 Mother bought a new hat to match her coat.
3 The sweets were divided among the four children.
4 The farmer found a tramp lying on some straw in the barn.
5 They were anxious not to lose their unbeaten record.
6 The painters are hoping to finish their work next week.
7 He had no excuse for being late for school.

d
1 vehicle
2 character
3 moustache
4 rhubarb
5 guest
6 antarctic
7 gnaw
8 rhythm
9 crumb
10 echo

e
1 Wallsend: Wallsend is situated at the eastern end of Hadrian's wall–hence the wall on the coat of arms. The eagle was also a Roman symbol.
2 Jarrow: The Venerable Bede, historian and theologian, spent most of his life in the monastery here, hence the reference to him in part of the shield of Jarrow's coat of arms.
3 Egham: There is a representation of Magna Carta on the shield because it was here where that document was signed in 1215.
4 Swindon: The locomotive in the top part of the shield refers to the town's importance as a railway engineering centre. The locomotive and wagon works were established here by the G.W.R.
5 Worksop: The forester holding a longbow would seem to be a reference to Sherwood Forest which originally stretched between Worksop and Nottingham.

f 1 adjective
2 noun
3 verb
4 adjective
5 noun
6 adverb
7 adverb
8 verb
9 noun
10 adjective

g 1 The special kind of alphabet that enables the blind to read by touch is called braille.
2 Deaf people communicate by such means as lip reading, sign language and the manual alphabet.
3 Lip reading is difficult because there are instances when different words produce the same lip movements.
4 Sign language consists of gestures, some of which are in the form of a simple mime.
5 A knight's outer garment is called a surcoat.
6 An achievement of arms consists of up to seven parts: shield, helmet, wreath, crest, mantling, motto and supporters.
7 The figures usually placed one on each side of the shield are called supporters.
8 The winged horse in Greek mythology that was for a time the mount of Bellerophon was called Pegasus.
9 The legendary creature that has the head and trunk of a woman and the tail of a fish is a mermaid.
10 The advantages of communicating by means of signs and signals are that these may be quicker and easier to read and in some cases visible over a greater distance than meassages in words. A further advantage is that many signs and signals do not depend on knowledge of a particular language.

h 1 Nile
2 Pergamum
3 English
4 Romans
5 Normans
6 Johann Gutenberg
7 Esperanto
8 Wednesday
9 Frigg or Frigga
10 September
11 New York
12 Portugal
13 Ecuador
14 Scotland
15 Pennsylvania

Using reference books *pages 74–75*

a 1 An encyclopaedia is a book or books containing information on many subjects.
2 Encyclopaedias are mainly intended for reference on particular points.
3 When using an encyclopaedia the first thing to know is how the information is arranged.
4 The OXFORD JUNIOR ENCYCLOPAEDIA has 12 main volumes and an index volume.
5 Each of the main volumes covers a group of related subjects.
6 OXFORD JUNIOR ENCYCLOPAEDIA Volume 1 (called Mankind) is about the people of the world, their customs, beliefs and religions.
7 OXFORD JUNIOR ENCYCLOPAEDIA Volume 3 (called The Universe) is about the countries of the world as well as stars, planets and other heavenly bodies.
8 In CHILDREN'S BRITANNICA all the articles are arranged in alphabetical order throughout the 19 main volumes.
9 CHILDREN'S BRITANNICA and OXFORD JUNIOR ENCYCLOPAEDIA each have the index in a separate volume.
10 A dictionary is an alphabetically arranged list of words, usually with their meanings and other details.

b 1 Cows, cattle, dairy products
2 Crocodiles, reptiles
3 Bed coverings
4 Planets, the solar system
5 Fruit growing, apples etc.
6 Crows
7 Inoculation
8 Australia
9 Railwaymen
10 Wood-wind, instruments of the orchestra
11 Dogs, pets
12 Turtles, tortoises

c 1 Vol. 2
2 Vol. 5
3 Vol. 9
4 Vols. 4, 7, 9
5 Vols. 1, 12
6 Vol. 8
7 Vols. 7, 11
8 Vol. 12
9 Vols. 3, 10
10 Vols. 10, 11
11 Vols. 7, 11
12 Vols. 2, 6, 13*

*the first part of the index volume includes some reference material

d 1 Vol. 8   7 Vol. 13
2 Vol. 19   8 Vol. 3
3 Vol. 9   9 Vol. 12
4 Vol. 16   10 Vol. 10
5 Vol. 6   11 Vol. 17
6 Vol. 8   12 Vol. 18

e 1 The advantages of an encyclopaedia of several volumes are that it will be able to give more information and can be used by several people at the same time. The main disadvantage is cost but there is also the point that it may be more difficult to find things in a multi-volume encyclopaedia.
The advantages of a single-volume encyclopaedia are lower cost and the fact that one can carry the complete thing more easily. It may also be easier to find one's way round a single volume. The main disadvantage is that it can give only limited information on many things while some items will have to be left out altogether. To make a worthwhile single-volume encyclopaedia usually means producing a very big book, so it may be better to divide it into more than one volume for that reason.
2 The pupil is asked to look at a multi-volume encyclopaedia for some information about who wrote it. This should yield the information that such a large work is almost certainly the work of a team of authors and editors.

Titles, contents and indexes *pages 76–77*

a 1 Our first guide when choosing a book will usually be the title.
2 ADVANCED ELECTRICAL ENGINEERING is likely to be unsuitable for beginners because the title indicates that it is at a higher level of difficulty.
3 TOP OF THE WORLD sounds as though it might be about Everest because Everest is the highest mountain in the world.
4 Illustrations in an adventure story can help to bring the story to life.
5 Illustrations are indispensable in books about such things as birds or trees.
6 Diagrams are often needed in books about scientific subjects.
7 Geographical topics probably require maps.
8 'Non-fiction' means books that deal with facts.
9 The contents of a book are found at the front and they are arranged in order of appearance.
10 The index is at the back of a book and is arranged in alphabetical order.

b 1 This extract is taken from the index to a book. We can tell this because the entries are arranged in alphabetical order.
(It is from EXPLORING THE WORLD by Patrick Moore. OUP)
2 Endeavour and Erebus are in italics because they are names of ships. The italics serve to distinguish them from other names.

3 Leif Eriksson was a Viking explorer.
4 The information given about Eskimos is in the form of illustrations.
5 Mount Everest appears to have its name back to front so that the key word (Everest rather than Mount) appears first.

c

For younger readers	*For older readers*
The little Dog	Knight Crusader
Two Bad Cats	The Xanadu Manuscript
The Little Fire Engine	Riders of the Storm
The Silver Christmas Tree	A Song for the Disco
Five Dolls in a House	Ever After
Mr Tall and Mr Small	A Journey of Many Sleeps

d

Fiction	*Non-fiction*
A Grass Rope	The Arab World
Prince of the Jungle	Collecting from Nature
Isle of the Sea Horse	People of the World
The Dark is Rising	All Made by Hand
Escape into Daylight	Exploring the Seashore
Cannibal Adventure	Bridges and Tunnels

e

Australia, exploration of	Hudson, Henry
Chrismas Carol, A	Hudson Bay
David Copperfield	Livingstone, David
Evesham, Vale of	Wind in the Willows, The
Evolution, theory of	Wren, Sir Christopher

Using books *pages 78–79*

a 1 People use books for reading or browsing for pleasure, for looking up a particular item or for studying for examination purposes.
2 Young people at school are encouraged to find things out from books and perhaps write about what they have found.
3 The least enterprising way of writing about something is simply to copy from a book.
4 It is helpful to read right through a passage first in order to get an over-all picture of what it's about.
5 Making notes is good practice in deciding which are the main things that must be included and which are the less important ones that can be left out.
6 The notes that have been prepared can be used as the basis of a written account.

7 The advantages of reading more than one account and then combining them in a piece of written work are that this is a way of combining the best points of each version and producing an account that isn't a copy of anyone else's work.
8 Browse means to read parts of a book here and there.
9 Version is used instead of account.
10 Blend means mixture.

b The solar system consists of the sun and its 'family' of planets and other bodies. The sun, at the centre of our solar system, is a star and though not the brightest star it is important to us because it gives us light and warmth. Without it the earth would be permanently cold and dark. The planets and other bodies travel round the sun, the path that each takes being called its orbit.

c 1 Read through a passage once or twice. Close the book and write an account from memory.
2 Read through the passage, making notes of the chief points. Close the book and write an account from the notes.
3 Read more than one account of a subject; then write a version combining the best points of each.

d Zebras are horse-like creatures standing about 1·2–1·5 m high at the shoulder. They were once found in Europe, Asia and North America, but are now confined to Africa, south of the Sahara. There are several species, all marked with dark stripes on a white background, a feature which seems to serve as a form of camouflage. Zebras are grazing animals, living in small bands. Their chief enemy in the wild is the lion, but many have been killed by man. Some species of zebra are now extinct.

e Some rules and recommendations about the care of books.
1 Always carry books closed and in a bag or case if outside in wet weather.
2 Do not eat and read at the same time.
3 Keep books away from young children and pets. (Of course books can be shown to young children, but the activity must be under supervision.)
4 Do not turn over a corner of a page to mark a place nor use the flap of the dust jacket for the same purpose.
5 Make sure that the hands are clean before handling a book.
6 Turn over a page from the outside edge towards the top corner.
7 Don't write comments or notes in the margin. (Unless it's your own book.)
8 Be careful when tracing maps, diagrams etc. Avoid pressing hard with a pencil.
9 Don't use books for resting things on (e.g. cups, vase, jar or bottle).
10 When replacing a book on a shelf where there are already other books use both hands and don't force a book back into position.

Using words *pages 80–81*

a 1 The horses galloped across the downs.
2 The injured player limped to the touchline.
3 Sally dived into the water.
4 The car swerved to avoid a pedestrian.
5 The weary hikers trudged along the dusty road.
6 The regiment marched proudly along the high street.
7 Adam jumped over the low wall.
8 The snake wriggled along the ground.
9 Paul slipped on the ice-covered path.

b 1 'What time does the programme end?' she asked.
2 'Half past ten, madam,' the manager replied.
3 'We shall win this match easily,' the captain boasted.
4 'You must let the cake cool before you put it in the tin,' she explained.
5 'It's my fault,' he admitted. 'I accept full responsibility.'
6 'Get off!' the man shouted as the children climbed on to his gate.

c 1 The car crashed into the tree.
2 I was astonished to find that the box was empty.
3 The children laughed at the antics of the clowns.
4 In his anger he struck a policeman.
5 The glass was shattered into a thousand pieces.
6 The vandals wrecked the building.

d 1 feeble, frail
2 stroll, wander
3 grip, clutch
4 laughable, humorous
5 uproar, noise
6 gleamed, twinkled
7 thump, strike
8 consider, study
9 connect, join
10 lively, active
11 haul, tug
12 rob, cheat

e Specimen answer; others are possible.
boom, cackle, clatter, click, clop, coo, hiss, hum, judder, pop, screech, splash, splutter, swish, twitter

Using words *pages 82–83*

a The two accounts of the football match are alike in that they both agree on the score, the order of goals and—to some extent—the manner in which they were scored. The essential difference is that each account is written with a distinct bias towards one side.

The first writer would seem to be a loyal supporter of the Reds, recording their clear win with the aid of such words as accurately, spectacular, fine and fierce.
The second writer, on the other hand, would seem to be in sympathy with the Blues and he explains their failure by references to such things as bad luck, the state of the pitch and one or two decisions that went against them.
Of the two accounts the first is probably the more accurate because it would certainly appear that the Reds were on top. Perhaps the most telling thing is that the reasons for the Blues' failure sound more like excuses.

In sections b, c and d the pupil is asked to write pairs of contrasting accounts about the same scene or event.

b 1 Two contrasting accounts of an incident at the end of a match, showing it as (a) a cheerful display and (b) a disorderly outburst.
2 Two contrasting accounts of a fire at a block of flats. The first to emphasise the calm, orderly way it was dealt with, the second making everything as dramatic and sensational as possible.

c 1 Two contrasting accounts of a holiday, the first looking on the more cheerful side, the second concentrating more on anything that went wrong.
2 Two contrasting accounts of a company's progress, the first optimistic in spite of some setbacks, the second pessimistic and full of foreboding for the future.

d 1 Two contrasting articles about fox-hunting: for and against.
2 Two contrasting articles about the proposed extension of an airport near a town or city: for and against.

e We are usually inclined to believe what we see in print because we think that most people will take reasonable care–as far as they can–to check the truth of what they write about. There are, however, limits to this because there are instances where it is not possible to find out exactly what happened, while in other cases there are conflicting accounts of what took place. Here, it is important for the writer to say what the doubts and uncertainties are. Another thing that should always be made clear is whether or not the writer is offering an opinion. Such an opinion may be based on fact but is not itself a fact.
It is sometimes difficult for a writer's own point of view not to influence what he/she writes. In some cases it may be an advantage for a writer to take one side of an argument since this may make for a more stimulating and readable piece of work. We should not expect our authors to be insincere in order to try to please everybody, but it is important for the reader to realise that other people may hold a different opinion.

A book that may be difficult to judge is the plausible one with a vigorous, racy style that quickly smooths over any obstacles and uncertainties. At first sight everything seems to be based on fact, but, on looking closer we aren't always so sure where the facts have come from.
The kind of book to be particularly wary of is that written by someone who claims special knowledge or experience that nobody else has.

Practice pages *pages 84–85*

a
1 Ducks
2 West Indies
3 Headwear
4 Drama, theatre
5 Swine
6 Sailing ships
7 Marsupials
8 Citrus fruits
9 Water supply
10 Masonry
11 Airport
12 Channel Islands
13 Toads
14 Ventilation
15 Wolf

b
1 Vols 7, 10, 13*
2 Vols 6, 7
3 Vol 10
4 Vols 1, 4
5 Vols 5, 11
6 Vols 1, 3, 4, 7, 12, 13
7 Vol 12
8 Vol 8
9 Vol 1, 2, 3
10 Vol 9
11 Vols 4, 7, 10
12 Vol 11

*the first part of the index volume includes some reference material

c
1 Vol 12
2 Vol 10
3 Vol 18
4 Vol 16
5 Vol 9
6 Vol 6
7 Vol 2
8 Vol 3
9 Vol 5
10 Vol 15
11 Vol 1
12 Vol 4

d
1 Keep your voices low,' he whispered. 'Somebody might hear us.'
2 'Here are the results of the competititon,' she announced.
3 'Oh please let me have it,' she begged.
4 'Finally,' the producer concluded, 'I would like to thank all those who have helped in any way.'
5 'Halt!' called the sentry. 'Identify yourself.'

e
1 I was positive that I had the right answer.
2 The smuggled goods were confiscated by the police.
3 The soldiers were ordered to attack.
4 We were baffled by the conjurer's tricks.
5 The cavalry charged towards the enemy guns.

f *For younger readers*
The Clever Mouse
The Dream Dragon
The House that Sailed Away
The Good Tiger
Giant Kippernose and Other Stories
Sam Pig Goes to Market

For older readers
The Stones of the Moon
Operation Midnight
Dolphin Island
The Fox Hole
Hounds of the King
A Kestrel for a Knave

g *Fiction*
The Cuckoo Tree
The King of the Copper Mountain
The Dangerous Ones
When the Wind Blows
Trouble on Sunday
The Conjuror's Box

Non-fiction
Our World
A Family in Greece
The Vikings in Scotland
The First Men on the Moon
Science and Crime Detection
Under the Sea

h Saturn, the second largest planet in the solar system, is unique on account of the three flat rings that surround it at the level of its equator. These are composed of small particles of matter and make the planet one of the most beautiful and spectacular objects in the sky. Because Saturn's axis is tilted we see the rings from different angles at different times. As well as the rings, Saturn has 10 moons, including Titan, the biggest satellite in the solar system and the only one with an atmosphere. Saturn is such a long way from the sun that it takes 29½ years to complete its orbit, as against one year for the earth, but a 'day' on Saturn is only about 10¼ hours long because the planet spins on its axis more than twice as quickly as the earth does.

i 1 A book or books containing information on many subjects is called an encyclopaedia.
2 The last volume of CHILDREN'S BRITANNICA consists of an index and maps.
3 Volume 2 of OXFORD JUNIOR ENCYCLOPAEDIA deals with animals and plants.
4 Volume 5 of OXFORD JUNIOR ENCYCLOPAEDIA tells about the lives of some famous people.
5 The index of a book is arranged in alphabetical order.

j 1 bright
2 sad
3 insolent
4 daring
5 annoyed
6 faithful
7 defeat
8 scream
9 obstruct
10 injure
11 revolve
12 jump

k 1 The contents were arranged at the front of the book.
2 The names in the index were arranged alphabetically.
3 The earth's orbit takes it round the sun once a year.
4 The stripes on a zebra seem to serve as camouflage.
5 Some species of zebra are now extinct.

Poetry *pages 86–87*

a 1 The special ways in which language is used in poetry include the use of rhyme and metre and the choice and arrangement of words.
2 Rhyme is the repetition of a sound, usually at the ends of lines but sometimes within lines.
3 Metre means the rhythm of a poem and the way in which the beats or accents produce this.
4 It is the choice and arrangement of words that especially distinguishes poetry from prose.
5 In a factual account of a pigeon we would expect to find the usual details of size, colour, flight, food and habits.
6 consult
7 communicate
8 combined
9 rhyme scheme
10 prose

b 1 size: small
colour: blue
shape: fat
posture and movement: they strut and stump about, their heads moving in and out as they do so
2 strutting, stump
3 the fat gentlemen
4 because they move out and in as though tapping at something
5 nails, walls

c 1 We could tell that the excerpt was poetry and not prose because of the way in which the lines had been broken up.
2 There is no rhyme scheme or pattern of rhymes in the poem.
3 humorous, lively, fanciful, clear
4 The picture is generally true.
5 Pomposity and a belief in one's own dignity and self-importance.

d 1 Kingfisher
2 Owl
3 Eagle
4 Skylark

e The complete poem PIGEONS by Richard Kell is in his collection DIFFERENCES published by Chatto and Windus. This poem also appears in THE NEW DRAGON BOOK OF VERSE published by OUP.

Poetry *pages 88–89*

a 1 The language of poetry is different from any other in the way it is used.
2 (Some) words are chosen for their sound as well as for their meaning.
3 Words help the poet to create word pictures that both nourish and exercise the reader's imagination.
4 The quality that the poet uses more than most of us is imagination.
5 A poem on its own is not enough. The reader must respond to bring the pictures to life.
6 Each time we read a poem we may find some extra quality in it.
7 Different readers may react to the same poem by interpreting it differently.
8 respond
9 interpret
10 vision

b The sea is like a big, hungry dog that rolls about on the beach all day, biting away at pieces of rock as if they were bones. And on stormy nights it is as though he gets up and howls and shakes his wet coat all over the cliffs. But on quiet days he seems to be just lying there with his head between his paws, hardly making a sound.

The two versions are alike in general outline and some of the detail, but are quite different in the effect they produce. The poem makes much the more striking picture, with its skilful use of words to suggest, first, the rush of the sea against the shore and then the very different picture of a calm sea in early summer. In the prose version the power is lost and the imagery seems out of place. It fails to come to life and does nothing for the imagination, while the marvellous contrast between the rough and the calm seas passes by in a matter-of-fact manner that we hardly notice. A reading aloud of the two versions is an effective way of confirming these points.

c Sounds: clashing teeth, rumbling stones, the sea-dog moans, the night wind roars, the sea-dog snuffs and sniffs, howls, hollos and (scarcely) snores

Movements: the sea-dog rolls, gnaws, licks his paws, bounds to his feet and shakes himself; the stones tumble, the moon rocks

The number and variety of sounds and movements are needed to build up the two contrasting pictures of a rough sea breaking over the beach and cliffs, and a calm sea in May or June. They are an essential part of the imagery of the poem and enable the poet to create a vivid and immediate effect with remarkable force and economy.

d The pupil is asked to write an essay suggesting why the sea and things to do with the sea have had a special fascination for poets.

e Some poems about the sea:

Pine Music by Kate Louise Brown
The Rime of the Ancient Mariner by Samuel Taylor Coleridge
maggie and milly and molly and may by e.e. cummings
Sea Song by A. Cunningham
The Old Ships by James Elroy Flecker
All day I hear the noise of waters by James Joyce
Sea Shell by Amy Lowell
Cargoes, Roadways, Sea Fever by John Masefield
White Horses by Irene Pawsey
Stones by the Sea by James Reeves
The Shell by James Stephens
Break, break, break by Lord Tennyson

Poetry *pages 90–91*

a 1 Coleridge said that poetry was 'the best words in the best order'.
2 The best way of discovering the nature of poetry is to look at some examples and see how poets use words to describe things and convey the truth of what they see and feel.
3 Things in nature–such as birds, trees and flowers–and the passing of the seasons are often seen by poets with a new awareness and insight.
4 The rose tree's scent draws thin in Autumn.
5 The wind blows 'with teeth of glass' in winter.
6 'The first sharp splinters of dawn' means very early in the morning when the darkness of the sky is first broken up by shafts of light here and there.
7 Holes in a roof are 'thatched with sunlight' because a person inside the building can see the sunlight through the holes.
8 A caterpillar 'tickles' the wall because its many legs lightly touch the wall as it moves along.
9 Rhyme and rhythm are effectively used to set the scene with a few bold strokes and to work up an immediate vitality that is both vivid and humorous.
10 The picture we get of Darius is of a fearsome character of great authority and importance.

b 1 convey 4 deserted
2 awareness 5 maintains
3 insight 6 vigour

c

1	a saucer of milk	a creamy sea
2	a grey squirrel	a small grey coffee pot
3	snow	crystal manna
4	a thrush's eggs	four blue stones
5	the moon	a child's balloon
6	inside a buttercup	like polished gold
7	fireworks	sudden fiery flowers
8	a dragonfly's wings	like spun glass
9	old sailing ships	like swans asleep
10	a swallow	a fish of the air

d The openings of the two poems are alike in the way they immediately build up a picture and an atmosphere. In the one we see straight away the imposing figure of Darius the Mede and at once we know who he is and what sort of person he is. In THE HIGHWAYMAN the opening is eerie and ominous and the appropriate setting for the tragedy that relentlessly follows.
The difference between the two is chiefly one of atmosphere. In spite of the forbidding figure of the king there is a strong undercurrent of humour in DANIEL that helps to give the poem its zest and energy. The opening lines of THE HIGHWAYMAN are full of movement, too, but the tone is hushed

and serious. The undertones here are real and threatening.
In each case we can judge from the opening lines what kind of action and events will follow. We know that the fearless Daniel will be thrown to the bad lions but will survive the ordeal, but we sense that the highwayman is doomed to die. Only the precise manner of his betrayal is yet to be revealed.

e Some of the things in nature that poets have written about:
animals, birds, flowers, harvest, insects, lakes, the moon, pets, rainbows, rivers, the sea, the seasons, the sky, stars, the sun, trees, weather (frost, rain, snow), the wind, etc.
The pupil is then asked to choose a favourite nature poem and copy it (or part of it) in an exercise book.

Books for young readers *pages 92–93*

a 1 Each year thousands of new children's books are published.
2 Books for children take account of their needs and interests.
3 About 200 years ago books available to children might include the Bible, stories of saints and martyrs, Aesop's fables and perhaps a few tales about King Arthur, Robin Hood and the Trojan War.
4 PILGRIM'S PROGRESS and ROBINSON CRUSOE were read by children, although they had not been specially written for them.
5 The first children's books included such things as instructions about manners and behaviour.
6 A LITTLE PRETTY POCKET-BOOK was different because it was intended to entertain as well as instruct.
7 A LITTLE PRETTY POCKET-BOOK was published in 1744 by John Newbery.
8 A LITTLE PRETTY POCKET-BOOK contained fables in verse, descriptions of games and a rhyming alphabet.
9 It was during Queen Victoria's reign that children's books began to look more like those of to-day.
10 Outstanding books of the Victorian age that are still read to-day include ALICE'S ADVENTURES IN WONDERLAND, BLACK BEAUTY, TREASURE ISLAND and THE JUNGLE BOOKS.

b 1	Myths and Legends	Irish Sagas and Folk-Tales
2	Historical novel	Bowman of Crécy
3	Animal story	Tarka the Otter
4	Fantasy and magic	The Phoenix and the Carpet
5	Detective story	A Hundred Million Francs
6	Humour	Professor Branestawm up the Pole
7	School story	Jennings and Darbishire

8	Space adventure	Threshold of the Stars
9	Ghost stories	Supernatural Tales of Terror and Suspense
10	Adult story, adapted	Gulliver's Travels

c 1 The Water Babies
2 Little Women
3 Black Beauty
4 The Jungle Books
5 The Wind in the Willows

d The pupil is asked to write brief summaries (as in section C) of one or two books.

e Specimen answers; others are possible

Joan Aiken	Midnight is a Place
	Tales of Arabel's Raven
	The Kingdom under the Sea
René Guillot	Companions of Fortune
	The Elephants of Sargabal
	The Great Land of the Elephants
C. S. Lewis	The Lion, the Witch and the Wardrobe
	The Magician's Nephew
	The Last Battle
Hugh Lofting	The Twilight of Magic
	The Story of Dr Dolittle
	Doctor Dolittle's Zoo
William Mayne	Follow the Footprints
	A Grass Rope
	A Swarm in May
E. Nesbit	The Princess and the Cat
	The Enchanted Castle
	The Railway Children
Mary Norton	Bedknob and Broomstick
	The Borrowers
	The Borrowers Afield
Willard Price	Amazon Adventure
	Gorilla Adventure
	Cannibal Adventure
Arthur Ransome	Swallows and Amazons
	Pigeon Post
	Great Northern?
Noel Streatfield	Ballet Shoes
	The Circus is Coming
	Thursday's Child
Rosemary Sutcliffe	Blood Feud

	The Eagle of the Ninth
	The Queen Elizabeth Story
Geoffrey Trease	The Hills of Varna
	No Boats on Bannermere
	The Baron's Hostage
Henry Treece	The Children's Crusade
	Viking's Dawn
	Hounds of the King
Alison Uttley	A Traveller in Time
	Sam Pig Goes to Market
	Little Grey Rabbit's Party
Ronald Welch	Bowman of Crécy
	Knight Crusader
	The Gauntlet
Ian Serraillier	The Enchanted Island
	The Challenge of the Green Knight
	The Silver Sword

Myths *pages 94–95*

a
1. The origin of the word myth is the Greek word 'mythos' which means speech or talk.
2. Myths began with the spoken word.
3. One reason why people carried out certain rituals was perhaps the belief that by 'acting out' certain things they could make them happen.
4. Another explanation of the origins of myths is that they were an attempt to explain things that people could not understand.
5. The purpose served by stories about monsters and other supernatural beings was that they may have helped primitive peoples to communicate their feelings about the mystery of life and why we are here.
6. When the old stories came to be written down the writers may have changed some of the detail.
7. traditional
8. rooted
9. rites
10. embodied

b The gods and the giants were often quarrelling and fighting with each other. One day the giant Thrym stole Thor's hammer, demanding the goddess Freya as the price of its return. Freya refused to marry Thrym and so an alternative way of recovering the hammer had to be found. At last, someone suggested that Thor, dressed up as Freya, should go to Giantland as if prepared to marry Thrym. Thor reluctantly agreed and Thrym laid out a great feast for his expected bride, but as soon as Thor got his hands on his hammer he revealed himself and killed all the giants who were there that day.

c According to Greek mythology Pandora was the first woman on earth. She had been given a box which the gods warned her not to open. In time, however, she was overcome by curiosity and finally lifted the lid. All the troubles and problems that now afflict mankind flew out. As quickly as she could Pandora shut the lid, just in time to prevent the escape of Hope.

d

Apollo–Greece	Vishnu–Hindu
Finn–Celtic	Siegfried–German (Teutonic)
Jupiter–Rome	Osiris–Egypt

e 1 **Argus**
Argus was a monster in Greek mythology. Some accounts say he had 100 eyes. Hera set Argus to guard Io, but Hermes killed Argus and cut off his head. It is said that the eyes were then transferred onto the tail of a peacock.

2 **Cerberus**
In Greek mythology Cerberus was a savage dog who guarded the entrance to the lower world. The creature had three heads and a serpent's tail.

3 **Chimera**
In Greek mythology Chimera was a fire-breathing monster. It had the head of a lion, the body of a goat and the tail of a serpent or dragon.

4 **Cyclops**
The Cyclops were a race of one-eyed giants in Greek mythology. They lived in Sicily where Odysseus encountered them on his long journey back from Troy. Another story tells how they were killed by Apollo for complicity in the death of his son.

5 **Fenrir** (or Fenris-wolf)
In Norse mythology Fenrir was a wolf monster. In the last battle with the gods Fenrir kills Odin, chief of the gods, but is killed by Odin's son Vidar.

6 **Harpies**
In Greek and Roman mythology the harpies were half birds and half women. They are perhaps best known for their habit of stealing food from people.

7 **Hydra**
In Greek mythology the Hydra was a monster with nine heads. If one were cut off two more grew in its place. Hercules, for his second labour, killed the hydra by burning each stump as soon as a head had been cut off.

8 **Jormungard**
The world serpent in Norse mythology. It grew to such a size that its body encircled the earth. At the last battle it kills Thor but is at the same time killed by him.

9 **Medusa**
In Greek mythology Medusa was one of the three frightful Gorgon sisters.

With writhing snakes for hair, Medusa was so revolting to look upon that anybody who looked at her was turned to stone. Medusa was eventually killed by Perseus who aimed his sword by looking in a mirror at his target.

10 **Minotaur**
In Greek mythology the Minotaur was a monster with the head of a bull and the body of a man. It was kept in a labyrinth where, from time to time, seven youths and seven maidens were sacrificed to it. This went on until the Minotaur was killed by Theseus who found his way out of the labyrinth by following a thread that someone had given him.

Practice page *page 96*

a

1	Prose	6	Prose
2	Poetry	7	Poetry
3	Prose	8	Poetry
4	Prose	9	Poetry
5	Poetry	10	Prose

b These notes give a brief indication of what the books are about.

1 A Midsummer Night's Death
A mystery. The verdict on a drowning is suicide but somebody has doubts about the matter.

2 Captain Cobweb's Cowboys
A wild west story that combines humour and excitement.

3 The Children's Crusade
A historical novel based on the ill-fated crusade of 1212.

4 Steam on the Line
An adventure story set in the early days of steam travel.

5 The Edge of the Cloud
An adventure story set in the early days of flying.

6 Run for Your Life
A thriller. Two boys discover a murder plot.

7 Goals in the Air
A story about a football team.

8 Boy Astronaut
A story about a boy who takes part in a mission to the moon.

9 The Foundling
A story about an orphan boy.

10 The Borribles
A fantastic story of how the Borribles go about saving their territory from an unfriendly invasion

c 1 Peter Pan 2 Gulliver's Travels 3 Robinson Crusoe

Extension Book 2

Introduction *pages 2–3*

a 1 Many of the farms of western Europe are among the most efficient in the world because they make the best of whatever land is available and make widespread use of machines, scientific methods and fertilisers.
2 The advantages of using machines on farms are that this takes out much of the heavy work and means that more work can be done with fewer men.
3 Scientific methods have helped farmers by producing better breeds of animals, and seeds that can resist certain diseases and pests.
4 The purpose of adding fertilisers to the soil is to provide extra 'food' in the form of nitrogen, phosphorus and potassium.
5 It is necessary for Britain to buy some foods from abroad because certain crops do not grow well or do not ripen in Britain's rather cool and damp climate.

b 1 sufficient
2 resist
3 granules
4 imported
5 damp

c 1 Housing, roads, sites for industry, coal-mining, quarrying, airports, caravan sites, playing fields.
2 Materials for clothing, bedding, carpets, shelter and medicine.
3 Climate, altitude, whether level or hilly, soil, size, drainage and the farmer's own resources, experience and preferences.
4 It can be argued that farming is the most important industry in the world because it provides essential food that enables other people to do their work.
5 Ways in which modern farms look different from those of about 100 years ago: larger fields; greater use of steel, concrete and other modern materials in buildings; more machinery about; probably no horses; fewer workers. The kind of farm likely to have changed least is probably the hill farm.

The tractor *pages 4–7*

a 1 The three forms of power mentioned in the opening paragraph are mechanical power, man-power and horse-power.
2 A tractor driver raises or lowers any implement that has been attached to his tractor by pulling a lever.
3 A tractor's engine may be used to drive such things as mowers, circular saws and pumps.

4 Most tractors have diesel engines rather than petrol engines because they are more efficient producers of power and therefore best suited for the kind of heavy work that the tractor will be called upon to do.

5 Improvements made to tractors that give the driver better protection and comfort include weatherproof cabs, complete with heater and a comforable seat. (Some tractors are fitted with roll-over bars which help to protect the driver if the machine turns over.)

b 1 tow
2 attached
3 fluid
4 stationary
5 pneumatic

c 1 P. A. S. means power-assisted steering. It helps the driver by making the steering lighter.

2 Rear-view mirrors give the driver better all-round vision and spare him the need for constantly turning his head to see what is going on round him. In the fields this helps him to do his work while on the road he can more easily keep a look-out for any following traffic. Headlights enable the driver to work late – very useful when he wants to make the most of a fine spell of weather.

3 The advantage of using automatic tractors is that fewer men would be needed to do a given amount of work. A possible disadvantage is that some farm workers might lose their jobs unless alternative tasks on the farm could be found for them.

4 A crawler or caterpillar tractor has a continuous track on each side instead of wheels, rather like an army tank. This kind of tractor is particularly suitable for use on heavy, wet soil. (There is an illustration on page 5 of the pupil's book.

5 One advantage in using horses to pull a plough is that they do not require expensive fossil fuel. Unlike tractors, they can get used to the task of pulling a plough and to following the commands of the ploughman.

d

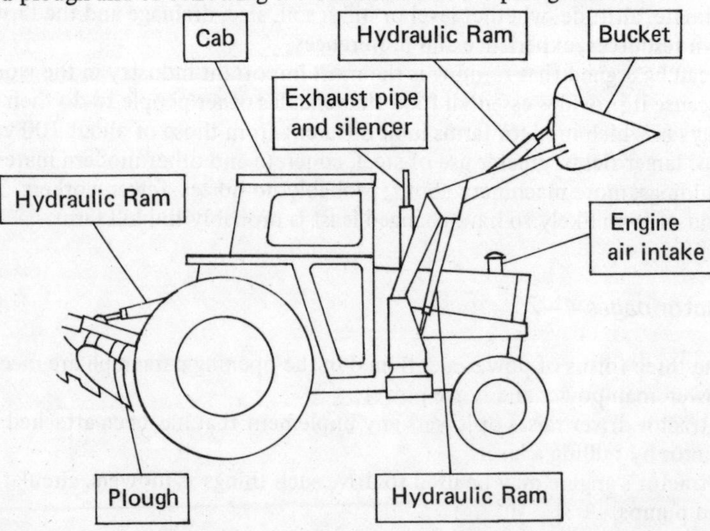

e The first illustration shows a disc harrow. After the ploughing has been done and a cultivator has been used to break up the lumps of soil a disc harrow is used to make a fine top layer of soil where seeds will grow well. The discs cut into the soil as they are pulled along.
The second illustration shows a crop sprayer. This is used to spray a crop with chemicals to kill weeds or pests, or control diseases.

Dairy farming *pages 8–9*

a 1 The two most common breeds of dairy cows in Britain are the black and white Friesian and the Ayrshire.
2 Two breeds of cattle that take their names from two of the Channel Islands are Jersey and Guernsey.
3 Cows are given additional food to help them give a good supply of milk.
4 Cows produce milk to feed their calves.
5 Young calves are fed on some of their mothers' milk, but are given milk made from milk powder as well. As soon as possible they are given solid foods such as concentrates, hay or grass.

b 1 The picture shows a milking parlour.
2 The cowman is wearing a clean white coat and cap and a plastic apron.
3 The part of the floor where the cowman stands is at a lower level than the part where the cows stand so that he has no need to stoop in order to do his work.
4 The cowman is fixing the cups of the milking machine on to the cow's teats.
5 The cowman can tell that milk is passing freely from the cows' udders by watching the glass jars to see that they are filling properly.

c 1 It is important for milking machines and other items of equipment to be kept clean because, unless great care is taken, milk can easily become infected.
2 Jersey and Guernsey cows give the creamiest milk.
3 A heifer is a young cow.
4 In order to give enough milk cows must have large quantities of water as well as sufficient food.
5 Hay and silage are made from grass and are used as food for farm animals during the winter. (Grass for silage is cut in May, while the grass is green. It is stored – packed as tightly as possible – in a clamp, pit, barn or a tower called a silo. Grass for hay is cut later – usually in June or July – when it has flowered and beginning to lose its greenness. It is then turned from time to time so that it will dry, baled and stored. The process of drying may be completed indoors.)

Diseases of cattle *pages 10–11*

a 1 Foot-and-mouth is the most contagious of cattle diseases.

2 The signs of foot-and-mouth disease in cattle are high temperature, lameness, excessive saliva in the mouth and the appearance of blisters on gums, tongue, lips and feet.
3 Cattle suffering from foot-and-mouth disease have to be slaughtered.
4 Other precautions to prevent the spread of foot-and-mouth disease include restrictions on people moving in and out of infected areas and the disinfecting of their footwear as they arrive and leave, and the disinfecting of farm buildings.
5 The effect of brucellosis on cows is that they give birth to dead calves.
6 Brucellosis is being overcome by testing all cows and slaughtering any that are infected.
7 Mastitis is an inflammation of a cow's udder and is caused by bacteria.
8 The effect of mastitis on cows is that they give much less milk than they should.
9 The best way for farmers to keep their herds free from mastitis is to follow a very hygienic milking routine.
10 Tuberculosis in cattle has been overcome by testing all cattle and removing any that show signs of having the disease.

b 1 contagious
2 excessive
3 slaughtered
4 epidemic
5 eradicate

c 1 'Cloven-footed' means that the hoof is divided. Cloven-footed animals include cattle, sheep, pigs and goats.
2 To ensure that our dairy herds remain free of tuberculosis all animals are tested from time to time by a veterinary surgeon.
3 The most serious of all the diseases than can affect cattle is foot-and-mouth.

Cereal crops *pages 12–13*

a 1 Cereal crops are important because they provide much of the food that is eaten by human beings and animals.
2 The biggest cereal crop in Britain is barley.
3 Most barley is made into animal food.
4 In Britain most wheat is grown in the east.
5 'Hard' or 'strong' wheat is best for making bread.
6 'Soft' or 'weak' wheat is used to make biscuits.
7 Britain buys some wheat from overseas because this is the 'hard' wheat that does not grow well in Britain but which is needed to make bread.
8 Oats is more common than wheat in Scotland.
9 Rye is used to make a dark-coloured bread.

10 Two cereal crops not grown in Britain but important in other countries are rice and maize.

b 1 Porridge, oatcakes and animal feedstuffs are made from oats.
2 Beer, whisky and animal feedstuffs are made from barley.
3 Wheat is used to make bread, biscuits, semolina, macaroni and spaghetti.
4 'Black' bread and some animal feedstuffs are made from rye.
5 Maize is used to make cornflakes, cornflour and popcorn.

c 1 Oats 2 Wheat 3 Barley

Potatoes *pages 14–15*

a 1 The parts of the potato plant that we eat are swollen underground stems or tubers.
2 The underground stems are swollen because the plant has made them to store food, mainly starch, for its own use.
3 Seed potatoes may be planted early in the year where the climate is mild, but in Britain the main crop is planted usually in March or April.
4 Potatoes can be planted by hand, but on farms machines are now more commonly used.
5 If growing potatoes are not well covered with soil they turn green and become unfit for human consumption.
6 A potato clamp is a kind of stack or heap of potatoes covered with straw and a layer of soil to keep out the frost.
7 An alternative way of storing potatoes is to keep them in special buildings.
8 The Irish potato famine in 1845–7 was caused by a disease called potato blight.
9 Potato plants grew in the highlands of South America before they were brought to Europe.
10 The South American Indians used potatoes by drying them to produce a kind of floury substance from which they made bread.

b 1 Potatoes grow best in loose soil because that enables the roots and tubers to develop.
2 Buildings for storing potatoes often have insulated walls to keep out the frost.
3 One of the most destructive of insect pests that attack potatoes is the Colorado Beetle.
4 The Indians living in the highlands of South America did not grow maize or wheat because it was too cold for these crops to grow.
5 Sir Walter Ralegh.

The farmer's year *pages 16–19*

a		
a	January	Lambing begins Hedging and ditching carried out
	February	Prepare ground for cereals – if weather permits Lambing continues Hedging and ditching continues
	March	Apply fertiliser to grass Continue preparing ground and sow spring cereals Plant early varieties of potatoes
	April	Plant main potato crop Sow sugar beet Dairy cattle put out to pasture Sow mangolds
	May	Spray cereal crops with weed killer Sow swedes Cut grass for silage
	June	Sheep shearing begun Sow turnips Hay making begins
	July	Hay making continues Spray potato crop against potato blight Sheep shearing continues Harvesting of cereals begins
	August	Harvesting of cereals continues Sow grass and clover seeds Sheep dipped
	September	Lift potato crop Harvesting of cereals complete Ploughing begins as harvest is cleared
	October	Sow winter wheat and winter oats Lift mangolds Ploughing continues Lift sugar beet crop
	November	Continue harvesting sugar beet and mangold crops Dairy cattle brought in for the winter
	December	Send sugar beet to factories, as required Prepare for lambing Christmas turkeys taken to market

b 1 A good time for the farmer to overhaul and repair some of his machinery and equipment would be late autumn or during the winter.

2 Tasks carried out on farms all the year round include:
   Feeding and caring for animals
   Milking cows
   Routine maintenance of machinery, equipment and buildings
   Clerical work – keeping records and accounts, filling in forms
   Paying farm workers
   Planning ahead; keeping in touch with prices, trends and developments

3 In the north of England or in Scotland some of the tasks set out in the chart above may be carried out later in the year. (For example, lambing may not take place until April or May.)

4 On a farm that concentrated on milk production a number of the tasks shown above (e.g. lambing, sheep shearing, growing potatoes) would not be carried out, but some crops (e.g. root crops) may be grown to provide food for the cattle.

5 Sometimes the farmer's year is shown as running from October to September because a great deal of preparation for the following year begins in Autumn as soon as the harvest is completed. (This applies to the arable farmer rather than the dairy farmer, whose work is spread more evenly throughout the year.) By about September–October most crops have been gathered in or are nearly ready to be lifted and so this, in a sense, means the end of the farmer's year.

The shepherd's year can be said to begin in Autumn because, in some parts of the country at least, that is the time when he arranges for all suitable ewes to be mated so that as many lambs as possible will be born the following year.

c *Winter – Hedging and ditching*

The hedger trims the hedge and then cuts and bends the branches over in such a way that they are woven among other branches so as to form a thick plait. The illustration shows how machinery can be used for some of this work, though hedging proper needs to be done by hand. Ditching – a less skilled but equally necessary task – is often done at the same time. The purpose is to clear the ditch of grass and weeds so that it forms an effective drainage channel.

Summer – Harvesting cereals

A combine harvester is being used. The straw is left behind in an even row ready to be picked up later by the baler.

Autumn – Ploughing

A tractor-mounted two-furrow plough is being used.

Spring – Planting potatoes

The tractor is pulling an automatic potato planter.

The Country Code *pages 20–21*

The six infringements of the rules shown in the picture are:

1 Walking through a field full of corn
2 Dog chasing sheep
3 Dropping litter
4 Leaving a fire unattended
5 Gate left open
6 Climbing over wall

Dangers and difficulties *pages 22–23*

1 The production of eggs, milk and meat depends on plants because hens, cows, sheep and pigs eat plants or things made from plants.
2 Too much sunny weather can be a problem for farmers because their crops need rain as well as sunshine.
3 Seed-eating birds (such as wood-pigeons, stock-doves, jays, crows and rooks) can be a serious nuisance to farmers. On the other hand some birds often help farmers by eating insect pests.
4 One result of myxomatosis was that foxes began to take more young lambs and poultry. This was because the number of rabbits available for them had been greatly reduced.
5 Other mammals that eat or damage the farmer's crops or property include hares, grey squirrels (the rare red squirrel is not a serious nuisance to farmers), stoats, weasels, moles, rats, mice and dogs.
6 A sow with piglets might become fierce at times because that is the natural way in which she protects her young.
7 A tractor might overturn when working across a hillside. To prevent this farmers sometimes work up and down the slope instead of going across it, or they may use a robot tractor (a tractor without a driver). Tractors can be made safer by being fitted with roll-over bars or with cabs that will not crush if the vehicle turns over.

Picture Question *pages 24–25*

Pupils' answers should be based on each group of six related illustrations which show the following:

1 Cows grazing in a field.
2 Cows being milked (in a rotary parlour).
3 Tanker driver taking a sample of milk (from storage tank for testing purposes).
4 Milk being drawn off from storage tank to tanker.
5 Bottles being filled by machines at the milk bottling plant.
6 Delivering milk to houses.

1 Poughing a field. The tractor is pulling a five furrow plough.
2 The tractor is pulling a cultivator whose strong metal teeth or spikes dig into the plough ridges and break them up into smaller lumps.
3 The tractor is pulling a seed-drill. The seeds are carried in a long box from which they drop into shallow furrows made by the drill.
4 Ripening corn standing in the field.
5 A combine harvester at work cutting the corn. The straw is left behind to be picked up later.
6 Storing the grain in silos.

Farming years ago *pages 26–27*

1 The illustration shows two men ploughing with horses. It is more usual nowadays to use a tractor-mounted plough, but horse-drawn ploughs may be used occasionally, especially in hilly districts.
2 The illustration shows a threshing machine (a machine for separating the grain from the husk) driven by steam. Many farmers would hire a machine like this at harvest time. More recently, reaper-binders have been used for this task, but nowadays most corn is harvested by combine harvester. A few reaper-binders may still be used but the method shown in the picture is no longer in use.
3 The picture shows somone milking a cow by hand. Most cows are now milked by machine and the older, much slower, method shown here is rarely used.
4 The picture shows someone shearing a sheep, using hand shears. It is more common nowadays to use powered shearing equipment, but shears may still be used where there is no convenient source of electricity.
5 The illustration shows someone making butter in a churn. This was a method used on the farm or in the home, particularly when people were making a fairly small quantity mainly for their own use. Nowadays butter is made in large quantities in factories.
6 The illustration shows someone cutting the corn with a scythe. This slow and laborious method is no longer used, most corn now being harvested by combine harvester.

Agricultural improvers *pages 28–29*

a 1 The most important reason for making farming more efficient is so that it can produce more food for people to eat.
2 Robert Bakewell was born in 1725 at Dishley in Leicestershire.
3 Robert Bakewell's particular interest was stock breeding.
4 Bakewell set about improving the quality of his cattle by careful breeding.
5 Bakewell worked with a local breed of cattle known as Leicestershire longhorns.

6 The result of his breeding methods was that he eventually produced animals that weighed almost twice as much as their ancestors.

7 Bakewell also worked with sheep and horses.

8 As other people got to know of Bakewell's work visitors from all over the world would call at his farm, in particular to see his bull 'Twopenny' and his ram 'Two-pounder'.

9 Bakewell made a lot of money by hiring out his bull and his ram (for breeding purposes).

10 The brothers Robert and Charles Colling carried on and developed Bakewell's work.

b Another man who is remembered for improving agriculture is Charles Townshend. He inherited his father's title of Viscount and took his seat in the House of Lords. In 1730 he gave up politics and retired to his country estate in Norfolk. There he became the first Englishman to grow turnips as a farm crop. Because of this he became known as 'Turnip' Townshend.

c 1 Before sufficient winter feed had been provided for cattle many of them had had to be slaughtered.

2 Growing a different crop in different years on the same piece of land does not exhaust the soil so quickly and cuts down the risk of disease. Letting a field lie fallow for a year means that no crops would be grown on it. Growing different crops in different years on the same piece of land is called rotation of crops.

3 Patrick Bell (1799–1869)

In 1826 the Reverend Patrick Bell, a Scottish Presbyterian minister, invented a reaping machine. The corn was not only cut, but left in bundles on the ground – an arrangement that made it easier to pick up afterwards and arrange into sheaves.

Jethro Tull (1674–1741)

Jethro Tull, a Berkshire farmer, invented the first really practical seed drill, which meant that crops (such as turnips) could be grown in rows. Previously the seed had been sown by throwing it by hand. Tull also devised a horse-drawn hoe and wrote a book called Horse-hoeing Husbandry.

Thomas Coke (1752–1842)

Thomas William Coke, later Earl of Leicester, inherited a large estate at the age of 24. He set about improving the soil, growing more and better crops and improving the quality of various breeds of sheep, cattle and pigs.

Arthur Young (1741–1820)

Arthur Young achieved fame as a writer on agriculture, persuading people to take an interest in improving farming by scientific methods. From 1784 he edited a series called 'Annals of Agriculture' which eventually ran to a total of forty-five volumes. In 1793 he became the first secretary of the Board of Agriculture.

Farming in other countries *pages 30–31*

1 Australia
2 New Zealand
3 Denmark
4 U.S.A.
5 Brazil
6 India

Extension Book 3

Introduction *pages 2–3*

a 1 flourishing
2 beneficial
3 contentedly
4 astonishment
5 forecast

b 1 The word spa comes from the name of a health resort and watering place in Belgium. Especially popular and fashionable in the 18th century its name has been generally applied to other similar resorts.
2 Builth Wells, Llandrindod Wells, Malvern Wells, Tenbury Wells, Tunbridge Wells, Leamington Spa, Woodhall Spa.
3 People sometimes drank sea water because they had been used to drinking spa mineral waters.
4 Specimen answer; other names could be used.
Aberdaron, Blackpool, Clovelly, Dawlish, Exmouth, Folkestone, Girvan, Hastings, Ilfracombe, Kirkcudbright, Llandudno, Morecambe, Newquay, Oban, Penzance, Rhyl, Southport, Torquay, Ullapool, Ventnor, Whitby, Yarmouth, Zennor.

The disappearing coast *pages 4–5*

a 1 hamlets
2 erosion
3 precarious
4 headland
5 shingle

b 1 An estuary is the tidal mouth of a river.
2 Fragile means easily broken.
3 Reasons why some parts of the coastline wear away include the following:
Some cliffs (e.g. those on east coast of Britain) are made of a softer material.
Effects of sea (waves and currents), heavy rain, wind and frost.
Effects of air pressure building up in rock crevices, causing rocks to break up.
4 To stop the coastline crumbling away promenades, sea-walls, groynes and breakwaters can be built, but the problem of erosion may then become even more serious at the point where such defences end.
5 The National Trust is an organisation formed for the purpose of acquiring

land and buildings of great beauty or historic interest so that they can be preserved in their original condition. The Trust is acquiring as much fine coastline as possible so that this will not be built on or spoilt in any other way. As Trust properties are usually open to the public this might mean more wear and tear on coastal paths unless care is taken to see that these are not over-used.

Defending the coast *pages 6–7*

a 1 subdued
2 massacred
3 secure
4 rebellion
5 fortified

b 1 Scotland was at no time fully under Roman control.
2 The Roman soldiers left Britain in order to defend Rome.
3 William of Normandy built castles in Britain in order to make his new kingdom secure against Saxon rebellion.
4 Pevensey castle enjoyed its period of greatest prosperity during the thirteenth century.
5 British, Canadian and U.S. servicemen were garrisoned in Pevensey castle during World War Two.

c 1 Most of the old Roman forts of the Saxon shore are now no longer at the water's edge because the channels and harbour entrances have long since become silted up.
2 William of Normandy is sometimes called William the Conqueror.
3 No doubt the Normans built their castle at Pevensey within the walls of an old Roman fort because the site was suitable (that's why the Romans built their fort there) and because the existing defences could be incorporated into the new structure.
4 The Pevensey gun was cast as part of the defences against an expected attack by Spain.
5 A pill-box is a small fortified position, often in the form of a circular gun emplacement.

Smuggling *pages 8–9*

a 1 illegally
2 prohibited
3 expert
4 seamanship
5 severe

b
1 It was necessary for smugglers to use isolated parts of the coast for their activities so that they would be less likely to be seen.
2 The haunts of smugglers are the places that they most often visit or use in connection with their smuggling activities.
3 A tax was put on such things as tea and tobacco in order to raise money.
4 The results of customs duties being imposed were that certain things became more expensive and people tried to smuggle goods into the country to avoid paying the duty.
5 The popular view of smuggling was that people were entitled to try it.
6 Smuggled goods would be offered to known customers to avoid the risk of dealing with people who turned out to be informants or agents.
7 People buying smuggled goods would ask no awkward questions because secrecy was an important part of such transactions.
8 The great age of smuggling (about 1700–1840) means that smuggling was then at its height.
9 More smuggling took place during the Napoleonic wars because Britain was then largely cut off from normal trading with the rest of Europe and smuggling was the only way of getting hold of certain goods.
10 Convicted smugglers were executed in public and their remains put on display as a warning to others.
11 The dead bodies were bound in chains so that as the flesh decomposed it would not fall apart.
12 A gibbet is an upright post surmounted by a short horizontal arm from which the bodies of executed criminals were hung.

c
1 Transported means taken to a penal colony in another part of the world.
2 It can be said that the government kept the smugglers in business in so far as it was the duties that the government imposed that made smuggling worth while.

A Smuggler's Song *pages 10–11*

a
1 A parent is speaking to a young girl.
2 'Watch the wall' is a way of saying 'look the other way' or 'don't look through the window'.
3 The gentlemen are the smugglers.
4 Baccy is short for tobacco.
5 The line 'Brandy for the Parson' tells us that members of the clergy were not above receiving smuggled goods.
6 A woodlump is a heap or pile of wood.
7 The words 'Put the brushwood back again' suggest that the barrels had been covered. This would have been done to hide them.
8 It was important not to call out 'Come and look!' in case the words were heard by a revenue man or soldier.

9 The horse would be tired because it had been working (with the smugglers) during the night.
10 The coat could have been torn while the wearer was clambering over rocks or among the undergrowth while it was dark and perhaps being pursued by the revenue men.
11 King George's men were soldiers.
12 'Dressed in blue and red' means wearing uniform.
13 It was important to be careful as to what was said to King George's men so that no details about smugglers or smuggled goods would be given away.
14 It was important to remember what was said by King George's men because their line of questioning might reveal how much they already knew or what lines of enquiry they were pursuing.
15 'Chuck you 'neath the chin' means a gentle touch or caress under the chin.
16 King George's men might make a fuss of the girl in order to win her confidence and make her forget to be discreet.
17 Signs of nocturnal activity mentioned in verse 5 include knocks, footsteps and whistles.
18 Trusty and Pincher are dogs.
19 Trusty and Pincher would appear to be well trained because they lie quietly when 'the Gentlemen' go by. Ordinarily dogs would bark and make for the door if they heard noises round the house.
20 The doll's cap was made of lace.
21 Valenciennes is in France.
22 The reward was for the girl doing as she'd been told.
23 The doll came from France because that was where the other smuggled goods came from.
24 The risk in the child having a French doll might be if anyone recognised it or asked her where she'd got it from.
25 It is true to say that people who don't ask questions will be told no lies to the extent that they are more likely to be told little or nothing – true or false – simply because they haven't asked.

b 1 The poem tells us that local communities kept any knowledge of smuggling very much to themselves.
2 The advantage in a child seeing and knowing as little as possible of any smuggling activities would be that it couldn't give very much away to a stranger.
3 It was necessary for the child to be told something because of noises in the night and other signs of smuggling, such as the barrels of brandy, the tired horse, the torn coat and the risk of inquisitive soldiers. A child would have to be brought up not to discuss these matters openly.
4 The pupil is asked to give his/her own reactions to being told to 'watch the wall'.
5 It is likely that smugglers could have been carrying letters for a spy during the Napoleonic wars.

Wrecks and wreckers *pages 12–13*

a
1 Many ships have met with disaster round our coast.
2 Survivors were sometimes in danger.
3 If a ship were wrecked people living near would set out for the shore.
4 The verger was watching a ship that had got into difficulty.
5 He could no longer restrain himself.

b
1 Many ships pass the Cornish coast because that is part of the approach from the Atlantic to the ports of southern and south-east England.
2 A false light could confuse sailors if they mistook it for a genuine one and so misjudged their position. Further errors based on this might lead them into difficulties.
3 Wreckers would use axes and crowbars to break up ships and large masses of wreckage into pieces of manageable size. Ropes would be used to tie things together into bundles that could be carried or hauled away.
4 The congregation was in a hurry to get out of the church in order to join in the plunder.
5 The parson shouted 'Stop!' so that the congregation would gain no advantage by making for the wreck ahead of him.

c
1 It is unlikely that fishermen would take part in wrecking because, depending on the sea for their livelihood, they would be more likely to have sympathy for any ships or sailors in difficulty. At such times it is almost certain that they would do what they could to help.
2 The reasons why ships (and particularly sailing ships) were often wrecked are many and varied. They include
   1 Strong winds
   2 Ship leaking
   3 Rudder failure or defective steering gear
   4 Errors of navigation
   5 Lack of accurate charts
   6 Unmarked hazards
   7 False lights
   8 Mistaking genuine lights
   9 Collision
   10 Not using the lead to take proper soundings
   11 Faulty chronometer
   12 "Taking a short cut"
   13 Cargo shifting
   14 A ship dragging her anchors
   15 Officers or other members of crew drunk and incapable. (Cargoes of liquor were sometimes raided, especially if damaged.)
   16 Faults in construction (e.g. rivets placed too far apart or wooden rivets painted over)

17 Engine room explosion, often leading to fire
18 (In war) Results of enemy action
19 Poorly trained crew
20 Overloading

Sea rescues *pages 14–15*

a 1 failed
2 disaster
3 launched
4 courageous
5 coxswain

b 1 The Forfarshire was driven on to the reef by the wind.
2 A reef is a ridge of rock at or near the surface of the water.
3 The Longstone lighthouse had been built to warn ships of the dangerous rocks in that area.
4 It might have been difficult to launch a lifeboat from the mainland because of the high wind and heavy sea.
5 Even if it had been possible to launch a lifeboat from the mainland Grace and her father were nearer the wreck. Also they had no means of knowing if anybody on the mainland knew that the Forfarshire had gone down and that there were survivors needing help.
6 All the survivors were not rescued together because the Darlings' boat wasn't big enough to hold them all.
7 'Grace's courage captured the public imagination' means that many people were thinking and talking about her brave deed.
8 Volunteer crews are people who offer their services entirely of their own free will.
9 More than 95,000 people have been rescued by men of the R.N.L.I.
10 The name Henry Blogg is commemorated in the name of the present Cromer lifeboat.

c 1 Paddle steamers are driven along by paddle wheels, usually placed amidships, one on each side of the vessel, though some river steamboats had stern paddle wheels. The other main method of driving a steam ship along is by means of the screw propellor, fitted to the stern of a ship. Paddle steamers continued in use for many years as ferries or pleasure boats operating near the coast, but even these are disappearing except for one or two specially preserved examples.
2 Cromer is in Norfolk.
3 The town where Grace Darling was born and where there is a museum named after her is Bamburgh (Northumberland).

Mary Anning *pages 16–17*

a 1 Ichthyosaurs were reptiles that had become adapted for living in water. They evolved about 190 million years ago, but became extinct about 120 million years later. With their streamlined bodies they looked something like dolphins, but were not related to them. Ichthyosaurs were good swimmers, flexing the body to drive themselves along and using their front limbs for steering. They would, however, need to come to the surface to breathe air into their lungs. They ate fish and molluscs. Ichthyosaurus itself was about 26 feet (8 m) long. Its remains have been found in England and Germany.

2 Dimorphodon, one of the earliest of the pterosaurs, was about 4 feet (1.2 m) long, with a wingspan of about 5 feet (1.5 m). The wings of pterosaurs were really sheets of skin held out by the legs, arms and the long fourth finger of the hand. The remaining fingers, sticking out in front of the wings like little hooks, may have been used to help the creatures climb to a position from where they could launch themselves. Their flight was probably more of a gliding or soaring movement rather than the true flight of modern birds. Like other pterosaurs, dimorphodon eventually died out. Its remains have been found in England.

b 1 A professional scientist is a person who has had the appropriate scientific training, acquired a proper standard of knowledge, and then follows a scientific occupation as a means of earning a living.

2 A geologist is a person who studies the structure of the earth's crust and the history of its formation and development.

3 Fossils are things or traces of things that have been preserved naturally for a very long time. In some cases animals have been preserved in frozen mud and insects have been trapped by resin which has hardened into amber. In other instances actual remains have been preserved in tar pits.

Many fossils are the remains of prehistoric animals and plants that have been preserved in rocks. It is usually the hard parts of an animal (such as bones, teeth, horns, shells) that become fossils, because flesh is either eaten by predators or soon rots away.

Most fossils have been formed under water. This is why shells are the most common fossils. But not all dead animals have become fossils. Fossilization happened when an animal was quickly covered or buried by a fine sediment (particles of rock, sand, clay etc., eroded from older rocks) and then left undisturbed. This would be more likely to happen in the sea or a river, because a dead animal would soon sink to the bottom and be covered by sediment. The sediment would have been carried along by currents in streams, rivers and the sea. Over many years the sediment hardened into stone and the trapped skeleton was petrified – that is, turned to stone. In other circumstances an animal might be buried in a swamp or it might fall into a river and be carried out to sea.

In course of time huge earth movements pushed the sea bed up above sea level to become dry land and even form mountain ranges. Sometimes rock containing fossils have become exposed to view. This could be caused by weather or the action of waves against a coastline. At other times human activity (coal mining, quarrying, making cuttings for roads, railways, canals etc.) has brought fossil-bearing rocks to light.

Fossils not only tell us a great deal about the animals and plants that lived long ago, they have helped scientists to date the rocks in which the fossils were found.

Piers *pages 18–19*

a 1 disembark
2 enlarged
3 accommodate
4 replace
5 survive

b 1 A ride in a stage-coach was likely to be a bumpy one because the roads at that time were not very good and because the springs of a stage-coach could absorb only a limited amount of movement caused by irregularities in the road's surface.
2 It was not possible for steamers to anchor close inshore because they had to stay further out to sea where there was sufficient depth of water to keep the ship afloat.
3 The first piers were originally built as landing stages.
4 As more people travelled to the seaside by rail paddle steamers were increasingly used as pleasure boats, taking people for short cruises.
5 Most piers were built during the 19th century.

c 1 Sailing ships were used before steamships.
2 amusement arcades
ballroom
bar
bingo
bowling alley
cafe
cinema
concert hall
disco
dolphinarium
fairground
helter-skelter
hotel
kiosks
leisure centre
maze
miniature railway
railway
roller-skating rink
seats
shops
slot machines
sports pavilion
springboards
sun lounge
theatre
toilets
trampolines
tramway
zoo

3 (a) Southend
(b) Blackpool

Tides *pages 20–21*

a 1 False
2 True
3 False
4 True
5 True
6 True
7 True
8 False
9 True
10 False

b 1 The tide has the effect of washing the beach each time it comes in.
2 It is safer to swim when the tide is coming in.
3 The importance of tides to shipping is that they enable vessels to enter and leave certain harbours in order to pick up and discharge passengers and cargo.
4 The power of the rise and fall of the tides can be used to generate electricity.
5 The Romans first learned about tides when they came to Britain because their native Mediterranean Sea was almost tideless.

Seaweeds *pages 22–23*

a 1 Seaweeds are unlike most garden plants in that they have no flowers, no clear division into leaves and stems and no roots.
2 The holdfast may be mistaken for a root.
3 The sea lettuce got its name because of its resemblance to lettuce leaves.
4 Brown seaweeds grow mostly between the tide marks.
5 It is the air bladders or blisters that enable the bladder wrack and the knotted wrack to float.
6 The bladder wrack is better able to resist being moved about by the action of the waves.
7 The red seaweeds are less frequently seen than the green or the brown because some of them occur in deeper waters.
8 An alternative name for carragheen is Irish moss.
9 Blue-green seaweeds are the least common.
10 The picture shows the bladder wrack.

b 1 Fronds are the leaves of certain flowerless plants.
2 Uses of seaweed:
Prevents erosion of seashore
Helps oxygenate water
Provides shelter (from sun, wind, waves and predators) and nesting material for some sea creatures

Food (especially in China, Japan and Hawaii)
Medicine (China)
A source of iodine
Extracts used in the making of such things as ice cream, jam, face cream, soap, toothpaste, paint, varnish, plastics, fertilisers and cattle food
Manure

Crustaceans *pages 24–25*

a 1 microscopic
2 protect
3 internal
4 expand
5 extricating
6 vulnerable
7 seek
8 refuge
9 crevice
10 brief

b 1 Some crustaceans that live in the sea are crabs, barnacles, shrimps, prawns, sandhoppers and lobsters.
2 Crustaceans are invertebrates.
3 A crab is least able to defend itself when it is moulting.
4 Other names used in the passage to mean the crusty skin of crustaceans are 'shell', 'hard covering' and 'hard outer coat'.
5 A number of crustaceans – such as sandhoppers, shrimps and prawns – act as scavengers.

c 1 The crayfish lives in fresh water. The woodlouse lives on land.
2 Camouflage means that the colour of a creature is similar to the colour of its background. Some animals can change their colour to blend with the background. Some crabs attach bits of seaweed or sponges to their shells and will change these if they move to a background of a different colour.
3 Aquatic means living in or frequenting water.
4 Barnacles fix themselves to such things as rocks, shells and piers.
5 The hermit crab.

Sea-shells *pages 26–27*

a 1 Molluscs do not have backbones.
2 Most molluscs are aquatic.
3 The shells of molluscs grow bigger as the animal grows.

4 There are more univalves than bivalves.
5 Bivalves are a double shell, hinged together.

b 1 Mother-of-pearl is the silvery iridescent lining of such shells as oysters and mussels. It is used in the making of buttons, cuff links and knife handles.
2 Most shells are broken by the action of the waves.
3 Sunlight causes the colours of shells to fade.
4 The statement that some molluscs bury themselves in the sand when the tide goes out suggests that they will re-emerge when the tide comes in again.
5 Piddocks and shipworms bore into wood to protect themselves from their enemies.

c Scallop Whelk
Razor Cowrie

Birds *pages 28–29*

a 1 frequent
2 carrion
3 forsaken
4 maintain
5 nape

b 1 The parts of the passage that tell us that the herring gull is a scavenger and a robber are the words "often preferring to eat scraps and carrion . . . and other birds' eggs."
2 When baby gulls peck at the red spot on the parent's bill they do this because of some inborn tendency to behave in this way.
3 The name 'black-headed gull' is not altogether a suitable name for this bird because the head is actually dark brown and even this colour disappears in the autumn.
4 Terns have been called 'sea swallows' because some of them are maritime or are frequently seen near the coast, and they have deeply forked tails rather like those of swallows. The nickname is therefore quite suitable.
5 A passage migrant is a bird that stays or rests in a place for a period of time en route to somewhere else.

c 1 Common tern.
Black-headed gull.

2 a Puffin
b Cormorant
c Gannet

Picture questions *pages 30–31*

1 Royal Sovereign Lighthouse. Completed 1971 to replace Royal Sovereign Lightship. Stands off Newhaven (East Sussex). Consists of a square, deep platform on top of a pillar, the roof of the platform serving as a flight deck for helicopters.

2 Lobster pots. Baskets in which lobsters are trapped. Pieces of dead fish and other bait are placed in the pots in order to lure the lobsters. Once inside, the lobsters cannot get out.

3 Groynes. Long, low walls made of timber (or other materials) running out to sea. Placed at intervals along a beach in order to check erosion and drifting of sand.

4 Launching a lifeboat down a slipway. This is a method of launching a lifeboat that is suitable in places where the lifeboat station is at a suitable height and where there is a sufficient depth of water at the point of impact to float the lifeboat.

5 Buoys. Buoys are used to mark safe channels and to warn of the positions of wrecks, sandbanks and shallow waters. Different shapes, markings and colours mean different things; some can be illuminated at night.

6 Martello Towers. Low circular forts topped by a gun platform built in 1804 along south and east coasts of Britain in case of an invasion by Napoleon. Named and modelled after a tower at Cape Mortella (Corsica) captured by the British in 1794.

Extension Book 4

Introduction *pages 2–3*

a 1 feast
2 friezes
3 permanent
4 replacing
5 withstand

b planned, used, give, customs, stay

c The ger or yurt is a kind of portable shelter that is used in Mongolia and other parts of central Asia. The framework consists of sections of expanding lattices or trellis work and these are opened out to form a circular wall broken only by a space for the door, which is often highly decorated. A series of willow rods forms the framework of the roof. Large pieces of felt or other material are then wrapped round the walls and over the roof framework and secured with horsehair rope. A small hole is left near the apex of the roof to make room for the stove pipe. All the materials needed to build a ger can be carried be two camels and it can be put up by a few people in half an hour. The shape and structure of the ger seem to have changed very little in hundreds of years so it is evidently suitable not only for the nomadic life but for keeping out the cold winds of winter.

d 1 Our other basic needs besides shelter are food, drink and clothing.
2 The features that most of our houses have in common include walls, floors, roofs, ceilings, doors and windows together with some arrangements for cooking, washing and sanitation.
3 Materials used to build our houses include bricks, stone, timber, tiles, slate, concrete, plaster, mortar, glass and plastic.
4 Materials used to build primitive huts and tents include stone, tree trunks, logs, branches, twigs, leaves, grass, straw, turf, rushes, reeds and other plants, earth, mud, clay and animal skins.
5 The advantages in building homes from materials that are found near at hand are that these are easy to find and so the task is likely to be done quicker – an important point if no other shelter is at hand. The disadvantages are that this may limit the choice of materials and may mean using things that are not really suitable.
6 Apart from architects and builders, professional people or tradespeople involved in the work of building houses include joiners, carpenters, tilers, glaziers, plasterers, plumbers, electricians and gas fitters.
7 The two reasons why the occupants of a house built by the joint efforts of

several people might provide a special feast are (1) as a celebration, and (2) as a way of thanking all those who took part in the work.

8 A party held to celebrate someone moving into a new house is sometimes called a house-warming party.

9 The main reason why nomads move about, often taking their homes with them, is to look for fresh pasture for their animals.

10 The advantages in a tropical hut having a tin roof instead of a thatched roof are that it is likely to last longer and be more efficient at keeping out the rain. The disadvantages are that the interior of the hut will be less cool when the sun is shining and much noisier during a rainstorm.

e 1 Felt is made from wool or hair, the fibres being matted together under pressure. It is used to make hats, billiard-table covers, slippers and chalkboard erasers.

2 Corrugated iron is sheet steel that has been bent into a series of parallel wavy grooves. This is done in order to stiffen it.

Çatal Hüyük, a prehistoric city *pages 4–5*

a 1 access
2 outskirts
3 pillaged
4 supported
5 abandoned

b found, hostile, unbroken, neighbourhood, country

c It used to be thought that the oldest cities in the world were those built about 5,000 years ago between the rivers Tigris and Euphrates, but recent excavations have uncovered the remains of much older settlements, such as Çatal Hüyük. Another ancient city that has been excavated is Jericho. We can read in the book of Joshua how the Israelites captured Jericho, but what the story does not tell us is that Jericho was a very old city even then. The famous walls of biblical Jericho have never been found – perhaps they have long since crumbled to dust. But archaeologists looking for them have discovered evidence of an earlier city.

d 1 It would have been difficult to build a sufficiently strong defensive wall surrounding Çatal Hüyük out of the materials available. A perimeter wall made of sun-dried mudbricks could quite easily have been breached.

2 Uniform means that many of the features of Çatal Hüyük (such as size of bricks and proportions of rooms and doors) conformed to one particular pattern. This implies orderly central planning and control of building work.

3 Broken bones were frequent because of people falling off ladders or from rooftops.

e 1 The method of dating ancient deposits of organic material is called radiocarbon dating or carbon-14 dating. It is based on the fact that, after death, the radiocarbon content decays at a constant rate.
2 Neolithic means of the later stone age or new stone age.
3 A shrine is a place where worship takes place or where devotions are made, often to a particular saint or god associated with that place.
A sanctuary is a holy place, the holiest part of a church or temple or a place of refuge.

Pompeii *pages 6–7*

a 1 artefacts
2 amphitheatre
3 mosaics

b 1 The ruts were caused by the wheels of carts that were used.
2 They stayed there because of the mild climate and the rich soil.
3 We can read accounts of the disaster that were written at the time.

c mosaics, coins, theatres, barracks, statues, murals, a forum

d 1 The work of archaeologists has contributed to our knowledge of the past by unearthing objects and remains and interpreting these to tell us more about how people lived and about the things that they made and used.
2 In the first century A.D. Pompeii was badly damaged by earthquake (63) and later (79) overwhelmed by a sudden eruption of Vesuvius.
3 After the eruption of Vesuvius in A.D. 79 the only parts of Pompeii that could still be seen were the tops of columns and the highest parts of buildings.
4 Apart from the risk of being buried by ashes and cinders the people of Pompeii were in danger of suffocation.
5 Some of the survivors went back to Pompeii in order to salvage any of their belongings.
6 The first methodical digging at Pompeii began in the eighteenth century.
7 The phrase 'in their original surroundings' means in the places where they used to be when Pompeii was a flourishing city.
8 The remains of Pompeii are open to the public.
9 Among the things that can now be seen at Pompeii are public buildings, houses, gardens, markets and shops. Some mosaics and wall paintings have also survived.
10 Pompeii's misfortune has been to our advantage in that the nature of the disaster of A.D. 79, which buried much of the city, was also the means of

preserving its remains, thus giving us a remarkably clear picture of the everyday life of the ancient Romans.

e 1 It is likely that people who hid in cellars would be suffocated by fumes. Entrances, stairways and windows would probably be blocked by ashes, cinders, stones etc. which would make escape difficult if not impossible.
2 Any upper parts of buildings made of wood would be burnt as a result of the eruption of Vesuvius, so we cannot be sure about this point.
3 Some people running away from Pompeii in A.D. 79 held pillows over their heads in order to protect themselves from falling ashes and cinders.

f 1 Other cities buried by the eruption of Vesuvius in A.D. 79 were Herculaneum and Stabiae.
2 The site of Pompeii is near the bay of Naples.

Roman remains in Britain *pages 8–9*

a 1 established
2 preserved
3 fragments
4 revealed
5 accidentally

b Throughout the Roman occupation most Britons continued to live in simple huts, in marked contrast to the Romans who had built far better homes for their own use. But after the Romans left Britain their buildings were eventually abandoned and fell into decay. One reason was that the incoming Angles and Saxons had little understanding of, and no use for, the amenities that the Romans had left behind. (They thought that the wonderfully straight Roman roads had been built by gods, not people.) It would therefore seem that Britain gained no lasting benefit from the ordered town life and superior buildings that the Romans had established. Nevertheless, the Roman occupation must have given the Britons at least a glimpse of a far more cultured way of life than they had ever known before.

c 1 It is usually more difficult to carry out excavations in areas that are now built up because most of the ancient remains have since been built on and may have been disturbed in the process.
2 'Romanized' Britons were Britons who had adopted Roman ways.
3 The Romans had previously built villas in their own country.
4 A farmstead is a farm complete with farmhouse and other buildings.
5 The part of the passage that tells us that wealthy or important Romans were looked after by servants who were looked upon as the property of their masters is the phrase 'quarters for slaves'.

6 The re-discovery of the Palace of Fishbourne came about when a workman digging a trench near Chichester found some fragments of coloured stone.
7 The term 'pro-Roman' means in favour of or supporting the Romans.
8 The phrase 'comparable with any even in Rome itself' means that the Palace of Fishbourne was as fine a building as any in Rome.
9 Friezes and mosaics were unknown in Britain before the Roman occupation.
10 It is likely that the skeletons found during the excavation of Fisbourne Palace were of people who had died during the fire that destroyed much of the palace in about A.D. 280.

d 1 Chedworth's quiet, secluded position could help a visitor picture what life was like in such a country house in Roman Britain because there are few intrusions there that might distract or disturb the imagination.
2 The archaeologists no doubt changed their minds as the size of the remains they were excavating became apparent.
3 The native Britons probably looked upon the palace of Fishbourne with awe and wonder, though some of them may have wondered why anyone needed so large and magnificent a house.

e 1 A pediment is a low-pitched gable, usually triangular in shape, placed over the front of a building in the Greek style.
2 Tesserae are small, cubic pieces of marble, glass or tile.
3 A hypocaust is a space under a floor along which air heated from a furnace is passed for the purpose of heating the room above it.

The Palace of Holyroodhouse *pages 10–11*

a 1 Holyrood Abbey is the older building because the Palace takes its name from the Abbey and not the other way round.
2 The phrase 'is of later construction' means 'was built later'.
3 The south-west tower was built to match an earlier feature of the building.
4 The Palace of Holyroodhouse has had an eventful history.
5 A treaty is an agreement between countries.
6 A punitive raid is an attack designed to punish someone.
7 There was a problem as to who should succeed to the throne of England in 1603 because Elizabeth had no children.
8 A civil war is an armed conflict between groups of people of the same country.
9 King Charles I was beheaded.
10 Charles II, son of Charles I, was restored to the throne after the death of Cromwell.

b Not all the buildings in the historic city of Edinburgh are connected with royalty. Some have associations with famous Scottish writers, philosophers and preachers such as Sir Walter Scott, David Hume and John Knox. One old house not far from Edingburgh castle was once the home of Bailey Macmorran. In 1595 he went to the old High School where students were on strike because they had been refused a holiday. When Bailey Macmorran tried to disperse the strikers one of them shot him dead. The house where Macmorran lived has been carefully restored.

c 1 Balmoral
2 The Palace of Holyroodhouse is the official residence of the reigning monarch in Scotland.
3 The title James I and VI means that James was the first king of that name to be king of England when he succeeded Elizabeth in 1603. He had been king of Scotland since 1567 and was the sixth Scottish king called James. Since the crowns have been united he is sometimes referred to as James I of England and VI of Scotland.

Mount Vernon *pages 12–13*

a 1 dedicated
2 successful
3 rebelled
4 deserted
5 courage

b 1 Members of the Mount Vernon Ladies' Association were no doubt keen to preserve the mansion and estate as a tribute to and in memory of the first president of their country.
2 The pupil is asked to express a preference for either Little Hunting Creek Farm or Mount Vernon as a name and to give a reason for the choice.
3 A 'gentleman farmer' is usually a wealthy or quite wealthy person who generally organises and supervises the farming activities on his land but employs others to do much of the day-to-day routine work.
4 The word that tells us that Virginia, Pennsylvania, Delaware and Maryland were once governed by another country is colonies.
5 The outcome of the colonists' fight against the British was that they won the war and became free to manage their own affairs.
6 George Washington retired twice – once after the war against the British and the second time after the completion of his term as president of the United States. (Actually he served two terms, 1789–93 and 1793–97.)
7 The attitude of the United States government and the state of Virginia towards buying George Washington's home would no doubt be very different today.
8 The attraction of visiting places such as Mount Vernon is to see the actual home where a famous or important person once lived. The attraction is even greater when such things as furniture, fittings and personal effects are arranged in such a way as to enable us to get a good idea of what life in such a house

was like. A visit may also add to our knowledge and understanding of the person who once lived there.

9 There are various reasons as to why the homes or birthplaces of some famous people have not been preserved. There may have been a lack of interest at the time. A building may have been pulled down to make way for something else, or in order to widen the road. In some instances it may have been that it would cost too much to repair the property or it may simply be that the person connected with a house or building may not have been appreciated until many years later, by which time it may have been too late to preserve their home or birth-place. In some cases we may not be exactly sure in which house a person was born.

10 'The Association's action saved Mount Vernon for posterity' means that the ladies of the association saved the house for succeeding generations to visit and enjoy.

c 1 The stripes in the United States flag stand for the 13 original colonies.

2 There are now 50 states in the United States and they are shown on the flag by 50 white stars on a blue background in the upper quarter next to the staff.

3 George Washington is the only U.S. president to have a state named after him.

Working at home *pages 14–15*

a 1 Raw wool is wool in its natural state before it has been cleaned or worked on in any way.

2 Semi-finished products are things that have been partly made but require further work to be done on them.

3 Carding means preparing wool for spinning by combing and straightening the fibres.

4 The advantage of using a spinning wheel was that a person using it could do other things as well. The disadvantage was that, having only one spindle, it could not do as much work as a jenny.

5 The advantage of using a jenny was that it could produce more thread than a spinning wheel. The disadvantage was that it needed a person's full attention.

6 The word attic could have been used instead of garret or loft.

7 Work in the home was affected by the seasons in that people would plant their crops and gather the harvest at the appropriate time and fit their spinning, weaving etc. in between.

8 Children were employed because there were no schools for them to go to and because it was important for all members of the family to help. It would not be possible to-day to the same extent because of the demands of education and the restrictions on child labour.

9 Later inventions for spinning and weaving that needed power could not be used in people's homes because they had no power to drive them.

10 The first powerloom factory in Manchester was burnt to the ground by an

angry mob because they feared that it would take from them work that they had been used to doing at home.

b In some trades, such as nailmaking and chainmaking, many people – including women and children – did their work in a small shed, workshop or forge at the back of the house. Because of the nature of the work, conditions inside were hot, cramped and very unhealthy. Nails were made from strips of iron which had to be heated in a fire so that they could be hammered into shape, pointed and cut to the required length, one end being flattened to form the head of the nail. In the case of chainmaking, sections of iron bars had to be heated, cut off, bent into the shape of a link, twisted round the last-made link in the chain and then closed. Heavy chains were made from thicker bars which needed more heat to be made workable. Because of this a full-time assistant – often a boy or a girl – would be used to work the bellows to fan the fire. Both nailmakers and chainmakers often had to work long hours for low pay.

c John Kay
Patented his flying shuttle in 1733. It enabled one person to operate a broad loom where previously two people had been required.
James Hargreaves
In about 1764 he invented the spinning jenny – a device that enabled one person to spin several threads at once, instead of the single thread of the spinning wheel.
Richard Arkwright
In 1769 he invented a spinning machine known as a water-frame – so called because it was operated by water power.
Samuel Crompton
In 1779 or 1780 he combined the best ideas of the jenny and the water-frame in a machine called the mule.
Edmund Cartwright
In 1785 he invented the first power-loom.
The flying shuttle and the spinning jenny could be used in the home, but the other inventions mentioned above needed power to operate them.

Picture questions *pages 16–17*

1 Houses situated under the flightpath near a busy airport. (Heathrow, London)
2 Houses without gardens. (Leeds)
3 Houses next to a flyover. (North Circular Road, London)
4 An example of ribbon development – long strips of houses alongside or near to a main road and following its course.
5 Slum dwellings. (Panama)
6 An example of a shanty town. (Rio de Janeiro, Brazil)
7 A modern high-rise development.

Understanding plans *pages 18–19*

a 1 The ground floor plan shows the downstairs part of the house.
2 The first floor plan shows the upstairs part of the house.
3 There are three bedrooms.
4 Bedroom 1 is the largest bedroom.
5 Bedroom 3 is the smallest bedroom.
6 Bedroom 2 has a built-in cupboard or wardrobe.
7 Bedroom 3 faces north.
8 The lounge could be described as a 'through' room. This type of room is so called because it runs through from one side of the house to the other.
9 The garage lies on the west side of the house.
10 The lounge is the biggest room in the house. This is because it is a room that is likely to be used by several persons – possibly the whole family – at the same time.
11 There is no room directly over the garage.
12 Bedroom 2 is directly over the kitchen.
13 The bathroom is directly over the entrance hall.
14 To get from the front door to the lounge one would enter the hall, take a few paces forward, turn left and walk forward to the lounge door.
15 To get from the front door to Bedroom 2 one would enter the hall, turn left immediately and climb the stairs. At the top of the stairs one would walk straight ahead towards the door of Bedroom 2.
16 The plan shows a detached house. It is detached because no other property is adjoining, and it is a house (and not a bungalow) because there is a first floor and a ground floor.
17 Four doors lead off the landing at the top of the stairs.
18 Three doors lead off the entrance hall.
19 The pupil is asked to say which bedroom he/she would choose for himself/herself and give reasons for the choice.
20 The bottom picture on page 18 shows the elevation (a representation of the front outside) of the house shown on the plans.

b 1 Delightful modern detached residence of style and character, close to all amenities and having the benefit of full gas-fired central heating. The well-planned accommodation comprises: entrance hall, spacious through lounge with views front and rear, large kitchen/diner with cupboards and shelves, three good sized bedrooms and bathroom with coloured suite. Garage. Well laid-out gardens front and rear. An ideal family home.
2 Compact, period house with easily-managed mature gardens. Situated in an elevated position and close to all amenities such as shops and bus stop. Very convenient for anyone working in the area and particularly suitable for first-time buyers looking for a substantially-built town house of modest proportions.

c 1 There is no section on page 18.
2 kit = kitchen
c/b = cupboard
ckr = cooker
w/r = wardrobe
fr = fridge
w.c. = water closet
a/c = airing cupboard
shr = shower

Falling water *pages 20–21*

a 1 Mr Kaufmann was evidently a wealthy man who was determined to have an individually-designed house of genuine character.
2 A department store is a large shop selling a wide variety of goods arranged in different departments – food, clothing, furniture, bedding, hardware etc.
3 Reinforced concrete is concrete made stronger by having steel bars or wire mesh embedded in it.
4 The part of the passage that tells us that Falling Water was an expensive project are the words 'cost an enormous amount of money'.
5 The part of the passage that means that Falling Water was generally looked upon as standing for all that was eccentric in modern architecure are the words 'for many people it became the symbol of way-out modernity'.
6 We can infer that Wright's Arizona house was a complex structure with a lot of detailed work in it because it was still unfinished over twenty years later when he died.
7 A civic centre is a large building or a complex of buildings in which the main public offices of a town or city are situated.
8 Some examples of Wright's non-residential designs are a temple, a factory, a museum and a civic centre.
9 So much reinforced concrete was used in the building of Falling Water because it was more suitable for the overhanging terraces or balconies which are a special feature of the house.
10 The advantages of owning and living in Falling Water would be that one would have a famous house and one that is quite unlike any other. The disadvantages might be that other people (sightseers, tourists etc.) would be curious to see it, since it is something of a landmark in the history of architecture, and its unusual position and structure no doubt make it difficult and expensive to maintain and repair.

b 1 It is difficult to assess Wright's influence on other architects.
Assess means estimate.
2 This is because his style was so very personal.
Personal means individual.

3 Wright expounded many of his ideas in books and speeches.
Expounded means explained.
4 He also founded a school where he could teach young architects.
Founded means established.
5 Some of his most fanciful plans were never carried out.
Fanciful means fantastic.

c Specimen answers; others are possible.
1 Hillcrest
2 Sea-view
3 Lakeside
4 Parkside
5 Woodland Cottage

d 1 It would not be possible for every family to have a house similar to Falling Water, even if they could afford it, because there are not enough distinctive and perhaps rather remote sites to go round. In any case there isn't enough land available to enable everyone to have a large enough plot so that the house on it can stand all by itself and not be closely overlooked by any others.
2 There could be several difficulties in trying to make all our houses blend with their natural surroundings. Few people can afford the expense of a uniquely styled house and so have to make do with a cheaper, more mass-produced product having many features in common with other houses. Long, low structures often blend best with their surroundings and do not obstruct the view of others, but such buildings need a lot of land and this is often in short supply. In some cases the natural surroundings may be less pleasing than those at Falling Water, and so an architect might wish to hide or ignore them. A special difficulty arises in towns and cities where there are few natural surroundings left to blend with, even if this were desirable. The fact is that most housing has to be near where people work, and this usually means putting a large number of houses on a given piece of land. The most likely place for building a house that blends with its natural surroundings is in the country. But then if too many people built houses out in the country there would soon be no countryside left.

Two poems *pages 22–23*

a 1 We are to understand that the town child lives in a house in a street.
2 The town child lives in a busy street.
3 'Crowded with feet' means that there are many people there.
4 The form of public transport mentioned that we rarely see nowadays is the tram.

5 The town child would prefer to see meadows and lambs instead of motor vehicles.
6 'The houses all wait in a row' no doubt refers to a continuous line of identical, or almost identical, houses. It may refer to a terrace or connected line of houses.
7 The town child doesn't like the sounds around him/her.
8 The one thing that the town child likes is the sky.
9 'Castles of clouds' may refer to the child's vision or daydream of what he/she would like to see instead of the mean street that has previously been described. These thoughts would seem to be prompted by the shapes, such as castles, that the clouds suggest.
10 The town child is able to use his/her imagination to escape from his/her surroundings by looking up to the sky and there picturing what he/she would prefer to see.
11 The country child lives in a house near a wood.
12 The country child would prefer to live in a street in a town.
13 It seems that the country child lives in a house that stands by itself because he/she wishes that someone lived near and says there is no one to play with.
14 The birds and the flowers help to provide company for the country child.
15 The country child would particularly like to see trams going along a well-lit street at night.
16 Wherever we live it is easy to think that there might be advantages in living elsewhere.

b 1 Here are some of the points that pupils' answers could include:

Living in a town

Advantages: Close to amenities – shops, schools, transport facilities, entertainment, hospitals, clinics, health centres, libraries, swimming baths. More things to do and more people to meet. Perhaps more jobs available.
Disadvantages: May become crowded and less healthy. Lots of bustle and noise. Traffic jams. Exhaust fumes and other forms of pollution. Effects of industry on people's lives. Little open space.

Living in the country

Advantages: Generally healthier, with life carrying on at a rather slower pace. People in small communities may be friendlier. Easy access to fields, woodland etc. and perhaps fine scenery. Opportunities for walks and picnics. Some things in the country (e.g. fresh fruit and vegetables) may be cheaper.
Disadvantages: May be too quiet for some people. Perhaps a long way from

large shops, schools and other amenities. Dependence on limited public transport, unless one has a car. Risk of feeling a bit cut off from the world. In some areas a real risk of being cut off caused by heavy snowfalls. Not much for young people to do after school or after work. Limited prospects for employment.

2 The pupil is asked to say where he/she would like to live.

3 Most people do not have much choice about where they live because in the first place they usually live with their parents and other members of the family. Later on, their choice of home is usually limited to one that is reasonably near their place of work and at a price that they can afford.

4 If everyone went to live in the country it would no longer be the country as we now know it because large parts of it would have become built-up and so indistinguishable from our towns and cities.

5 In 1700 most people in Britain lived in the country because the population was then much less. There are now so many more people in Britain that there wouldn't be room enough for all of them to live in the small scattered rural communities that we find in the country. The increase in the population since 1700 has been accompanied by the growth of towns and cities, which is where most people live.

Conversions *pages 24–25*

a
1 familiar
2 established
3 octagonal
4 hexagonal
5 mock
6 ceased
7 derelict
8 purchased
9 huge
10 adapted

b
1 Turnpike Trusts were set up to deal with the construction and maintenance of roads.
2 A toll is a charge or tax for the use of a road or bridge.
3 When a traveller had paid the toll the toll keeper would raise the barrier or open the gate.
4 Toll houses were built close to the road and near the barrier to make it easier for a keeper to see anyone coming, collect the toll and open the gate.
5 Toll gates could be a nuisance to travellers because they would have to stop, wait for the keeper to appear, pay the toll and then wait until the barrier had been raised or the gate opened.

6 An octagonal or hexagonal house would give the keeper a better view of the road because he would be able to keep a look-out in different directions.
7 The phrase 'sympathetically converted' means that the windmill was altered with a real feeling for and understanding of its original purpose and appearance.
8 It would be better for a windmill converted into a home to have its internal machinery removed so as to make more living room inside.
9 The mill at Morcott has been restored in such a way that, from the outside, it still looks like a working windmill.
10 The phrase 'in good order' means in good working order and able to fulfil their original purpose.

c 1 Toll houses can be a problem when someone wants to widen the road because they are built so near to it.
2 It would seem that people go to the expense and trouble of converting mills and other buildings into dwellings partly because of the challenge that this presents and partly so as to have a home that is unlike most others.
3 The cottages were called Mill Cottages.
4 The problem in using a tollhouse as a home are (usually) its nearness to the road and the hexagonal or octagonal shape of the rooms, making it difficult to fit carpets and arrange furniture. The problems in using a windmill are the height of the structure (more difficult to paint and maintain), the need for more than one staircase and the problem of fitting carpets and furniture into circular rooms. The problems of using a church as a home are the lack of interior walls that could divide the place up into manageable rooms, and the height of the building – this presenting heating problems unless an upstairs is made out of the otherwise wasted upper part. In some cases there is the additional problem of being surrounded by a graveyard.
5 The sort of schools that might become available for conversion into homes are usually the small country schools that have been closed because of falling numbers and/or reorganisation into larger units.

d 1 (a) fantail
(b) oasthouse
(c) mews
2 In the first place windmills were used mainly for grinding corn and for pumping water from wet ground. They are not much used now as their ability to produce enough power is rather uncertain, especially in light wind. Since about the end of the 19th century they have been overtaken by other forms of power – steam, oil, electricity – although there are a few places in the world where improved types of windmills are still used.
3 Listed buildings are buildings that have been declared as having special historic or architectural interest or importance. They are protected against demolition or alteration unless the consent of the local planning authority is obtained.

Safe as houses? *pages 26–27*

a 1 hazards
2 maintained
3 widespread
4 havoc
5 lethal

b 1 An open fire is an exposed fire in a domestic fireplace.
2 Domestic appliances that can cause a fire if carelessly used include electric fires, electric blankets and paraffin heaters.
3 Natural occurrences are events that are caused by nature and not by people.
4 Many people survived the earthquake by being out of doors because they were not killed or trapped by buildings (such as the houses they lived in) falling or collapsing on top of them.
5 Services to the home that can be disrupted by an earthquake are water, gas and electricity.
6 The two things that may cause a fire and make it difficult to control are (1) the fracture of a gas main, and (2) the fracture of a water main.
7 Apart from the fire hazard the other problem that arises when water supplies are disrupted is the lack of clean water for drinking.
8 The tropical regions are those parts of the earth that lie between the tropics of Cancer and Capricorn.
9 Some hurricanes cause no damage to property because they do not reach land.
10 The dangers mentioned in the passage that people can cause through their own carelessness are fire and, to a lesser extent, flood. (People do not actually cause floods, but it is sometimes possible for both individuals and the community to take measures to reduce the effects of floods.)

c 1 **Uses of fire** (apart from providing warmth and for cooking):
To provide light.
For burning rubbish.
For heating water.
For religious and ceremonial purposes.
For signalling purposes (e.g. warning beacon).
As a defence against wild animals.

2 **Ways in which people can accidentally cause a fire in the home:**
Dropping a lighted match.
Knocking over a stove, heater or fire.
Leaving a chip pan unattended while cooking.
Smoking in bed.
Throwing away cigarette ends that are still burning.
Playing with matches.

Mis-use of fireworks.
Too many appliances on one plug.
Careless storing of inflammable items.
Clothes left too near a fire in order to dry.
Heaters placed in draughty places or too near curtains.

3 **Measures that can minimise the worst effects of floods**:
Making observations and keeping records of weather conditions etc. so as to be better able to predict floods and warn people.
Improving methods of reaching and evacuating flood victims.
Flood-proofing of buildings – raising buildings off the ground or building them of waterproof materials.
Controlling flow of river waters by means of artificial lakes and dams.
Dredging river mouths and keeping river beds free of silt.
Increasing the height of river banks.
To prevent flooding by the sea: Building dykes, breakwaters and sea walls.

4 Heavy lorries can be a danger to houses either by running into them or by shaking the structure of the houses as they pass by. (These factors particularly apply to narrow streets where the houses are near the roadway.) Lorries carrying dangerous loads can be a further hazard if they skid or are involved in traffic accidents. Insecure loads can be a nuisance if they drop off and in doing so they may occasionally damage property.
Aircraft can be a danger to houses by crashing into them. Houses near airports or in areas where low-flying manoeuvres are carried out may be at risk.

d 1 Some famous fires:
Year
64 Rome
1666 Fire of London
1871 Chicago
1906 San Francisco

2 Hwang Ho or Yellow River

3 Earth tremors are occasionally felt in Britain.

4 Houses may be affected by subsidence when the ground settles as a result of mining activity underneath. Walls and ceilings sometimes crack, and in extreme cases houses may become unsafe and have to be demolished.

Homes throughout the world *pages 28–29*

Answers may include some or all of the following points, together with any other relevant details of style, period, structure, materials used etc.

1 Britain
Little Moreton Hall (also known as Moreton Old Hall), Cheshire.

Tudor, 16th century.
Timber-framed, spaces between filled with brick or plaster.
Upper floors jutting out, slightly overhanging the storey below.

2 Holland
17th century town house.
Tall, narrow frontage, stepped gable (sometimes called crow steps, corbie steps or corbie stones) and asymmetrical arrangement of door and windows at ground level are special features of this type of building.

3 Germany
16th century half-timbered house.
As in many other houses made of wood, or partly of wood, the timbers are used to good decorative effect.
The steeply sloping roof – typical of this mediaeval style – is a practical feature in a region where heavy falls of rain or snow may be expected.

4 Indonesia
Dyak Longhouse
Made of bamboo; roof made of grass and leaves.
The structure, large enough to house an entire village, rests on wooden piles several feet high.
Access by means of ladders.

5 Mongolia
Ger or yurt.
A trellis framework covered with layers of felt, canvas or hide.
Portable.
Used in towns as well as by nomads.

6 Japan.
Traditional style house.
Built on a wooden frame and featuring sliding outer doors or panels that can be opened or shut according to the time of day or the weather.
The projecting roof serves the purpose of protecting the outer walls.

7 Switzerland
Chalet.
Built mostly of wood.
Features of chalets include small windows, low ceilings and overhanging roofs supported by brackets.

8 Venice
Part of the Ca' D'oro Palace which overlooks the Grand Canal.
Notable features of this famous Gothic palace (now a museum) are its graceful lines, decorative detail – the tracery is characteristically Venetian – and slender pillars.
Ca' D'oro means house of gold.

Making a house into a home *pages 30–31*

a 1 good taste
2 a comfortable look
3 an inviting atmosphere
4 a personal touch
5 handed down
6 taken into account
7 at ease

b 1 Town planners plan towns or parts of towns as a whole so as to avoid the worst effects of piecemeal, random or higgledy-piggledy development. The various requirements of housing, education, industry, transport etc. are worked out so that different needs and interests are taken into account in order to provide a balanced and harmonious whole.
2 Plumbers install pipes for bringing pure water to houses and for taking away soiled water.
3 Among the most important items to put into a house are: furniture, fittings, household linen, bed coverings, carpets, rugs, mats, curtains, cutlery, crockery, household and kitchen utensils, cleaning materials and equipment, tools.
4 The 'do-it-yourself' approach can give people greater satisfaction than paying somebody else for their services because it gives a sense of achievement, adds a truly personal touch to the work and almost certainly costs less.
5 The disadvantages of the 'do-it-yourself' method of home improvement are that it usually takes longer, makes many demands on a person's spare time and may not always compare with the best that an experienced tradesman could do.
6 People can get pleasure from thinking about how to furnish or decorate their homes by working out different ideas and schemes and imagining how these would look.
7 A colour scheme is a plan which takes into account how the colours and patterns of various things in a room (such as curtains, carpets, furniture and walls) will blend together in a way that is pleasing to the eye.
8 A photograph, an ornament, a cut glass tumbler, a clock, a lace tablecloth.
9 Another thing that would tell us that a house was unfurnished would be the hollow sound – caused by lack of carpets, curtains and furniture. A new house is also likely to have a distinctive smell about it (new wood, plaster etc.), while the absence of fittings (e.g. curtain rails) would suggest that the house had never been occupied.
10 Pupils are asked to give their views as to whether it is possible for a person to be too houseproud.

c Assuming, for the moment, that houses could have thoughts about the people who live in them, pupils are asked to suggest what views might be expressed by:

1 A new and unoccupied house, wondering who will come to live in it.
2 A house already occupied, giving its opinions about the people who live there.

Extension Book 5

Introduction *pages 2–3*

a 1 symbols
2 intelligible
3 conform
4 originated
5 surmise
6 co-operate
7 emphasise
8 aid
9 rehearse
10 imparting
11 vital
12 transporting

b 1 The word language comes from the Latin word lingua, meaning the tongue.
2 Language began in a spoken form.
3 Language can be used to our disadvantage if it is used to tell lies or in any ways corrupt or undermine our highest values and principles.
4 A meaning of the word communication – other than the giving and receiving of information – is transport of goods or people by road, rail, sea or air.
5 Ways in which the bus (or the people in it) going along the road would depend on, or make use of, words include the following:
people looking for direction indicator on bus
asking for tickets, stating destination
looking for street names etc. as the bus went along
driver observing any information on road signs as he went along (e.g. diversion, traffic control)

c 1 One's mother tongue is one's native language.
2 If we say that a person has a smooth tongue we mean that his soothing, eloquent way of speaking may be used to flatter or deceive the listener.
3 If we say that a person has a sharp tongue we mean that he has an abrupt or severe way of speaking or expressing himself.
4 Keeping a civil tongue in one's head means being polite in one's manner of speaking.
5 A person who speaks with his tongue in his cheek is not sincere in what he says.
6 The expression 'hold your tongue' means 'say nothing'.
7 A tongue-twister is a short sequence of words difficult to say quickly and clearly. Some examples are:

(1) She sells sea-shells on the sea shore and the shells she sells are sea-shells I'm sure.
(2) Peter Piper picked a peck of pickled pepper. Where's the peck of pickled pepper Peter Piper picked?
(3) A bloke's back brake-block broke.
(4) The sixth sick sheik's sixth sheep's sick.
(5) Around the rugged rock the ragged rascal ran.

d 1 Language is the most common method of communication.
2 We cannot be sure how human speech began.
3 More complicated messages can be conveyed by language than by cries and calls.
4 Speech came before writing.
5 The earliest available evidence of language is written.
6 As new ideas have developed the number of words in a language has increased.

e 1 throat, larynx, vocal cords, hard palate, soft palate, nose, nasal cavities, mouth, tongue, teeth, lips.
2 Reasons for learning a foreign language:
It enables us to communicate with more people.
It enables us to read the literature of another country and enjoy such things as films, plays and television programmes made there.
It helps us to understand the point of view of other people and to know more about their customs, traditions and way of life.
It can make travel abroad easier and more enjoyable.
It may help us to understand more about our own language, especially if the two languages are related.

The Pony Express *pages 4–5*

a 1 The word in the opening paragraph that means the central area of the United States is Midwest.
2 The word in the passage that means the same as horses is mounts.
3 It was necessary to have stations every 10–15 miles because that was about the distance that a man would ride a horse at speed before changing to a fresh mount.
4 The Pony Express used rough beaten tracks known as trails.
5 The Pony Express service required careful organisation and planning so that horses and men were in the right place at the right time. Food and accommodation also had to be provided.
6 The phrase 'in the saddle' means on horseback.
7 It was necessary for a keeper to have a fresh horse ready for immediate use whenever a rider appeared so that the rider could change mounts quickly

and be on his way. This routine would be varied when a fresh rider would be taking over.

8 A Pony Express rider might have to face attack by Indians or robbers.

9 If there was no fresh rider to take over the same rider would have to continue with the journey, carrying the mail to at least the next station.

10 The name of the method of sending messages by electricity that is mentioned in the passage is the telegraph.

b 1 Pony Express riders carried the mail in leather pouches.

2 The Pony Express service was paid for by the charges made for carrying mail.

3 When the Pony Express service closed down its promoters lost money because they had spent a lot before the service began, providing horses, saddles, stations, food etc. When the service closed down after a few months they had not had time to recover their investment.

4 The extension of the telegraph would not have had the same effect on stage coach services to the west because stage coaches carried passengers.

5 The Pony Express was a relay system in that each rider covered only part of the journey before being relieved by someone else.

c The old idea of the Pony Express was briefly revived in Britain in October 1979 in order to see which was quicker – the present-day Post Office or a man on horseback. Early one Monday morning at Elstree in Hertfordshire two letters, one stamped first-class and the other second-class, were posted in the usual way. At the same time a third letter was handed to a 'Pony Express' rider to see if he could beat the modern system. All three letters were addressed to the same person in Kenilworth. After changing to a fresh mount every ten miles or so the tired rider delivered his letter at ten past eight in the evening, nearly fourteen hours after he had set out on his 100-mile journey. Sixteen hours later and the first of letters that had been sent by post arrived at its destination.

d 1 The early North American trails were used by Indians, explorers, pioneers, trappers, settlers, traders and cattlemen.

2 The advantages that a single rider on horseback would have over a group travelling by stagecoach or waggon would be speed, independence and the ability to travel in places unsuitable for stagecoaches and waggons. A single rider would also present a less conspicuous target and have a better chance of hiding in case of danger.
The advantages that a group of people would have over a single rider would be that they could help each other, look after anyone who was ill or wounded and take it in turn (especially at night) to watch out for danger.

e The Pony Express has become so well-known because it is often seen as part of the attempt to tame the 'Wild West' – an ever-popular subject and part of the stirring story of the exploration of new territory and the extension of the frontiers of civilisation. The picture of the solitary rider pitting his skills, determination and pioneer spirit against dangers, known and unknown, is one that stirs the heart and rouses the imagination of most of us. Like the 'Wild West' itself the Pony Express era may have since been enlarged and over-dramatised, but it remains a fascinating episode with associations that go far beyond an attempt to improve communications. Its few short months of triumph and its eventual replacement by the much less romantic telegraph line may also be part of its enduring appeal.

Telegraph and telephone *pages 6–7*

a
1 achieved
2 familiar
3 converted
4 upheld
5 demonstrate

b
1 The telegraph was first known as the electric telegraph.
2 The word semaphore is used to describe a method of signalling consisting of a post with movable arms.
3 The word cable is used to mean an insulated bundle of telegraph wires.
4 The first attempt to lay a cable under the Atlantic was unsuccessful.
5 After about forty years the telegraph became rather less important because of the invention of the telephone.
6 The telephone has become such a well-known way of talking to people at a distance because it is convenient, easy to use and suitable for installation in almost any building.
7 Other words that could have been used in place of device are contrivance or invention.
8 Alexander Graham Bell is generally acknowledged as the inventor of the telephone.
9 Bell was involved in a number of lawsuits in order to defend his claim to be the inventor of the telephone.
10 Bell visited Britain in 1877 in order to demonstrate his invention.

c Samuel Morse

d The Great Eastern was the largest ship of the 19th century. She was so big that she was launched sideways. The vessel was driven by paddle wheels and propellors, as well as carrying sails. It was a remarkable ship, but it was not a success. It was underpowered, it was too big for many of the world's harbours and it never carried its full complement of passengers. It was designed for service to the far east but was soon transferred to the transatlantic service. It was withdrawn after only eleven voyages and eventually became a cable-laying ship.

e 1 The machine is called a teleprinter.
2 The name of the service is Telex.

f The building shown on page 6 of Extension Book 5 is the Post Office Tower in London. It is used for transmitting and receiving telephone conversations and television programmes.

Communications satellites *pages 8–9*

a 1 artificial
2 orbiting
3 elsewhere
4 reflected
5 amplify
6 located
7 huge
8 altitude
9 synchronised
10 stationary

b 1 Communications satellites are used to pass radio messages, telephone conversations and television programmes from one part of the world to another.
2 Direct transmission of television pictures across the Atlantic is not possible because the Earth's surface is not flat.
3 Signals from one place are sent up to the satellite which then passes them down to somewhere else, the satellite acting as a link between the two places.
4 Later communications satellites were an improvement over earlier types because they amplified the signals they received before re-transmitting them.
5 Radio waves weaken as they are travelling to a satellite and back to earth.
6 Television pictures from the United States to Britain are first sent to the satellite over the Atlantic Ocean and from there re-transmitted to Britain.
7 The first communications satellite was called Echo because the messages it received were, in a sense, repeated or reflected in much the same way as an echo is a repetition of a sound.
8 Signals sent to Echo had to be strong so that, even when they had become somewhat weakened, they would still be audible.
9 A satellite completes one orbit of the earth at the same time as the earth rotates once on its axis at a height of 22,300 miles (35,980 km).

c 1 One satellite can serve only part of the world.
2 A synchronous satellite completes one orbit in a day.
3 The earth spins round on its axis from west to east.

d 1 Space exploration, royal tours of overseas countries, Olympic Games, World Cup games, Test Matches and other forms of international sport.
2 The International Telecommunications Satellite Consortium.

e 1 Communications satellites are unpowered.
2 Communications satellites are unmanned.
3 Goonhilly Downs.

Fingers, hands and arms *pages 10–11*

a 1 One person is pointing out something to the other, perhaps giving directions or, more likely, drawing attention to some feature or incident of interest.
2 One person is waving good-bye from the open window of a railway carriage.
3 One person is greeting another by offering an outstretched hand for the other to take and shake.
4 The little girl is working out a sum or problem by counting on her fingers.
5 As the referee admonishes the player – presumably for misconduct or dissent – the player appears to be using his outstretched hands and forearms in a placatory manner towards the official.
6 A beggar holds out an upturned hand for alms.
7 The soldier in the foreground raises his hands as a sign of submission or surrender.
8 The priest raises his hands in order to bless the person who is kneeling before him.
9 The person on the right is using the open arms and hands as a way of inviting the other person into the room and allowing her to go first. Quite possibly the man has just opened the door and his invitatory gesture would follow easily and naturally from that.

b 1 Tom is an experienced card player.
2 There was fierce fighting at close quarters between the Romans and the Gauls.
3 After paying all expenses we had only a few pounds left.
4 Mrs Brown looked after her mother in every possible way.
5 The unruly pupils were disciplined by their new teacher.
6 Mr Roberts will make an attempt at doing almost anything.
7 The new team manager was given complete freedom of action.
8 I cannot undertake any additional work as I am fully occupied.
9 The 'hands' on a ship are members of the crew.
10 If you win 'hands down' you win easily or comfortably.
11 A high-handed person is arrogant and overbearing.
12 If you wash your hands of something you have nothing more to do with it and accept no further responsibility for it. (See Matthew, chapter 27, verse 24.)

c 1 She was only a very young child when her father died.
2 The people were very angry about the new laws.
3 The police caught up with him at last.
4 Our host gave us a hearty welcome.
5 He kept his relatives at a distance.
or
He was not on close terms with his relatives.
6 The widow was glad that her sons were too young to take part in the fighting.
7 The enemy had a large army.
8 The people made ready for war when a neighbouring country threatened invasion.
9 The defeat of the invader was a great military achievement.
10 The defenders surrendered when they ran short of food.

d 1 Long before the examination she had mastered all the main facts.
2 I couldn't say exactly what was the cause of the trouble.
3 I was sure that my younger brother had taken some part in it.
4 I was too awkward and clumsy to thread the needle.
5 She could handle her father so that he did just what she wanted.
6 He swore that he never touched the jewels.
7 She had been working all day but no one did anything to help her.
8 There was no proof of his involvement but several people had indicated or hinted that he was implicated.

e Specimen answers; others are possible.
David was asked to keep an eye on his young sister.
The batsman lost his head and was run out.
My heart sank when I saw the damage that had been caused.
We thought we might have to pay through the nose because it was so late.
I thought he was pulling my leg, but it turned out that he was perfectly serious.
I was given the message by word of mouth.
They were determined not to knuckle under to his threats.
The gruesome details were enough to make one's hair stand on end.
The two horses were neck and neck at the finishing post.
I made no comment so that I wouldn't put my foot in it.

Spelling *pages 12–13*

a 1 Effective communication depends on people using the same words to mean the same things and arranging the words in such a way that others can understand them.
2 Effective communication is further helped if everyone spells words in the same way.

3 Correct spelling is something that we have inherited in the sense that it has been passed on or handed down to us by others.
4 'Odd' is used to mean strange, unusual, extraordinary or peculiar.
5 Some people might spell what as wot because that is how it sounds.
6 English spelling does not always follow the way words are spoken.
7 The silent letters are h (in aghast), g (in gnash), p (in pneumonia), b (in dumb) and w (in wrench).
8 When letters are transposed they are put in the wrong order.
9 Amateur typists are people who have not been trained to type properly, using all the fingers of both hands, and who do not type letters, manuscripts etc. for a living.
10 Someone might confuse seen with scene or right with write because these pairs of words sound the same.
11 Context means those parts of a passage that come immediately before and immediately after a particular word or phrase, so helping us to decide its meaning.
12 Someone might write ave instead of have or ammer instead of hammer because they drop the 'h' in speech and so leave it out in writing.

b 1 quarter
2 chord
3 chemist
4 elephant
5 amphibian
6 architect
7 sculpture
8 moustache
9 optician
10 sabre
11 pneumatic
12 liquid
13 mosquito
14 neighbour
15 night
16 plumber
17 mountain
18 initial
19 foreign
20 blancmange

c 1 welcome
2 holiday
3 until
4 pronunciation
5 coconut
6 maroon
7 forty
8 quarrel
9 wilful
10 colossal
11 although
12 catarrh
13 necessary
14 sorrowful
15 guarantee
16 beginning

d 1 illegal
2 traveller
3 territory
4 surrender
5 likeable
6 sincerely
9 guitar
10 guest
11 island
12 salmon
13 coffee
14 thumb

7 mathematics
8 hymn
15 campaign
16 dispatch

e 1 seize
2 fiend
3 feint
4 receive
5 fruit
6 potatoes
7 guide
8 flying
9 nuisance
10 Tuesday
11 February
12 ghost
13 Wednesday
14 crescent
15 estuary
16 ghastly
17 syringe
18 abscess
19 gauge
20 fluorescent

f 1 aluminium
2 centre
3 mollusc
4 pyjamas
5 programme
6 defence
7 manoeuvres
8 favourite
9 neighbourhood
10 catalogue

Although there could be complications in the change-over period it might not be a bad idea if Britain adopted some U.S. spellings, partly for convenience and partly to standardise all texts written in English. Spellings such as pajamas, catalog and center certainly look more logical and less complicated. In some instances (e.g. maneuvers instead of manoeuvres) the U.S. spelling may partly obscure the origins of the word (in this case the French word manoeuvre) but this might be a small price to pay for greater simplicity.
It is interesting to note that many British dictionaries give a second spelling of certain words, either as the U.S. version or as an acceptable alternative, so smoothing the way for any widespread adoption.

g The pupil is asked to write a paragraph or prepare a talk on the importance of correct spelling.
The following points might be included:
Correct spelling as a courtesy to the reader.
There is (usually) only one correct spelling of a word, but there are many possible incorrect versions, including some that have minimum resemblance to the correct form.
Some incorrect spellings may give rise to misinterpretation and misunderstanding.
Incorrect spellings may discourage someone from reading a piece of work.
Too many incorrect spellings may interrupt the continuity of what is being read, especially when the reader has to stop to decipher certain 'words'.
On the other hand:

A few minor spelling errors are not going to ruin a skilfully presented argument, a well told story or an interesting or vivid piece of writing.
Some notable writers have been poor spellers. The quality of their work has survived this weakness. After all, someone else can correct the spelling, but few people can produce a really original and lasting piece of writing.
It is always better to risk a few spelling mistakes if one is attempting to widen one's vocabulary or extend the range of one's expressive powers. The spelling can be checked later as a separate exercise.

Overworked words *pages 14–15*

a over and over again
from time to time
coming to mind
no doubt
after a while
on our guard

b clichés

c
1 The house was expected to be ready on time.
2 More people live in Tokyo than in the whole of Switzerland.
3 His cruel remarks made me angry.
4 I was sorry to see her go.
5 I think you should sell it as soon as possible.
6 We could not understand how they found out.
7 The success of the company was due to hard work.
8 I will keep the book until you want it back.
9 She had saved a little money but it wasn't enough to buy the house.
10 I was angry but I tried not to show it.

d
1 Nowadays many people travel by air.
2 Only a few pupils came by bus.
3 There was some milk left in the jug.
4 The house cost about £40,000.
5 Many people were made homeless by the earthquake.
6 He carried an umbrella although the sun was shining.
7 We hope to hear better news before long.
8 Occasionally I go to the swimming baths.
9 There is a bus stop near the school.
10 The garages were behind the flats.

e
1 super
2 fantastic
3 fabulous
4 terrific
5 diabolical
6 definitely
7 ghastly
8 incredible
9 frightful
10 rotten
11 tremendous
12 terrible
13 dramatic
14 livid
15 fiendishly
16 frantic
17 gorgeous
18 massive
19 sensational
20 stupendous

f
1 Other words that could be used instead of nice are kind, friendly, delightful and considerate, but the exercise is particularly designed to draw attention to the less common use of the word to mean such things as subtle, fine, precise, punctilious and fastidious.

2 Some alternative words for said:

acknowledged	confessed	indicated	reiterated
admitted	confided	inquired	rejoined
advised	confirmed	insisted	relented
affirmed	contended	interrupted	remarked
agreed	contradicted	laughed	repeated
alleged	cried	maintained	replied
allowed	declaimed	mentioned	reported
announced	declared	mocked	requested
answered	declined	mumbled	retorted
appealed	demanded	murmured	revealed
argued	demurred	muttered	roared
asked	denied	observed	scoffed
asserted	disclosed	ordered	scolded
avowed	divulged	pleaded	screamed
bawled	drawled	pledged	shouted
begged	echoed	prayed	sighed
bellowed	ejaculated	proclaimed	snapped
beseeched	enquired	promised	snarled
boasted	estimated	pronounced	sneered
bragged	exclaimed	proposed	sobbed
called	explained	protested	stated
challenged	gasped	questioned	suggested
chuckled	granted	quoted	surmised
claimed	groaned	ranted	taunted
commanded	grumbled	reasoned	urged
commented	guessed	recanted	uttered
complained	hinted	recited	vowed
conceded	howled	refused	whispered
concluded	implored	refuted	yelled

Using words *pages 16–17*

a
1. The notice is used to warn people of the dangers of live electric wires overhead.
2. The label on the bottle gives a brief indication of the contents (medicine) and directions for use, such as how much, how often and when.
3. The writing on the envelope is the name and address of the person to whom it should be delivered.
4. The notices here are signposts placed at the approach to a road junction. Both primary routes and local direction signs are shown here as well as a smaller sign showing the way to a railway station. Details on the road signs include road numbers and distances in miles.
5. The bus indicator shows the service number and the vehicle's destination.
6. This illustration shows the name of a street.
7. The sign in the window or door indicates that the premises are closed.
8. Illustration eight is an example of a label on an item of pre-packed food. These labels give such details as the sell-by date, weight, price (of the actual package) and price per pound of that particular commodity.
9. The notice in the shop window is for the purpose of announcing that the goods on display (and others in the shop) are to be sold at reduced prices.

b
1. recipe
2. invitation
3. catalogue
4. prospectus
5. birthday card or greetings
6. programme
7. Highway Code
8. brochure
9. guide
10. manifesto

c
1. Peter said we would lose, but he had to admit that he was wrong.
2. I copied the sentence out exactly as it was written.
3. Young Jimmy always liked to make the final remark in any discussion or argument.
4. The book was claimed to be the most up-to-date on astronomy.
5. Sara spoke to Linda before going into school.
6. To put in a good word for someone is to speak well on their behalf.
7. A person of few words is someone who says very little.
8. To give one's word is to promise.
9. To break one's word is to break a promise.
10. Taking the words out of someone's mouth is saying what the other person was about to say.

d Examples to show how words (spoken or written) are used to

instruct: various forms of education and training

entertain: books, magazines, newspapers, plays, films, concerts, radio and television programmes

persuade: advertisements, salesmanship, articles, political pamphlets, speeches and broadcasts

inform:	letters, messages, reports, books, newspapers, magazines, documentary programmes, operating manuals and instructions for such things as cars and household appliances, forecasts, the giving of advice or directions
warn:	notices indicating danger or poison, oral warnings, meteorological warnings (of gales, floods, ice, fog)
encourage:	support – often oral – to individuals, groups and teams, messages of support
command:	giving orders – usually oral – especially of a military kind
promise:	pledges – usually oral – to do or not to do something; a formal vow given on joining an organisation
inspire:	slogans, speeches, messages – oral and written – designed to lift the spirit, raise morale and create a feeling of well-being and readiness to do a certain thing
protest:	letters, speeches, placards, banners, newspaper articles, slogans expressing dissent or disapproval

e The word propaganda most often means a way of giving news and passing comments in such a way that one point of view is presented in the best possible light and at the expense of any others. Alternative views are usually left out altogether or are misrepresented. There is no serious independent criticism. Open and free discussion is not permitted or is actively discouraged. This kind of propaganda may sometimes distort the truth, but often it will rely on selection and presentation in order to put across a certain point of view and exclude others. Nowadays propaganda usually means political propaganda and is favoured in those countries where only one political party is allowed. Because of this the word has acquired a mostly unsavoury reputation, but it must be remembered that some propaganda campaigns (e.g. against smoking) may be genuinely aimed at the public good.

Oratory is the art of making speeches in a grand and eloquent manner, usually with the intention of persuading people to support a certain point of view. Orators take great care to select, arrange and speak their words so as to command attention and rouse the feelings of those who are listening. It is a form of public speaking that really needs a large 'live' audience to be fully effective as it draws some of its inspiration and strength from the immediate reaction of others.

Slang *pages 18–19*

a 1 informal
2 literary
3 dialogue
4 intimate
5 derived

6 originated
7 familiar
8 vigorous
9 pitfalls
10 appeal
11 novelty
12 clique
13 unintelligible
14 precise
15 hinder

b 1 Members of the criminal fraternity would use their own distinctive kind of slang so that any discussion of plans (if overheard) would mean very little to others.
2 'American English' is English as spoken in North America.
3 'Old hat' means out of date.
4 The words that would describe most slang words and expressions are brief and forcible.
5 Heavy use of a certain kind of slang may identify the user with a particular clique or social group, whether he belongs to it or not.

c 1 apples and pears
2 Cain and Abel
3 plates of meat
4 butcher's hook
5 mince pies
6 trouble and strife
7 sky rocket
8 France and Spain

d 1 The slang expression 'cased the joint' would be inappropriate as part of an official police comment on a robbery.
2 The slang here is acceptable as the report refers to a young man's appointment as conductor of a symphony orchestra.
3 The expression 'bumped off' is out of place here in an otherwise serious comment on Elizabeth's dilemma.
4 "Scram!" is quite suitable here, as that is the sort of word a night watchman might use to deter intruders. He was angry, too, so a more refined expression would hardly be appropriate.
5 As this is a straightforward reference to a law and its terms, the word 'bangers' is not really suitable.

e 1 racing
2 flying
3 radio
6 journalism
7 sport and popular entertainment
8 the railways

4 the criminal underworld
5 the theatre
9 the armed forces
10 music (trumpet playing)

f 1 yob — a lout, loafer or layabout (Back slang for boy)

2 bobby — a policeman (from Sir Robert Peel, Home Secretary in 1828 when Metropolitan Police Act was passed)

3 bunkum — claptrap, humbug (from Buncombe County, North Carolina, U.S.A., whose member made a long-winded speech in Congress, explaining that he spoke 'for Buncombe')

4 pal — a mate, friend or partner (from a Gypsy word)

5 titfer — a hat (from Cockney rhyming slang tit for tat)

6 brass tacks — actual practical details or serious business (Rhyming slang for facts)

7 skint — broke, hard up, destitute (from skinned)

8 showbiz — the entertainment business, especially popular variety and musicals (from show business)

9 ad-lib — to improvise or extemporise, especially to fill in time (from Latin ad libitum, meaning at pleasure)

10 bread — money (Compare bread as a staple article of diet with money as an equally important means of subsistence; compare 'bread-winner')

Advertising *pages 20–21*

a 1 Some things that might appear in an advertisement for a concert that would not be considered as persuasion or inducement are: a straightforward and unadorned list of items, names of performers, time and place of performance and prices of admission.

2 A hoarding is a large screen or fence of boards.

3 Big business means that it is a large-scale and well organised enterprise with a lot of money involved and many interests at stake.

4 The other word in the passage that means advertising is publicity.

5 'On the credit side' refers to those points that can be made in favour of advertising.

6 Commercial television finds the money to pay for its programmes by charging people who advertise on its channel.

7 'Carried away' means to be so excited by something that we suspend all self control.
8 Television advertisements may act in favour of care of the teeth by advertising toothbrushes and toothpaste, so drawing our attention to the need for regular dental care. They may act against this interest by promoting the sales of things that may harm our teeth.
9 Medicinal products are various kinds of medicines.
10 Impartial advice is opinion or counsel that does not favour one point of view more than another.

b 1 'You can count on our calculators' means (1) you can use them for reckoning purposes, and (2) you can rely on them.
2 'Our houses are worth looking into' means (1) the houses are worth examining, and (2) they are deserving of close investigation – with a view to eventual purchase, of course.
3 'Stocks are moving fast' means (1) that sales are good, and (2) the bicycles run freely and easily.
4 'Top gear' is often used in a mechanical sense, referring to the gear in which a vehicle makes most progress and achieves its maximum speed. 'Gear' in the advertisement means clothes and 'top' in that connection means the best.
5 The double meaning here is (1) interesting sounds, and (2) an idea or notion that creates a favourable impression – something that seems attractive and pleasing.
6 'Give your teeth something to smile about' means (1) clean them so that they will look attractive, and (2) give them something to be pleased about.
7 'Drive home a bargain to-day' means (1) complete a favourable transaction, and (2) buy a car and – literally – drive it home by controlling its movements.
8 'Pictures' here means the photographs you take, but the expression 'getting someone into pictures' means getting someone into the work of performing in cinema films. The phrase is used to catch the attention and is not meant to be taken literally.
9 'Stop at the lights' can mean stop when the traffic lights turn red, but in this sense it means go to see the decorative display of lights at Blackpool.
10 A soft option is an easy alternative and using a water softener is an easily carried out alternative to putting up with hard water.
11 'The raining champions' means that the wipers are excellent in the rain. The play on words is on the similar-sounding 'reigning champions' – meaning the current leaders in a particular field.
12 'Ahead of hair' means that a wig will provide a head of hair and will even be in advance of the natural covering.
13 Here the play on words is on 'turkey' and 'Canaries'. The suggestion is that we should forego the traditional Christmas at home and go on holiday to the Canary islands instead.
14 Here the play on words is between the old saying 'Give a dog a bad name' and 'Give a dog a good mane' by taking it to the canine hairdresser.

15 The saying 'Crime doesn't pay' is altered slightly to read 'Grime doesn't pay', grime meaning dirt.
16 'Smooth your cares away' can mean to make light of or overcome your troubles, but here we are urged to use face cream in order to remove what may be the results (i.e. lines and wrinkles) of the burden of care.
17 To cover all someone's needs is to provide for their general requirements, but here it can also be taken in a literal sense as the people who sell and fit carpets do actually cover floors with them.
18 To take into account is to take into consideration. The bank or building society asks us to do this by opening an account with them.
19 'People who are going places' is a phrase used to mean people who are getting on well in the world. The other meaning is that the removal firm can provide a service for those who are changing their residence.
20 'L' stands for 'learner' in the sense that it is the initial letter of that word. In the sense in which it is used here it doesn't also stand for 'long' because (the implication is) the learner will not take long to pass the driving test as a result of the driving school's expert tuition.

c 1 Bold headlines; eye-catching layout; skilful use of photographs, drawings, charts and cartoons; emphasis on a competitive price; special offers – often of limited duration so as to draw early response; use of personalities who are said to use and recommend a particular product; quotations from the letters of satisfied users; convenient coupon to fill in, cut out and send (no need to write a letter); use of freepost.
2 Sponsorship in advertising means that a certain firm or company will promote or support a particular event, such as a concert, sporting occasion or race. The sponsor's name is usually mentioned in programmes, prospectuses, fixture lists, on any equipment used and in announcements and may even be part of the name or title of a particular event.
3 The main advantage of having advertisements on television is that the revenue from them pays for the programmes. Some people may also find it a way of keeping up-to-date with what is available in the shops and elsewhere. The main disadvantage is that, by appearing at times other than between items, advertisements can seriously interrupt programmes. This can be unfortunate where continuity and atmosphere are important, a carefully-planned build-up of dramatic tension being easily broken by an advertisement for soap powder. Regular viewers may find the repetition of some advertisements tedious, to the point where the message is lost on them through overstatement. There is also the point that commercial television may be less able to cater for minority tastes, since these attract smaller audiences and therefore fewer people to see the intervening advertisements.
4 There are advantages for the reader who may be looking for information about the kinds of things that are often advertised in such publications. The magazine will offer him a kind of handy pack of items to look through. The disadvantages are mainly for the person who wants to read only the articles

and features. These tend to be broken up ('turn to page 54') and interleaved with advertisements that one does not wish to see. The advantages for the advertiser are that the advertisements tend to look as though they are part of the magazine, sharing its general style and perhaps cashing in on its reputation, while the general reader can hardly avoid seeing at least some of them – perhaps when he is looking for something else or finding his way from one part of an article to another. A possible disadvantage for the advertiser may come about if readers shun the glossy magazine as little more than an advertising supplement, looking rather to the main body of the newspaper for serious information and comment.

5 aggressive advertising
advertising that is carried on with great vigour, energy and initiative, often forcibly addressing and challenging the listener or reader
seductive advertising
advertising that is presented in an alluring and enticing manner, using soft words, soothing phrases and gentle tones
factual advertising
advertisements that concentrate on actual facts and figures (such as performance, capacity, economy and other measurable items)

Words that may be confused *pages 22–23*

a 1 The manager was poring over the accounts.
2 A series of pillars supported the roof.
3 The rebel leader made an inflammatory speech.
4 The bugler sounded the lights out.
5 The mayor opened the new theatre.
6 An eclipse of the sun is an impressive sight.
7 He wore a toupee to cover a bald spot.
8 The guerillas were armed with modern weapons.
9 The gardener had left his secateurs on the lawn.

b 1 The giant panda is a very rare animal.
2 One player was sent off for a flagrant breach of the rules.
3 The yeti is sometimes called the abominable snowman.
4 She was wearing a 22-carat gold ring.
5 The young actress had been taking elocution lessons.
6 The British coal industry was nationalised in 1946.
7 John has chosen architecture as his vocation.
8 He made a great fuss over quite a paltry sum.
9 He switched off the lights in order to conserve energy.
10 The artist mixed his colours on a palette.
11 Rubies are among the rarest of precious stones.
12 He washed his overalls in a strong detergent.
13 I was misled by his ambiguous instructions.

14 A dinghy is a kind of small boat.
15 The second edition of the encyclopaedia contained many improvements.
16 He was presented with an inscribed pewter tankard.

c 1 Daniel has a loose tooth.
2 I held the bag tightly as I didn't want to lose it.
3 Her promotion meant an increase in salary.
4 We can eat celery raw or cooked.
5 Jane was popular with all the boys.
6 The poplar is a kind of tree.
7 Mr Brown is an antique dealer.
8 The antiquated stove was not very efficient.
9 The boy had a nasty abscess on his neck.
10 An abbess is the chief nun in a convent.
11 A nuclear war could threaten the survival of the human race.
12 The zoo was noted for its humane treatment of its animals.
13 The jumbled message was barely intelligible.
14 An intelligent person understands things quickly.
15 The traffic warden offended everyone by his officious manner.
16 The steward was wearing an official badge.
17 There was an appreciable improvement in the weather.
18 An appreciative audience listened intently.

d Specimen answers; others are possible
1 The sorcerer was studying a book of magic spells.
The waiter brought an extra cup and saucer.
2 The poet laureate wrote a foreword to the new anthology.
I looked forward eagerly to her next visit.
3 Jane passed her driving test at the first attempt.
I will call for you at half past seven.
4 She looked through the book before deciding to buy it.
The car was given a thorough overhaul.
5 We made good progress along the dual carriageway.
Arrangements were made for the two men to fight a duel.
6 The players were responsive to the captain's influence.
The people responsible for the catering arrangements were given a special vote of thanks.
7 An aqueduct is an artificial channel for conveying water.
A viaduct is a kind of bridge for carrying a railway or road across a valley.
8 A tarantella is a lively dance.
A tarantula is a large spider with a slightly poisonous bite.
9 Access to the beach was gained by means of a steep, narrow path.
Passengers were charged extra for their excess luggage.
10 In our search for the watch we decided to retrace our steps.
Due to a fault in the mechanism the plane could not retract its undercarriage.

Other causes of confusion *pages 24–25*

a 1 The unruly schoolboy was suspended by the head teacher.
2 As I watched through a hole in the fence I saw my neighbour watering his garden.
3 The police are looking for a man about six feet tall who has a broken arm.
4 St Leonard's is a large boys' school.
5 The eggs were stamped by the farmer on the day they were laid.
6 Measles is commonest in young children and among people who live in large towns.
7 There was too much water in the jar.
8 Jimmy didn't come to school in the morning because he had a sore nose. He didn't come in the afternoon because of the wet weather.
9 We beat Parkside at football last week.
10 Last season they scored the fewest goals of any team in the league.
11 In case the dog had fleas we didn't allow it to sit on the sofa.
12 Mr Williams was a much-respected member of the community who, on retirement, went to live in the country.
13 Thank you for the car insurance form which I have now signed.
14 Later on we met Mr Smith who, with his wife, was waiting for a bus.

b 1 There were about forty-odd people at the meeting.
2 Mr Johnson has a fleet of twenty six-ton lorries.
3 The candidate used a loud-speaker.
4 The wanted man was wearing a light-blue shirt.
5 There was nobody in the house.
6 Only a handful of coins was left behind.
7 A man-eating tiger had been seen near the village.
8 Mr Thompson is a greengrocer.
9 My answer was altogether wrong.
10 Mother doesn't drink anything besides tea.
11 We went into the house to have a look round.
12 By two o'clock I was almost ready.
13 Mrs Fisher went to see her grandchildren.
14 Grace Darling's father was a lighthouse keeper.

c 1 One of the survivors was able to recount her experiences in great detail.
2 The election result was so close that a re-count was ordered.
3 Mrs Price decided to have her old sofa re-covered.
4 The police recovered most of the stolen property.
5 The club was disbanded in 1960 but re-formed ten years later.
6 The method of voting was reformed so that more people could express their opinions.
7 Several players remarked unfavourably on the state of the pitch.
8 The groundsman re-marked the lines at half time.

d 1 This means that only her son (and nobody else) cuts the grass on Saturdays.
2 This means that it is her only son (she has no other sons) who cuts the grass on Saturdays.
3 This means that he only cuts the grass on Saturdays – he does not sweep it, roll it, water it or anything else.
4 This means that he cuts only the grass on Saturdays – he doesn't cut anything else.
5 This means that he cuts the grass only on Saturdays – he doesn't do it on any other day.

e Specimen answers; some variations are possible
Only Clive's sister is studying French and German.
Clive's only sister is studying French and German.
Clive's sister is studying only French and German.

Mr Davis only cleans his car at weekends.
Mr Davis cleans only his car at weekends.
Mr Davis cleans his car only at weekends.

Only Mrs Young takes Class Four for music.
Mrs Young takes only Class Four for music.
Mrs Young takes Class Four only for music.

Latin *pages 26–27*

a 1 extensively
2 acquired
3 remote
4 tongues
5 survived

b 1 The word 'Latin' comes from Latini – the name of the tribe who first spoke the language.
2 Latin grew in importance because Rome (where the language was spoken) became more important.
3 It would be convenient to have Roman law in Latin so that the law would be the same throughout the empire.
4 'Subject people' were races and tribes conquered and ruled by the Romans.
5 Becoming Romanised means adopting Roman ways, customs, habits, manners, dress and (to some extent) language.
6 The Celtic languages of western Europe suvived in places such as Ireland, Scotland and Wales because they were not conquered, or were only partly conquered, by the Romans. Distance and mountainous terrain made Roman occupation difficult to achieve and maintain.

7 An alternative name for classical Latin is literary Latin.
8 An alternative name for common Latin is vulgar Latin.
9 Literary Latin was used by authors such as Virgil, Ovid and Livy.
10 Common Latin would be used by people who could neither read nor write.
11 Countries became separated from Rome after the break-up of the Empire because the system of central administration and authority had broken down.
12 Location variations of common Latin developed into such languages as French, Italian, Spanish, Portuguese and Romanian.
13 Important institutions or bodies whose use of Latin helped to keep it alive were the Roman Catholic Church, schools, universities and monasteries.
14 The phrase in the passage that means 'now in general circulation' is 'in current use'.
15 Synonyms are words that have the same meaning as other words in a language. There are so many of them in the English language because English is a mixture of many languages and has borrowed widely from others.

c

1 a.m.	ante meridiem	4 i.e.	id est
2 p.m.	post meridiem	5 e.g.	exempli gratia
3 etc.	et cetera	6 cf.	confer

d

1 post mortem	after death
2 via	by way of
3 incognito	under an assumed name or title
4 verbatim	word for word
5 versus	against
6 viva voce	oral (by the living voice)
7 terra firma	dry land
8 vice versa	the other way round
9 per cent	in the hundred
10 per annum	by the year

e

1 ad infinitum	to infinity, for ever
2 in memoriam	in memory of
3 tempus fugit	time flies
4 nil desperandum	nothing is to be despaired of
5 pro patria	for one's country
6 sotto voce	in an undertone
7 Dei gratia	by the grace of God
8 Deo volente	God willing
9 in loco parentis	in the place of a parent
10 status quo	the existing place of affairs (in some cases the previous or former state of affairs)

f The letters on the pillar box stand for Elisabeth, Regina, meaning Elizabeth, Queen.
The second illustration shows the coat of arms of Worcester and the motto Civitas in bello et pace fidelis, meaning The city faithful in war and peace.

Communication without words *pages 28–29*

a 1 The label on the garment gives instructions on how to wash it, the upper figure showing the washing machine setting for the appropriate washing process and the lower figure showing the water temperature in degrees centigrade. Although some words are included the system also uses symbols to show such things as whether an article is suitable for machine-washing, whether it may be treated with bleach, whether it is suitable for dry cleaning, the correct setting for the ironing process and whether tumble drying is appropriate or not.
2 The red cross on a white background shows that the man belongs to the Red Cross organisation for looking after the sick and wounded in war.
3 Illustration three shows a page of music, the symbols indicating the pitch, duration, speed etc. of the notes to be played.
4 The numbers on the label indicate the price of the shoes in pounds sterling.
5 The picture shows a clock face bearing the Roman numerals for 1 to 12.
6 Picture six shows a gantry or platform on which stand several railway signals of the old-fashioned semaphore type.
7 The triangular sign warns drivers to expect traffic merging from the left along the road indicated.
8 This illustration shows a weather map and includes symbols for rain, sunny intervals, cloud, temperature in centigrade, wind speed in m.p.h. and wind direction.
9 The picture shows a radar screen. This kind of equipment is used to control air traffic, detect aircraft movements and as a navigational aid for ships.

b 1 a pistol or whistle
2 a gun salute
3 a whistle
4 an alarm clock or telephone call
5 chimes, strikes and the noise made by cuckoo clocks
6 doorbell or knocker
7 a bugle
8 a drum or drums
9 a hunting horn
10 a bell

c The picture was put there in case the spacecraft should eventually reach a civilisation outside our solar system. If successfully decoded it would tell the people there something about where it came from and who sent it. The man and woman represent the people of Earth, the representation of a spacecraft shows how the plaque got there (the spacecraft itself might be damaged), while the ten circles of varying size stand for the sun and the nine major planets of our solar system – the arrow indicating the path of the spacecraft from Earth. The atomic code for the hydrogen molecule is included because hydrogen is the simplest of all atoms, the diagram showing one proton and one electron. The pattern of lines radiating from a point like the spokes of a wheel show that the spacecraft originated in a world that had its own star system.

d
1. Two plus two equals four.
2. Angle ABC plus angle BAC equals angle ACD.
3. a squared multiplied by a cubed equals a to the fifth power.
4. An atom of carbon plus, or reacting with, a two-atom molecule of oxygen produces a molecule of carbon dioxide.
5. This is a short extract from a knitting pattern; p = purl, tog = together and k = knit.

e
1. I can come to your house next Sunday.
2. Specimen answer; others are possible

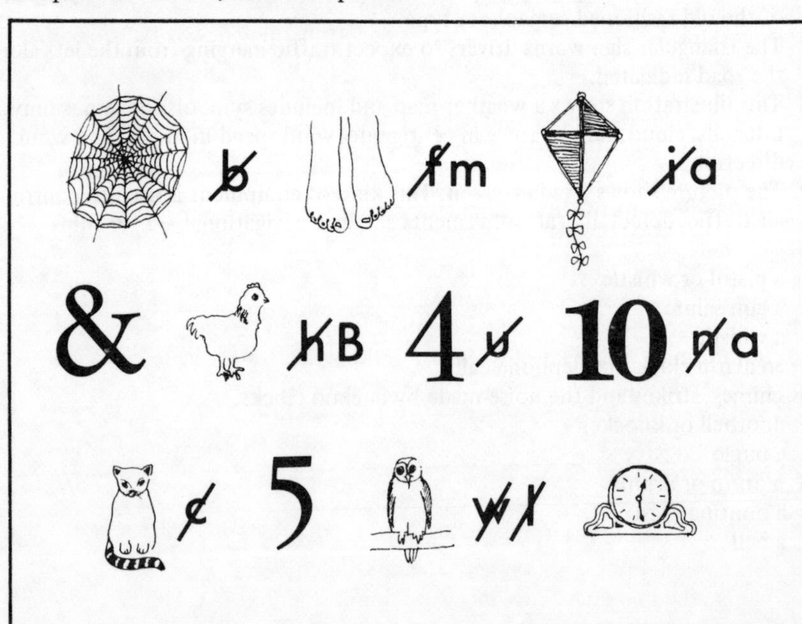

Why write? *pages 30–31*

a 1 The word used to mean fictitious tales told in prose and usually long enough to fill a book is novels.
2 Before they actually begin writing a book authors often spend a lot of time planning their work. They may also visit foreign places and talk to people who have special knowledge or experience.
3 When we say that writing is a vocation we mean that the people who do it feel a special call or inner summons to do it.
4 When we say that a story has pace we mean that events in it happen quickly, one after the other.
5 The incidents in a story are the things that happen or take place – events, occurrences, pieces of action.
6 The other word used to mean a story or tale is yarn.
7 The persons in a play or story are usually called the characters.
8 In the sense in which it is used here, to attack means to criticise adversely.
9 The phrase 'will win a wider audience' means 'will gain or attract more readers'.
10 The expression 'rooted out' means eradicated, destroyed or exterminated.
11 The word used to mean people who study prehistoric remains is archaeologists.
12 The two ways of finding out about the past that are mentioned are (1) digging up remains, and (2) studying old documents.
13 The word in the passage that means limited or restricted is confined.
14 The phrase that means talent for devising something new is flair for originality and invention.

b Among the reasons why people write non-fiction books are the following:
1 to explain how things work
2 to entertain
3 to tell us about the lives of famous people
4 to inform us about other countries and peoples
5 to provide information for the 'do-it-yourself' enthusiast
6 to explain and interpret current events
7 to make a scholarly contribution about some topic or person
8 to inform us of the latest research or discoveries about a subject
9 to suggest suitable hobbies or leisure activities
10 to help people look after themselves, improve their health etc.
11 to teach people who want to study or develop their professional skills
12 to suggest new or unfamiliar dishes and explain how they are prepared

c 1 Alice in Wonderland by Lewis Carroll
2 The Swiss Family Robinson by Johann Rudolf Wyss
3 Winnie-the-Pooh and The House at Pooh Corner by A.A. Milne
4 The Tale of Peter Rabbit by Beatrix Potter

d Science fiction stories are stories that combine an imaginative approach with a scientific basis or background. The imaginative approach enables a writer to place his or her stories at any time in the future (and occasionally in the past) and anywhere in the universe. The strange worlds of distant galaxies are a commonly-used setting, but science fiction stories may also deal with visitors from other worlds to our own planet.

The scientific basis or background, often carefully researched and well thought out, means that the events of the story are as plausible and practicable as they can be in the light of present knowledge and experience.

People write science fiction stories because there is great interest in such things as space travel and space exploration and the question, so far unanswered, as to whether there is any form of life as we know it elsewhere in the universe. In some cases science fiction may actually anticipate events that lie many years ahead. In recent years there has been a great upsurge in the popularity of science fiction stories due, in part, to such things as the moon landings, space probes and artificial satellites. But the idea of writing imaginative stories about the future is by no means new. A Greek writer called Lucian wrote about imaginary trips to the moon – over 1800 years ago. In the more recent past Jules Verne (1828–1905) and H.G. Wells (1866–1946) produced important works of science fiction.

The difference between science fiction and fantasy is that, while science fiction tries to present what could possibly happen, and sometimes explains how, fantasy deals with the impossible and the unattainable and is not intended to bear any close resemblance to reality.

e The Little Red Engine
The Famous Five
The Secret Seven
Noddy
Jennings
Sam Pig
William
Babar the Elephant
Biggles
Bobby Brewster
Worzel Gummidge
Tim

It is possible that people write several books dealing with the same principal characters and often the same kind of situation because the popularity and success of the first book encourages them to add to the series. Indeed they are sometimes asked to do so. It may also be convenient to use the same general background and location instead of working out a new setting altogether. In some instances authors may genuinely feel that they cannot get all their ideas into one book, so subsequent books in a series may continue the story or the careers of certain characters and develop the idea.

Apart from convenience for the author and the opportunity it gives him or her to exploit an idea, there is an advantage for the reader who, having enjoyed a particular book, merely has to look out for others in the same vein and with a title that usually suggests a common lineage.

Notes

Notes